Women without Children

Women Without Children

Nurturing Lives

Yvonne Vissing

Rutgers University Press

New Brunswick, New Jersey, and London

Library of Congress Cataloging-in-Publication Data

Vissing, Yvonne Marie.
   Women without children : nurturing lives / Yvonne Vissing.
      p.   cm.
   Includes bibliographical references and index.
   ISBN 0-8135-3080-6 (alk. paper)
   1. Childlessness—United States.   2. Women—United States—Psychology.
 3. Women—United States—Attitudes.   I. Title.
   HQ755.8.V57   2002
   306.87—dc21   2001048610

British Cataloging-in-Publication information is available from the British Library.

Manufactured in the United States of America

For Fran

Contents

Preface

This social scientific book looks at how a select group of women have made lives without children, and it uses their stories to illustrate issues that childless women face daily. This book also explores the social expectation of motherhood and how it plays out in these women's individual lives. Here, in their own words, I present their view of their lives and the concerns that they regularly experience as childless women. What factors contributed to their childlessness? How do they interact with others who have children? How have they emotionally resolved their childlessness if they had anticipated one day becoming mothers? What benefits and drawbacks have they found to not having children? If they had hoped for children, how have they coped with menopause and the realization that motherhood is now unlikely? And after their deaths, in what ways do they hope and expect to be remembered? This book offers insight into the personal and social experiences of these women and presents the full implications of their childlessness—the sacrifices as well as the opportunities.

Little has been written about how childless women feel about their childlessness, what experiences may have contributed to their childlessness, and what being childless has meant at different stages of their lives. Yet women without children confront challenges, overcome obstacles, and evolve over time in ways that are unique to their childbearing status, and because childlessness is a growing trend, more women undoubtedly will encounter these challenges.

I thank the women who participated in this study for sharing their stories. Great appreciation is given to Ellen Levine, who saw the potential for this book and helped it find the right home. I also thank David Myers and the staff at Rutgers University Press for their faith in this book. I have greatly appreciated the help and support of the administration of Salem State College, the sociology department chairpersons Ken MacIver and Arthur Gould, and the summer 1997 writer's workshop at Salem State College. I also thank Kathy Smith, Quixada Moore-Vissing, and Kathryn Gohl for their fine editorial assistance. I give very special thanks to Jeffrey Salloway, who greatly encouraged my writing and research. To all of my family, especially Wizard, Kiki, Chris, and Leah, whose love and patience helped me complete this project, I extend my love and appreciation.

I hope this book will endow those who are childless with emotional support and those who are not childless with knowledge and sensitivity on this topic. Today's childless women are blazing a trail for other girls and women who may choose or be forced to walk a childless path. I hope that by sharing the experiences of some of these childless women, this book will make that journey less difficult for those who follow.

Women without Children

Introduction

Even though she has been my best friend for twenty years, Fran has never volunteered information about what it means for her to be childless. I have never felt comfortable asking. Instead, over the years I have inferred her feelings from watching fleeting looks or stiffening muscles. I have learned to examine her silence. What I have discovered is that despite all her joys and successes, not having kids is a source of discomfort. I avoid conversation about it, as I would avoid touching a bruise or a scab. For better or worse, she has no biological children—and never will. Her childlessness is a problem for me. I have children and she does not. Although we can talk everything else in the world, this is the one area in which our relationship can be awkward. My motherhood is an open book, a regular part of our every conversation, yet her childlessness seems to be off limits. I think she understands my most heart-felt emotions, but I'm not sure that I have understood hers. While I suspect that not having children sometimes makes her sad, I really don't know to what extent that is true. It could be that she masks her distress—or it could be that she is quite comfortable about not having children and that it is my discomfort with the issue that has caused the void in our conversation around this topic.

Honest communication about childlessness is unusual. I have found that other women without children do not easily volunteer information about the meaning of childlessness in their lives. For instance, consider the experiences of another friend, Joy, who has wrinkle lines from laughter and salt-and-pepper hair, and relishes her husband's home-made wine. She had hinted that something was missing in her life, but her cheerfulness enabled us to be easily swept into other topics of conversation. Yet one day, in a vulnerable moment, she talked openly about difficulties conceiving—how they had gone from doctor to doctor in search of "something, anything, that we could do to get pregnant." She detailed their strategies: doses of vitamin E for them both, boxer shorts for her husband, sexual positions that encouraged conception, and "saving up" to have intercourse "when the time looked promising." I had not known she had been trying for years to conceive.

Around the time I learned I was pregnant, I called Jana, an old friend I had not seen in a long while, to tell her my news. When she picked up the phone, I learned that Jana had just come from the clinic and was recovering from "another" abortion—I had not known until then that she had undergone any. "I haven't told people—it's not something you advertise," she said. She felt she had done the right thing to terminate the pregnancy. Still, "the right thing was hard to do." I hung up without telling her I was pregnant.

I hesitated to tell another friend, Beth, about my pregnancy because I knew she didn't want kids. She had often asked, "Why would anyone want them? They cost so much and limit your time, your relationships, and what you can accomplish." If I told Beth I was excited about being pregnant, I feared she would criticize me. She would not understand my decision to be a mom, and I wondered if I really understood her decision not to be one. So I said nothing until my blossoming belly revealed my secret.

My relationships with these women had one thing in common: silence about the meaning of children. I finally confessed my uneasiness about the subject to a childless friend, Barbara. I admitted that I often talked about my own kids to mask feelings of discomfort, as if my words enabled her to share motherhood vicariously. I had assumed she felt distressed about her childlessness, but I had never had the courage to ask. I justified my silence by thinking that if I didn't ask, then she wouldn't have to think about it. Yet, Barbara told me, "I think about being childless all the time. There isn't a day that I don't wish I had a child. I can talk about it because it's such an ever-present part of who I am. Having children is a regular part of your life. You accept your motherhood and go on doing the day-to-day things of your life. So do I. I accept that I will never have children of my own. I chose to be childless. But you know, I still wish that I had a child, but I also know that by not having one I've been able to do other, wonderful things." What a curiosity—she simultaneously felt both remorse and celebration over her choice to be childless.

What is the meaning of childlessness in women's lives, and how do they construct lives challenging the expectation that all women are, or should be, mothers? To understand what childlessness means to some women, I interviewed a select group of 125 childless women (for more information about how these interviews were conducted, see "About the Interviews"). The women included in this study may have never had a child; they may have become pregnant and, because of miscarriage or abortion, not carried the child to term; or they may have borne a child who died shortly after birth. This book does not focus on women who have borne a child and put it up for adoption, women who have adopted other women's children, or women who have borne a child and experienced secondary infertility. My focus is on women who have chosen not to have children and on women who thought they might have children but never did.

I began interviewing women in my own circle of acquaintances and then broadened the field by asking these women to recommend others. Because the initial women interviewed were middle to upper-middle class and usually college educated, their circles of acquaintances most likely were as well. As a result, not all classes of childless women were included, and the experiences of those who were cannot be taken as representative of all women. This book has come out of my research and interviews, and does not necessarily reflect the views of all childless women. Instead, I focus on how this group of childless women has described their own lives and emotions. This book explores their particular sense of what childlessness has meant in their lives.

Although men who have not become fathers may experience some of the same issues and emotions as these childless women, their experiences were not included in this book either. Men are socially defined by their careers, not by their reproductive roles, so the issue of childlessness is not as central to their lives as it is to women's, for whom nurturing children is such a central aspect of their traditionally prescribed social role. For women, childlessness has fundamental implications for their identity.

The stories told by the women I interviewed describe a type of life journey that has not been well chronicled. The women tell about moments of anguish and contentment, times of frustration and reflection, instances of sadness and delight, and periods of confusion and determination. As mature women, they were able to share with me their insights and candid confessions about the celebrations and challenges they had experienced. Now that they have moved beyond that period in their life when motherhood could have occurred, they have had the opportunity to reflect on what childlessness has meant to them in its totality. Their experiences may be uniquely their own, but perhaps their stories will offer a perspective for debate and dialogue. The following pages relay the stories they have shared, stories that impart valuable knowledge about how they have built lives without children.

CHAPTER 1 Childlessness in America

They are married and single, heterosexual and lesbian. Some are infertile and some have been pregnant. Some have chosen and some have not chosen to be childless. But for most, childlessness is an ambivalent experience; it is part of an active and ongoing process in which not having children is an outcome. Consciously or not, most women make decisions that determine whether they will have children. Women choose what types of partners to have as well as the extent of their commitments. They choose, except for instances of rape, how well to know partners before becoming intimate with them. If they decide to be intimate, they choose what kind of contraception to use, and if they conceive, they choose whether to go through with the pregnancy. If they decide to carry the pregnancy to term and the baby lives, they have other choices: they can keep the baby, let family members care for it, or put it up for adoption. If they cannot get pregnant and want children, there are choices of infertility treatment: they can use fertility drugs, be implanted with eggs, or hire a surrogate to carry the child. They themselves can become a surrogate mother, have a child, and give it to another woman who will call herself mother. They can adopt children, acquire stepchildren, become godparents, or choose careers that incorporate children into their lives. They may choose to let relationships, jobs, or school come first. They can let people and circumstances take precedence over their desire to have children. And they may simply choose to not have children.

The cultural mandate that women are supposed to become mothers is etched into most women's psyches. Girls are socialized to believe that they will have children, and they learn at an early age how to act in nurturing ways that can be described as motherly. They may nurture children, family, friends, colleagues, animals, flowers, organizations, professions, or social causes. The "female as nurturer" and "nurturer as mother" mandates are disseminated by books, toys, television, music, role models, and culturally explicit messages.[1] Because it is virtually impossible to avoid these messages, women have to find some way of reconciling issues surrounding their femininity, the assumption that they should nurture others, and their status as mothers or nonmothers. What is nurturing like for women who don't have children? What are the private emotions childless women experience? How does childlessness influence women's success, productivity, and willingness to nurture? These questions, and others, are explored in this book.

Today's childless women have important stories to tell—and many of their stories pertain to the ambivalence they feel about motherhood. Women who were interviewed for this study, such as Ramona, asked, "Where is the place for women who sometimes feel sad, and other times feel relieved that we don't have children?" The emotions surrounding childlessness are complicated, and none of the literature has adequately addressed them. Mica explained that "most of the women I know are like me—we have times when we don't want kids, and times when we wish we did. There are times we hurt so much inside because we don't have them, and other times when we are delighted we don't have to be bothered with kids. We don't feel just one way or the other."

The ambivalence these women feel was born out of a variety of social phenomena. Advances in medical technology have made it possible to create, postpone, and terminate pregnancies. Remarkable advances in science and reproductive therapy have been readily accepted as legitimate and even miraculous. Changes in the economic structure of American society have made it necessary for most women to work, and alterations in the roles of women have resulted in their greater pursuit of professional occupations. Lack of high-quality, affordable, available child care may have deterred women who might want children. Ideological conflicts tug at women who want to pursue both professional and maternal lives when they find economic and relationship barriers to "having it all." Also, demographic trends indicate that more women see childlessness as a preferred lifestyle. Couples feel less compelled to marry, and when they do marry, childbearing need not be an automatic outcome. When women consider having children, they may try to analyze how the number of children may affect their quality of life. Because "the speed of life has increased," as Maura, a deliberately childless woman explained, "it's important to parcel out a little bit of time just for yourself, for recreation, for pursuing personal interests, and for having a little quiet time." For these and other reasons, it became an acceptable social behavior for women en masse to decide to have babies later in life. At about the same time, it became more fashionable and acceptable to remain "child-free." As a result, childbearing has perhaps never been a more complicated decision.

Childless women such as Lucy pointed out how "there may be more of us childless women around, but that doesn't mean that we're seen to be as acceptable as women who are mothers." Western society continues to define women on the basis of their sexual and care-giving roles, so women who opt out of motherhood flout convention and may even be seen as deviant. Merely because they have no children, these women may be at risk of having their own lives viewed as incomplete.

Within most cultures, motherhood is exalted, whereas barrenness is a source of shame. History and myth have contributed to the stigma of childlessness. Greek mythology gives us examples of perfect women—goddesses—and they are beautiful, loving, and sexual, like Aphrodite, and fertile, like Artemis. Mothers are supposed to be devoted to their children, as Demeter was to Persephone. Then there is the virgin goddess Hestia, sister of Zeus, known as the goddess of the hearth and home, who reinforces the ideology that even though women are not married or are without children, still they are expected to take care of others.

Fertility is promoted in biblical writings. Adam and Eve were instructed to "be fruitful and multiply." Sarah, who became pregnant in her eighties, gave every woman who wanted children hope that such miracles could also occur for them. Infertile women could become pregnant through the use of outside intervention, as in the book of Genesis, where mandrake is used by Leah as an infertility cure. According to 1 Timothy 2:15, a woman becomes more blessed through childbearing: "Women will be saved through bearing children." If women do not have children, they may suffer dire consequences, religious tenets hold, as in Genesis 30:1, where Rachel pleads, "Give me children or I die!"

Yet biblical passages also convey another view of childless women. Whereas the previous quotations describe the importance of having children, other passages, such as those in Isaiah 1–10, celebrate the importance of women who do not have children. The following passage from Isaiah encourages childless women to be joyful, not sad, for they are blessed with the opportunity to love others in ways that surpass the care provided by mothers:

> Sing, O barren, thou that didst not bear.
> Break forth into singing, and cry aloud
> Thou that didst not travail
> For more are the children of the desolate
> Than the children of the married wife,
> Saith the Lord.
> Enlarge the place of thy tent
> And let them stretch forth the curtains of thy habitations, spare not,
> Lengthen thy cords, and strengthen thy stakes.
> For thou shalt spread abroad on the right hand and on the left
> And thy seed shall possess the nations,
> And make the desolate cities to be inhabited.
> Fear not, for thou shalt not be ashamed,
> Neither be thou confounded, for thou shalt not be put to shame
> For thou shalt forget the shame of thy youth,
> And the reproach of thy widowhood shalt thou remember no more.

This passage challenges the negative stereotypes of "barren" women. But it also mandates that barren women must care for others if they are not to be ashamed, and thus it too reinforces the ideology of female as nurturer. Yet it also empowers by declaring that barren women have a vital role in improving the world because "more are the children of the desolate [barren] than the children of the married wife." These competing views—the duality of the meaning of fertility—are ingrained parts of the female experience.

Despite the benefits childless women have provided to others across time, fertility has remained the symbol of true womanhood. Women's fertility was of utmost importance in building the United States. Colonial America's family systems were characterized by Christianity, patriarchy, subordination of women, and family-centered production, and most families averaged seven or eight children.[2] The boast "Our land free, our men honest, and our women fruitful" exemplified the link between childbearing and the new American experience. Girl children were valuable only in their potential to bear more children.[3] The childless woman was regarded as useless and despised as a piece of land that would yield no crops. The same word was given to both— barren. Religious imperatives encouraged large numbers of children in colonial America. Because Puritans could not know if they were to be saved by God, they looked for visible signs that would give hints of what their future might be in heaven. Having many children was regarded as a sign of great blessedness. If a woman had no children, it could mean she was being punished for some indiscernible sin or that she was not acceptable for entry into heaven. But if "spinsters, widows and those wives who were naturally barren" would devote themselves to doing "good works and serving others," according to theologian Cotton Mather, they might get into heaven by pursuing a "path to spiritual fruitfulness in all good works of piety and charity."[4]

Having children was not just a spiritual issue but an economic one as well. During the early years of the nation, children were a cheap source of labor—they worked in the fields for farming families and in factories for urban ones. Having many children was also desirable because infant mortality was high; having many children increased the chances that there would be someone who could provide for the rest of the family—especially as the parents became older and unable to work. Before social service and economic systems were created to assure that older persons' needs would be met, aged parents were

entirely dependent on their children for care. Lack of children jeopard-
ized one's future standard of living.[5]

Having children, aside from being an economic issue, promoted the
values of productivity that were essential to the rise of the new nation.
Mothering became part of the Cult of True Womanhood ideology that
emerged in response to the industrial revolution. This ideology, which
linked femininity and the preservation of Puritan values, was expressed
in motherhood, with the mother becoming the "virtuous guardian
angel of the home."[6] As historian Diane Eyer expressed it, "The idea of
motherhood as a powerful and almost sacred institution appealed to
both men and women, expert and layperson alike. All women were to
derive total fulfillment from complete devotion to their children and
husbands. To be a wife and mother was the biological destiny for which
their instincts had prepared them."[7] Toward the end of the eighteenth
century, as marriage became romanticized and sentimentalized, childlessness took on the aura of personal tragedy. The Victorian era developed a new ideal of femininity that made strict distinctions between
proper male and female functions.[8] Appropriate women's behavior
emphasized motherhood and the stay-at-home guardian of family,
home, and hearth. This new ideal of motherhood was made possible
by its opposite—working-class mothers and children who were
employed outside the home as domestics for middle-class families or as
factory workers. This gender role resulted from the increased standard
of living generated by the industrial revolution.

Love, not utility, became the foundation for marriage, and a growing emphasis on domesticity resulted. Home became the center of life,
and the housewife was responsible for making family life a source of
fulfillment. During this time, women increasingly focused their identities on the quality of motherhood, not necessarily on the quantity of
children born. Thus, between 1800 and 1900, fertility dropped by half,
to 3.5 children per woman.[9] Having fewer children allowed women
more time to concentrate on mothering. It also opened the door to
women's greater participation in the world outside the family, which
included involvement in the temperance, antislavery, and women's
emancipation movements. Child protection later became part of this

Progressive movement, and public education for all was seen as a way to provide children with the information, skills, and values they would need as adults.[10] But women's rights remained in the vanguard.

By the end of the nineteenth century, in response to economic and social oppression, the women's rights and suffragist movements had grown viable. Led by such women as that inspiration to mothers, Elizabeth Cady Stanton, and her childless colleague, Susan B. Anthony, the movements encouraged women to consider options besides marriage and motherhood. If women did have children, the leaders argued, they needed help to raise them; if women did not want children, they should have reproductive options such as access to birth control. The women's emancipation and suffrage movements attempted to embrace the needs of a wide range of women from different incomes and backgrounds—they imposed neither motherhood nor childlessness as an ideal. All types of women were regarded as important to the growth of the nation, and choice was regarded as an essential part of freedom in this democracy.

Faced with powerful contradictions between the romantic ideal of the family and the reality of discrimination against women, nineteenth-century feminists constructed both pro-family agendas and newly envisioned forms of family. Motherhood moved to center stage. During the early twentieth-century wave of immigration, white middle-class women were encouraged to "save the race" by procreating. In 1914 the U.S. Congress passed a joint resolution making the second Sunday in May Mother's Day. The resolution proclaimed the American mother as "the greatest source of the country's strength and inspiration" and lauded her labor as "doing much for the home, for moral uplift, and religion, hence much for good government and humanity."[11]

Yet many in the first wave of feminism believed that having children without proper support could oppress women, because motherhood allowed a woman less time and fewer resources and opportunities to pursue nondomestic concerns. This opposition to motherhood was not readily embraced by society at large. Freud, whose ideas had developed and become popular in the decades following World War I, used biological differences to explain male and female psychic development.

According to Freud, "A girl deprived of a penis substituted a desire to bear her father's child; in the healthy adult woman this desire was transferred to another male. If adult women did not seek to become mothers, they were suffering from unresolved penis envy and a masculinity complex."[12] Freud's disciple Helene Deutsch argued that female sexuality was really a desire for motherhood and that not bearing children would create psychic suffering and damage in women.[13] This view was further advanced by those who argued that motherhood was a cornerstone for healthy psychic development and that one of the ills of the twentieth century was women's failure to accept motherhood as the ultimate goal of their lives.[14] These theories were clearly influenced by the social milieu of the day, during a time when the stay-at-home mother was the ideal.

The history of womanhood in the United States illustrates that conditions of childbearing and economics have gone hand in hand. When the Great Depression of the 1930s resulted in a paucity of jobs for both men and women, there was a vested interest in keeping women in the home and out of the workplace. But World War II shattered gender discrimination on the occupational front. When men went away to war, women were needed to keep the nation's infrastructure operating, and they entered the workforce in unprecedented numbers. Women, embodied by the caricature of Rosie the Riveter, found themselves enjoying productive work outside the home and being paid for it. While men were at war challenging powerful international adversaries, women transformed the internal structure of America—and their psyches. Women who had begun working while their husbands were off at war did not want to abandon their jobs when the men returned. Despite ebbs and flows, women have not left the workplace since.

The end of World War II saw servicemen returning home and the birth of the baby boomer cohort. These children were born into an era of industrial expansion, an era that saw an increase in real wages and personal savings. The economic good times resulting from this growth also ushered in consumerism and materialism.[15] Consumerism was a hallmark of nuclear families in the 1950s, when televisions, automobiles, electrical appliances, and houses were purchased en masse. Having children was the American way, and girls learned that motherhood was natural and inevitable—until the 1960s. In the 1960s, civil rights and women's rights legislation occurred side by side. The women's movement of the next decades encouraged women to see each other as sisters. Although some asserted that the single experience women shared was their capacity to mother,[16] others responded that the experience most women shared was domestic enslavement and oppression. Now called feminists, writers of this second wave, such as Betty Friedan, Shulamith Firestone, and bell hooks, suggested that it was oppression, not maternity, that bound women together.[17] Traditional mothers of the 1950s who had worked hard cleaning and cooking and caring for their families were redefined as domestic slaves who earned no wages. By the end of the 1970s, motherhood had been reevaluated. Many feminists considered motherhood a dirty word that described a social arrangement of entrapment and victimization. To those who viewed motherhood as responsible for the subservient condition of women, women and men alike had been brainwashed by a pro-natalist view that having a child is the natural, normal, and right thing to do.[18]

As life in a single-paycheck family became increasingly difficult, women found they were unable to give up their roles in the workplace but that the one role they could sacrifice was motherhood. Some women purposefully set out to purge themselves of the harmful effects of female socialization and to become androgynous; to be liberated, they severed themselves from the childbearing role. By the mid-1980s, mothering no longer defined women's lives.[19]

Women entered the workforce in droves as a result of the women's movement. To achieve economic parity, women found they had to control their childbearing potential. During the 1960s when the birth control pill became widely available, young women seized it as a method to control their reproductive lives. Women were now able to explore their sexuality without becoming pregnant, allowing them to break out of the 1950s mold and to establish a new view of themselves as liberated individuals who were able to explore their own potential. By controlling their reproduction, they subsequently controlled their social options and economic lives. And they began to question whether they really wanted children. Out of this changing social view of women came an attack on procreation itself.

Ultimately, both the pro-natalists and anti-natalists influenced women's psyches. "It was impossible not to get caught up into the motherhood future, and it was equally as impossible not to get swept up in the feminist future," said Monica, one of the women interviewed for this study, who described herself as ambivalent about having children. Women shared what were often conflicting messages, which helps explain why they were ambivalent about both their feminine/feminist precepts and their interest in having children. Meredith Maran writes that "in part because they got us when we were so young, and in part because the mass media have been obsessed with defining and exaggerating codes of masculinity and femininity, they have ensnared us in an endless struggle for gender self-definition. What a woman has to do, on her own, is cobble together some compromise between these [feminist and feminine characteristics]."[20]

"We were sold schizophrenic messages in a variety of ways, like in the ad slogan, 'I can bring home the bacon, fry it up in the pan, and never, ever let you forget you're a man,'" said Leanne, another woman interviewed for this study, who had planned to have children but then didn't. "In an odd sort of way, these messages made me confused about what kind of woman I was supposed to be. How does a woman work, cook, be a seductress and a mom all at the same time?" Her experience was common, according to author Susan Douglas, who describes how the mass media sold females "representations of happy brides and contented moms" on the one hand and images of liberation, freedom, excitement, and self-directed empowerment on the other.[21] According to Douglas's analysis,

> In a variety of ways the mass media helped make us the cultural schizophrenics we are today, women who rebel against—yet submit to—prevailing images about what a desirable, worthwhile woman should be. We are ambivalent toward femininity on the one hand and feminism on the other. Pulled in opposite directions—told we were equal, yet told we were subordinate; told we could change history, yet told we were

trapped by history—we got the bends at an early age, and we've never gotten rid of them. . . . I am simultaneously infuriated and seduced. I adore the materialism; I despise the materialism. I yearn for the self-indulgence; I think the self-indulgence is repellent. I want to look beautiful; I think wanting to look beautiful is about the most dumb-ass goal you could have. On the one hand, on the other hand—that's not just me—that's what it means to be a woman in America. American women today are a bundle of contradictions because much of the media imagery we grew up with was itself filled with mixed messages about what women should and should not do, what women could and could not be. This was true in the 1960s, and it is true today. The media urged us to be pliant, cute, sexually available, thin, blond, poreless, wrinkle-free, and deferential to men. But the media also suggested we could be rebellious, tough, enterprising, and shrewd. Since the 1950s women have been indelibly imprinted by (mass media) and we have our parents who raised us, socialized us, entertained us, comforted us, deceived us, disciplined us, told us what we could do and told us what we couldn't. And they played a key role in turning each of us into not one woman but many women.[22]

The mixed messages that women received made it difficult for them to decide whether to have children. Women in this study, such as Kris, wanted to be "fully female—in every way. I want to be successful in my career, I want a man to adore me, I want children crawling over me, I want to be a pillar of my community, I want it all." Natalie was clear about wanting the benefits of both family and career, and she didn't want to sacrifice one side of herself for another: "I was a successful professional, and I wanted a family. Seems reasonable, eh? But time-wise, it wasn't." She felt she had to choose one or the other, "but when you shut one door to go through another, even if you like where you've gone, there's always a sense of curiosity, maybe even regret, that you didn't take the other one." Melinda, who wanted a child and couldn't have one due to infertility, explained that "there's something wonderful and magical about having a child. It's something that women can do that men can't. Having babies unites all people in a spiritual way that really puts women above men, of having the ultimate experience. As a woman, my body can open a door of creation that men can't. Why would I want to deny myself this experience?" Other women, such as Betsy, who "just ended up without kids," felt that it was hard to fit into a mold of what women were supposed to be. Betsy described herself as "Definitely feminine, but definitely a feminist. I guess you could call me a feminine feminist. I was a Playboy Bunny and a go-go dancer. I like clothes, hair, makeup, jewelry, ballet, dance, and beauty. Some of these things people would see as opposite feminism. I'm artistic and beautiful. I make my own decisions. I'm a leader at work and at school. But sometimes I do feel conflicted." Many women, like Betsy, did not see themselves as either a traditional feminine woman or a feminist. Often, women such as Kendra regarded themselves "as both. I'm the master of my destiny and my body. I enjoy being a woman. Like in the Rogers and Hammerstein way, I'm strictly a female female. But I'm also a bright woman who has her own business, and I refuse to be discriminated against because I've chosen to be both kinds of woman." Mary recalled, "Women in my mother's generation stayed at home. But our generation's view was to work and have a family. Both are important." Veronica alleged that "neither the feminine nor the feminist script were totally acceptable to me. They are both part of the whole me, so it seemed stupid to label myself as one or the other. Both postmodern feminism and postmodern femininity need to be explored as part of the same dynamic rather than as opposite, competing ideas." Childless women felt they were part of a new cultural revolution—one in which femininity and feminism were integrated "as they damn well ought to be," according to Mary. These women are not alone in this view. American women today consider home and family just as important as career. They want both quality and quantity time with their children as well as time and support to pursue their professional goals. They long for balance in their lives, unlike their grandmothers who sacrificed careers for home and mothers who sometimes sacrificed homes for careers.[23]

The stories told by Betsy, Mary, and Veronica reverberate with the notion that the social forces promoting motherhood and careerism have not been integrated. The result is that economic institutions continue to impose expectations on women either that they remain childless or, if they have children, that they minimize their involvement in the workforce. "Frankly, it's almost impossible to shatter the glass ceiling if you've got kids," Donna said. "The good ol' boys come up with all kinds of reasons for inhibiting mothers' ability to climb up the corporate ladder. I've watched them chip away at moms' self-esteem, make them feel guilty, pile up unreasonable workloads and then snap them, even though they still do a good job getting things done." Corporate institutions are committed to maintaining a culture based on masculine values. Their primary goals are power and profit, not family well-being. Most offer no universal daycare for working parents. Maternity and paternity leaves are often unpaid.[24] Even though it is illegal, some women are fired, demoted, or denied benefits simply because they are pregnant; others who are expecting may experience discrimination on the job.[25] There is also a widening gap in income levels between parents and nonparents, with parents tending to have lower incomes. Then when the expenses of children are added, parents' income levels fall further behind those of their child-free counterparts.[26] "I don't want to be working all the time to pay for the things a kid needs and be so stressed out when I drag home that I don't have time to enjoy them," Maggie confessed. For women the penalties for having children are so intense that many have either opted out of motherhood completely or decided to postpone childbearing until a better time. But, as women such as Veronica noted: "I decided to wait for kids until I had my house in order—good job, stable relationship, right place to live. By the time those things happened, it was too late."

The effect of the compartmentalization, not integration, of women's lives can also be seen by looking at this trend in reverse. Increasing numbers of high-powered, well-paid women have decided that the corporate fast track is counterproductive to child rearing—they cannot work and have children. Some have opted to leave the workplace "and have a normal family life"; some have opted to stay in the corporate world and remain childless. "There are really no in-between options. You either work and do not see your child or you don't work at all. I'm not surprised that women are leaving the workplace. I don't want things to go back to the 1950s when women felt they had to stay home, but jobs are so demanding these days that it is hard to find one where you can be home for dinner every night."[27] Both Diana Baker, who earned $890,000 as chief financial officer of the *New York Times*, and Brenda Barnes, president of PepsiCo North America who walked away from a $2 million salary, resigned to stay home with their children and live saner lives.[28] "I can understand that," Natalie, a deliberately childless woman in this study, said. "The work world has turned either/or: either you make your work your priority or you have kids. For women who want to succeed and shatter the glass ceiling, you've really only got one choice. And that choice doesn't include kids!"[29]

Themes of feeling caught in a childbearing dilemma were repeated by many women I interviewed. "The pressures to make an active choice about whether or not to have kids were so intense that I think I numbed out," confessed Abigail. "Instead, I just let myself get swept up in the currents of life and I allowed myself to go with the flow of wherever I was taken, instead of strategically deciding 'yes' or 'no.'" Abigail was surprised when she decided that she did want children and then couldn't have them. "I'm embarrassed to admit it, but part of me feels as though I'm not a 'real woman' because I can't have kids. I feel like there's something wrong with me, like I'm being punished for something—but I don't know what." Another woman, Janice, confessed that "Most of the time I'm cool about not having kids—but that's when I'm not feeling vulnerable. On those days, you get hit, like on Mother's Day. That's the one day of the year when I feel like Hester Prynne, wearing a scarlet letter on my chest, as if everyone can just look at me and tell that I'm not lucky enough to be a mom. I feel different, left out, and sad, I guess." This experience of feeling successful in some roles— especially occupational ones—and insecure in the "real woman" role was common. Christine found that there was only one definition of success that really mattered—and that was her ability to have children: "I was the second highest paid female banking executive in my state. I owned my own home, had beautiful clothes and furniture, I went to exotic places and knew interesting people. Yet it all meant nothing. Every time I saw family, all I'd hear was, 'When are you going to get married and have kids?' Even when I married, I really wasn't accepted as having 'made it' unless I became pregnant."

The tension or distress women experienced over childlessness could not be explained merely by demographic, economic, or historical trends. Women's reproductive roles are political with personal ramifications. Whether she is childless or a mother, a woman's reproductive status impacts the way she is treated by institutions and by others. It also effects how women view themselves. Childless women are still stereotyped as pitiable, full of regret or remorse, and some women do feel sad that they did not have children.[30] Sherri, like other women I interviewed, cried when she shared her stories about how much she wanted children and how hard it was for her to accept that she would never have them. But for every childless woman who grieved, there were others like Monica or Mica who were blatantly ambivalent about children, or women like Nance who had actively sought not to become mothers. "It's hard when you tell somebody that you don't have kids and that's the way you want it," said Nance. "They get this look on their faces like, 'You're so selfish,' or 'Why are you so mean?' I am not selfish, and I'm not mean! I'm not sure I can say the same about them, though. You know, I've had people come out and ask me if I hated kids. I'm childless by choice, but I love kids. I just don't want to have any." This reaction corresponds to stereotypes, which portray childless women as selfish, hard-hearted, or even anti-child.[31] But the childless women I interviewed did not define themselves in this way.

More often, they defined themselves as content with their choice to be childless, even though it was not always an easy decision. "When I tell people I'm glad I don't have kids, they can think I'm selfish or mean if they want, but I do a tremendous amount to make the world a better place, more so than many people with kids," Maura alleged. "It's too hard to be Superwoman and do it all." Janice, who felt conflicted about whether or not to have kids, reflected that "when I was a kid I learned two different messages about being female, and you couldn't have one if you had the other. Like being a good mother meant giving 110 percent of your time and energy, and that motherhood was a woman's ultimate and most fulfilling task. And yet we were encouraged to go to college and pursue a career, and to be independent, liberated women. If you didn't, then you'd bought the status quo and would turn out to be 'just a mother.' But if you were a career woman who didn't have a family, then you were a ball buster, or an empty woman who had nothing except work." Many women were like Maggie, a school administrator, who said, "I don't know if I can do both home and career. I can't be all-nurturing at home and a machine at work. I'm a whole person. I'm a perfectionist, who wants to give whatever I do my all. If I have kids, I know that my kids would have to come first and my job would suffer. If I have a family, I'll never be able to get back into the professional fast track. The professional world simply has no sympathy for sick kids or soccer games. I felt I had to make a choice." And she did. She chose to be childless. She was not alone in her decision.

Today, within certain social sectors, being child-free is in vogue. Organizations such as the National Childfree Association and Childless by Choice provide information to both those who have chosen childlessness and those who are undecided and want more information as to whether to become parents. They enhance awareness of childlessness as a legitimate lifestyle and provide support to those who have no kids. Such organizations were created in response to the discrimination felt by childless people in employment and social situations specifically because they had no children. "It's nice to belong to groups like this because they understand and can support you," a professional woman, Gail, acknowledged. But some childless-by-choice people view children as oppressive, time- and money-sucking obstacles to personal and professional achievement.[32] The focus of this anti-natal view is on the personal empowerment, pleasure, independence, and productivity that may result when one does not have children. The child-free movement has also attracted people who are rabidly anti-child, as shown in a statement by Sylvia: "I can't stand kids and can't stand people who can't talk about anything except kids. I don't want to live near them or sit near them when I go to the restaurant or the movies. And people who plead special privilege at work just because they have kids drive me nuts. Sometimes I want time off too, so why should they get it more than me, just because they chose to have kids?" Sylvia is not alone in her response. There is now a national movement to make employment practices and taxes "equal" for those who do not have children.[33]

But other deliberately childless women such as Josi argued that there is a big difference between being child-free and anti-child: "I know women who have no kids who feel like they're getting a raw deal because the world doesn't put them first. I don't have kids either, but I think that society has to bend to put kids first—I mean, if you don't take care of kids and make sure they get what they need, how can they become productive adults?" This tension between the pro-child and anti-child advocates is part of a growing social trend. Those who believe it is society's obligation to nurture all children debate with those who believe that children are choices and therefore solely a parent's responsibility. There are those who believe that preventing pregnancy is a sin and that motherhood is everyone's business and responsibility. In some areas of the world, not having a child may be the politically correct action and women who have children—especially female children—may be harshly penalized. Having children, or not having them, has become a political as well as a personal issue.

In the last two decades, childlessness has been transformed from what was commonly regarded as "a private trouble" into a "public, social problem."[34] The reasons for this are complex. It used to be that if a woman had difficulty conceiving, it was a private matter between her and her husband, and perhaps her doctor. But today, a highly publicized, multimillion-dollar industry has been developed to assist those with "reproductive failure." Before 1968, the term "childlessness" was listed in the literature only as a cross reference to "sterility."[35] Inability to have children was treated as either a medical or a psychosomatic problem, and the term "infertility" became a dominant entry in the medical literature.[36] But as infertility has grown into a profit-making business, difficulties conceiving have become "hot." Reproductive difficulties have become open topics of conversation, just as the term "infertility" has become a household word and people with the problem are encouraged to "do something about it."[37] Infertility clinics have popped out across the nation. For those who cannot conceive, adopting children has become a fashionable and convenient way to acquire children. There are a variety of private and public clearinghouses and abundant information on how to locate children to adopt.

In addition, there are now more women who have not married or had children but who may have them in the future—or they may not. There are increasing numbers of women who have married and have decided that they do not want to have children. The child-free are members of a large and increasingly vocal group. There are more DINKs, or couples with double income and no kids, who do not want to jeopardize their lifestyle by the expensive proposition of childbearing, and more LINKs, or people with low income and no kids, who feel that they cannot afford to have children.

Being childless is becoming normative. Even national talk-show hosts such as Oprah and Rosie O'Donnell have commented on their own childlessness, and in doing so they have helped put that topic on the table for public discussion. "Almost everyone knows someone who can't have kids," said Nance, a deliberately childless woman. "Today people spill their guts to therapists, to their doctors, to women in their support groups, and even to total strangers or reporters about the intimacies of their ovaries; things that women wouldn't dream about saying in my mother's day, women talk openly about today." Ellie "found it useful to talk with other women who weren't sure whether they wanted to have kids. I'm not sure, and by talking with them it helps me sort through my own position." An infertile woman, Sherri, confessed that "I find comfort in having the opportunity to talk about my experiences and look forward to hearing what other childless women have to say." So did women like Josi, for whom childlessness was a deliberate choice. The childless women I interviewed wanted to know what other women experienced, how they felt, and how they dealt with the flood of emotions and situations associated with not having children.

Although the topics of infertility, reproductive therapies, surrogate mothers, adoption, and childlessness have become popular, childless women themselves are still largely invisible.[38] Even though nonparenthood may be an emerging lifestyle actively selected by some, it is not necessarily understood. Indeed, public attitudes toward childless women are often insensitive, as Abigail, another study participant, learned: "People can be so rude! They'll make nasty comments not just behind my back, but to my face, about my body, my relationships, or how they think my work-life has affected my not having kids—as if they really knew anything about any of them!"[39] Women who choose not to have children are often regarded as selfish, maladjusted, unhappy, hedonistic, irresponsible, immature, abnormal, and unnatural.[40] Despite their increased numbers, they are still seen as sad, unfulfilled, lonely in their old age, or spinsterish: "My roommate, who bent my ear off after her boyfriend dumped her, didn't like the advice I gave her, so she turned to me and blinked, 'Well, at least I'm not going to be an old maid like you are!' I was so hurt, but that's how she saw me— never married, no kids, and living alone for the rest of my life, with just my houseplants," Mica confessed. Such stereotypes may be far from true. In a recent study, however, four hundred undergraduate students were asked to evaluate several types of women: the voluntarily child-free, those with only one child, those with two, and those with eight children. Which group did they evaluate most negatively? Child-free women.[41]

The old stereotypes about childless women do not mesh with the realities of contemporary women, who may have rich social lives, productive careers, leisure time, and discretionary dollars. Yet the stereotype of the pitiable and selfish childless women is hard to erase, even when it is inaccurate. Not surprisingly, although childlessness is a common experience, most women interviewed admitted that they did not talk frequently with others about the causes, or consequences, of it. A childless woman, Irena Klepfisz was one of the first to write

> out of my need to express some of my feelings and conflicts about being a woman who has chosen to remain childless, as well as to break the silence surrounding the general issue of women without children. That the silence has persisted despite the presence of the women's movement is both appalling and enigmatic, since the decision not to have a child shapes both a woman's view of herself and society's view of her. I have read a great deal about woman as mother, but virtually nothing about woman as non-mother, as if her choice should be taken for granted and her life was not an issue. . . . And though I have heard strong support for the right of women to have choices and options, I have not seen any exploration of how the decision to remain childless is to be made, how one is to come to terms with it, how one is to learn to

live with its consequences. I feel very strongly that in celebrating a woman's liberation from compulsory motherhood, we have neither recognized nor dealt with the pain that often accompanies such a decision. I hope to break the silence.[42]

The childless women interviewed were pleased to have the opportunity to share their stories because, as Josi stated, "It's been a long journey for me to come to grips with why I felt the ways I do about not having kids. I wish other women had talked with me, so that I could understand the pros and cons of what I was getting into. Maybe by telling our stories, other people will become wiser, more sensitive to what it means to be childless."

CHAPTER 2 **The Pushes and Pulls of Childlessness**

Picking the wrong lover. Being afraid. Allowing jobs or school to take precedence. Not having enough money. Having a rocky relationship. Having no relationship at all. There is no single reason why women are childless. Every woman I interviewed had her own story to tell, such as Sarah's tale of infertility, Melanie's of a husband who doesn't want kids, Zoe's of being too involved with her career to have time for babies, or Betsy's of never meeting the right guy. Some women, like Maura, actively chose not to have children: "I looked at who I was and who I wanted to be, and I had a life plan that simply didn't include motherhood." The active selection of childlessness as a lifestyle could be as simple as "some of us just never wanted kids," as Sylvia asserted, to very complex reasoning. Maggie admitted that "part of me wanted kids—I'd had a great home life and wanted to pass it on. But there were other parts of me too, parts I didn't feel I could develop or give to others if I decided to have kids. It took me a while to decide what to do. But ultimately, when I looked at it that way, my choice became clear." Natalie acknowledged that "making the choice wasn't easy. I put a great deal of thought into not having kids. I wonder if mothers really thought about their childbearing decisions as much as we child-free types have. Most of the time, women who become mothers don't actively choose to be—it just happens to them." Josi mused, "Getting pregnant without thinking about it is so easy. A moment of passion and wham!—you have to figure out after the fact what you're going to do.

It's not that way for women who've decided not to have kids. We've thought long and hard about it." Among the women in this study, those who purposefully chose to be child-free were more likely than women who had not chosen their childlessness to feel that they had control over their own destiny. They tended to be more confident of themselves and satisfied with their life outcomes.

As the women in this study discussed why they remained childless, common themes emerged. Some women said that they were voluntarily childless, whereas others indicated that they were involuntarily childless in that they felt pushed into their childless state. Most, however, explained that their decision was an outcome of weighing conflicting reasons about why they wanted or did not want children. Reasons for childlessness ranged from children being too much effort— "Kids deserve more than I'm able to give" (Jane), to the preference of an adult lifestyle—"I want to come and go as I please doing the things I enjoy" (Nance). Often relationships were key in women selecting childlessness, either because the relationship was not right—"His temper is a problem, his willingness to be domestic is an annoyance, and I'm not confident I want to have children with someone like him" (Veronica), or because the relationship was very right—"Life together with just the two of us is so wonderful; why would I want to risk it?" (Barbara). Career priority was central to Maggie's decision; she "chose to become a teacher for other people's kiddos instead of filling the school with kids of my own." Rhonda had economic concerns: "it's hard enough for me to survive on my income, much less supporting a family on it." Ability to parent was another consideration, whether for biological reasons like Rose's: "I found out at age fourteen that I'd probably never be able to have children, and decided then that I'd create a good life for myself without them," or for mental health considerations: "I've got no business having kids—I was poorly parented and felt that I wouldn't be a good mother, even if I tried," said Valerie.

Although some women purposefully chose to remain childless, most did not. Strategic choice entails sorting through alternatives and actively deciding which course of action is best. Most women who said they were voluntarily childless actually chose after the fact, when it appeared that having children was not an option for them. "I never said I chose not to have kids until recently," Natalie confessed. "It was only when I realized I never would that I said, 'Oh, I chose not to.'" The notion that choice was not usually proactive but reactive was repeated by other women. "I never really chose to be childless. I let other people and situations make my decision for me. But in doing so, I chose. All the women I know who don't have kids chose, on one level or another," said Amanda. "Everyone chooses," Mica agreed. "Whether you actually say the words or not is irrelevant—it's your behavior that tells the true story. Even infertile women could choose to adopt, use reproductive therapies, or decide they didn't want the childbearing experience. It's just that most of us don't admit we've chosen until down the road when out decisions are staring us in the face." As Amanda and Mica indicate, most childless women made their choices years before on a subconscious level or in a passive way. "I think we'd grown up in a time when we didn't have to make our own decisions," Mica continued. "It was simply easier to let others decide for us, or to let life run its course and sweep us along with it." Kendra, who was ambivalent about whether or not to have children, reflected on "how when I was little, I did what my parents told me to do. Then teachers decided, or I let my friends guide my actions. Later, I let my male friends dictate the nature of my relationships, and essentially that of my life. I don't know why I let them. I think I grew up believing that other people knew more than I did, or that they made better decisions. So while part of me wanted a child, I let other people's agendas speak to that part of me that didn't. The result? I haven't had kids, and I'm torn about it. I didn't know I was choosing, and even today, I don't know which way I should have gone." This theme was repeated over and over. Veronica explained how "I engaged in haphazard decision making because I thought I didn't know what I wanted. Even though I always had boyfriends, I never fell so in love that I wanted to get married. When I finally did fall in love, he didn't want to marry me. I seem to choose people who are unavailable, men who clearly aren't right for me. Circumstances never worked out, and I felt I had all my choices taken away from me. But I now I ask myself, did I subconsciously choose? Was it that I didn't really want

marriage, so I picked nonreceptive partners? By doing so, it took the
heat off of me. As I get older and the patterns kept repeating, I had to
stop and ask myself, 'Why?'" Missy summed up the feelings of many
childless women: "If I'd really wanted a child, I would have found a way.
There are women who've adopted or spent thousands for infertility
treatments, women who've broken off relationships in search of new
ones that could give them family, women who have jumped through
fiery hoops, letting nothing stop them from getting a child. While part
of me wanted a child, I guess I didn't want one badly enough. But I
wasn't able to be straight enough with myself back then to have even
realized that's what I was doing—avoiding having a child."

Although some women actively decided to remain childless and
other women did so subconsciously, others, such as Ellie, decided not
to decide for a while: "I knew I couldn't handle having a child back
then, so I put having a child on hold until I got my life in order. I didn't
expect things would never fall into place to allow me to have a baby."
Most women had not made a conscious decision to remain childless.
Rather, it was an outcome that occurred over time. They viewed their
childlessness as a temporary state in which childbearing was postponed
until a later time when they anticipated that relationships, lives, or
desires would be more conducive to parenthood. Author Rosemarie
Nave-Herz found that "temporary childlessness often coincided with a
traditional view of the mother role and at the same time with strong
work orientations of women. The professional woman and the traditional mother role often seem mutually exclusive. Some couples try to
solve this conflict by postponing having children in the hope of remov-
ing the conflict later. But for other couples this problem will solve itself
involuntarily later when time has run out for them."[1] Women found
their decision to temporarily remain childless to be a perfect solution.
They did not deliberately choose parenthood or childlessness; rather,
they spent years suspended and waiting. "For me and Little Orphan
Annie," mused Lucy, "tomorrow was always a day away." "I just didn't
see how women who work full time, have husbands and kids, and a
home to keep up kept from going out of their minds. There's no balance, no time for yourself or having the luxury of time to do the little

things right," said Claire. "Maybe later in my life, when I'm happily married, and my career is more stable, I thought then I'd have a child." Only she didn't. Allowing time or other people to dictate their life course permitted women to "never have made a decision about having kids" (Jane). Women such as Amanda, Mica, Lucy, and Jane indicated that their choices were made at a level that they themselves weren't aware of until later in life.

Childbearing decisions are complicated. Women have many choices about what they will become, as Sylvia, a deliberately childless woman pointed out: "There's this presumption that you'll be married with kids, that you'll have a career, be a civic activist, and have hobbies. It's all too much! Just because I'm biologically able to have kids doesn't mean that I will or should. Someone once used this analogy—Could I build a house? Sure, but will I choose to do all the things I could do? No! We're always choosing the directions of our lives," she said. Many factors influenced women's decision—or unwillingness to make a conscious decision—about having a child. The women I interviewed women shared common experiences such as relationships, self-defined role prescriptions, biological capability, career demands, financial security, lifestyle, and perceived competence, all of which influenced their desire for a child. Because of these multiple, and sometimes competing, factors, most of the women felt ambivalent, pulled and pushed by different forces that encourage both motherhood and childlessness.

When women are considering whether to have children, "there are forces that pull you toward wanting to be child-free," Natalie explained. "There are things that are so exciting to do, things that are so important, goals you want to accomplish, that you don't have time to think about kids. It's not that you don't want them, because having kids can be a cool thing to do. It's more about being drawn more to other things besides having children. So for me, I was simply drawn more toward other things than having kids." Pulls, then, were forces that encouraged women to engage in meaningful activities that they deemed to be more important and satisfying than motherhood.

Pushes, on the contrary, were factors that discouraged women from having children that they may have wanted. When a woman felt pushed into being childless, she felt that she "didn't have control. The situation dictated what happened to my life." Veronica explained her frustration of being pushed into childlessness: "I always thought I'd be a mom. But first I went to school and then started my career, where there were hurdles to jump before I had the latitude to have children. The relationship I thought was stable turned out not to be, and I didn't want to have a baby alone. By the time I got everything together, my clock had run out and I couldn't get pregnant."

Whereas pulls were positive forces that encouraged women to seek something other than motherhood, pushes were negative forces that dragged women who wanted children into childlessness. Often, it was more the woman's perception of an event than the event itself that determined if it was a push or a pull. Consider the difference between Dawn and Belinda. Dawn's relationship with her partner is all important: "I love him so much that I'd do anything for him. He has children from a previous marriage and doesn't want more. Sure, I'd have liked to have had kids. But I honor and respect his decision. Living with him is so much better than being with anyone else, and we're having so much fun together, why would we want to upset the apple cart by bringing a baby into the equation?" Belinda, however, found that "Carl doesn't want kids and I do. What he wants always seems to come first, and I keep hoping that he'll change his mind and want kids as much as I do. I resent that he's always so careful not to have 'an accident,' as he calls it. We could make such beautiful babies together." In these cases, both women would have liked to have had a child but neither man wanted children. But Belinda resents Carl and mourns not being a mother, whereas Dawn sees her relationship as one of growth and fulfillment. Dawn has experienced her relationship as a pull toward something more important to her than having children, whereas Belinda regards herself as being pushed into childlessness.

Similarly, a job can be perceived as a pull or a push, as exemplified by Del's and Wendy's experiences. Del was excited to work because she "always knew I'd have a profession, that through my work I'd make the world a better place. I don't mind the night meetings and the long days. What I do is worth it. Having a child could be wonderful, no doubt about it. But I'm having a wonderful time building my business. I travel all around the world. We're at a very exciting phase of organizational development, and I wouldn't have the time or the energy to devote to motherhood right now. Whenever I try to cut back on time, my employees call and tell me that they need me, that my vision and skills are critically important." But Wendy felt "angry at work. I thought that when I got a job I'd make enough money to afford having a child. But we never made as much as we thought we would, and car and house and bills just kept piling up, so we never could get ahead. There was this unwritten rule at work that if you had kids, you'd never get promoted. My supervisors, who were always male, ridiculed women when they worried about sick kids, or had to leave early for a kid's dentist appointment. Today they call this the mommy track or the glass ceiling, but when I was trying to decide whether to have kids, they made it pretty clear that I'd never get ahead if I got pregnant." For Del, career was a pull toward a liberating lifestyle of childlessness, whereas for Wendy work was a demanding push that made her unable to have children.

Pulls toward childlessness could be building a career, pursuing an education, maintaining a desired lifestyle, supporting existing relationships, or building dreams. Women who felt pulled toward childlessness talked about their rich and interesting lives: "It's hard to be a mom and spend months sailing for the America's Cup competitions or hiking the Appalachian Trail," said Rose. Women preferred having time to cultivate their own social, physical, cultural, or intellectual pursuits: "Every morning I work out at the gym then I meet friends for lunch. In the afternoons I work at the museum and I'm on several boards of directors. When I get a free evening, I want to curl up with a good book and a glass of wine. Now where in all that would a child fit in?" Layne asked. Natalie felt that "there are so many wonderful and exciting things to do, sure bets. It isn't that having kids wouldn't be fun, because they could be. But they might not be. And there are so many other things I like to do that I know will be rewarding. I guess I've chosen the other things, not because I want kids less, but because I want other things more." Natalie and Rose confirm that lives of childless women can be fascinating and wonderful. They saw themselves as making personal investments for not only their future but also the future of their friends, families, organizations, and communities.

Whereas relationships and occupations sometimes discouraged women I interviewed from wanting a child, so too could a woman's perception of her ability to mother. Women who grew up in families in which there was conflict, abuse, alcoholism, or other types of dysfunction tended to feel that they might be inadequate parents themselves; family dysfunction, therefore, was regarded as a push factor in the creation of childlessness. Like Jane, some women wanted children but felt they should not have them: "My dad was sexually abused by his father and my mom's mom was emotionally abusive. As a result, my folks couldn't relate to us kids at all. Mom had lots of anger and was physically vicious to my brother. I was afraid I could be violent to children and I wouldn't be a good parent. Child abuse is part of my past, and I wouldn't want to inflict it upon other children. I'm not patient and don't want to raise a child to have the same feelings I had as a child."

Another commonly cited reason that pushed these women into childlessness was a genetic, biological factor or health problems. Dawn found that her diabetes made it difficult for her to become pregnant, Grace had uterine cancer that had resulted in a hysterectomy, Inez was born with a chromosomal disorder she feared would be passed on to her offspring, and Sarah had endometriosis. As a result of their conditions, they became infertile, unable to bear children they had dreamed about having. "It's unbelievably difficult to be at war with your body, wanting children and finding that it won't let you," Dawn admitted. On the other hand, some women found that their bodies worked fine but that their husband's did not. Olivia miscarried several times, perhaps because her husband "was exposed to massive amounts of Agent Orange when he was a solider in Vietnam. Everyone from his battalion has deformed children. I'm sure that has a lot to do with us not having kids."

The ultimate push into childlessness was the loss of a child. Joanna talked about her miscarriage: "We were so excited about having the baby. But the pregnancy wasn't proceeding right, and I stayed in bed for weeks, trying to buy time to get the baby bigger so maybe I wouldn't lose it. But I miscarried anyway." Sherri had several miscarriages "and figured out that my body wasn't ever going to let me carry a child to term." In some cases, women like Anne bore children only to have them die in her arms shortly after birth. "We'd prepared the nursery but my sons died before we were able to take them home." The emotional difficulties they experienced as a result made this form of childlessness "the most difficult of all."

It seemed that the women who chose to remain childless were the most satisfied with their lives, whereas the women who were pushed into childlessness were the least satisfied with theirs. Even though all women experienced pushes and pulls toward childlessness, most were childless because they "were just too damned ambivalent about having kids to decide one way or the other" (Missy). Their ambivalence showed up as doubt, hesitancy, indecision, or uncertainty about what course of action to pursue. In my interviews with these women, they discussed their mixed feelings, their vacillating emotions: sometimes they really wanted a child, sometimes they definitely did not, and sometimes they didn't care one way or another. Because their emotions were so complex and often contradictory, deciding whether to have children was difficult. Letting nature take its course was easier. "Ambivalence is about wanting kids and not wanting them. Ambivalence is about wanting a career and wanting to stay home. Ambivalence is wanting both a rich family life and a full career life. Ambivalence exists because neither home nor the career would feel entirely comfortable," according to Mica. Ambivalent women tended to be reactive rather than proactive. They were more likely to make decisions about childbearing on a subconscious level, decisions that resulted in "accidentally" becoming pregnant or in remaining childless even though they said they wanted to have children.

"I don't think we even knew that we were ambivalent. Feeling conflicting emotions was part of our female experience. We didn't know how to talk with one another about contradictory feelings," Nicole reflected. Because, in the interviews, women were not disclosive about ambivalent feelings, the "maybe of having a baby" was an unexpectedly difficult topic to discuss. Ellie, as she completed her master's degree, confessed that "I can't talk about it sensibly. Part of me wants to go with my boyfriend and get married and have babies as soon as I can. It doesn't matter if I complete my degree or work in a high-power job. The other part of me doesn't want to be dependent on any man. I want a career and life that's all mine. Children would get in the way of that. So I don't know what I really want, or what I should do. And nobody can tell me what will be the right thing."

Little information is available about the ambivalent experiences of childless women.[2] Yet "ambivalence was a major part of my experience," said Ramona, and it seems that ambivalence around the issue of motherhood is nothing new. When the authors of the book *Why Children?* explored the personal experiences of both mothers and non-mothers, they found that ambivalence creeps into the lives of all women—especially those who want kids but cannot have them.[3]

Many of the women I interviewed experienced multiple pushes and pulls toward childlessness. Usually there was not just one single reason for her decision. Because multiple factors intertwined, "I weighed the pros and cons. I looked at the reasons why I wanted kids and the reasons I didn't. I tried to decide which was most important," reflected Sonya. They weighed each of the factors that made them lean toward, or against, motherhood. "Some reasons were clearly more important to me than others. For instance, I felt I could manage my job situation, but I wasn't sure of my relationship. These were the two most important factors for me. While I had other considerations, like my social life and my family, it really came down to these two," Veronica observed. "For me, it wasn't my job or relationship, but my freedom, my lifestyle," stated Janice. What one woman saw as important, another may not have—but every woman had priorities that influenced her desire for childbearing.

Often a woman decided on temporary childlessness as a way of juggling the multiple pull or push factors. This is shown in Deborah's statement: "I'm in medical school and there's not enough hours in the day. There's so much to learn and do at this stage in my life. I feel like a sponge, soaking up gallons of information. Maybe I'll reach a point of saturation, but it hasn't happened yet. Whatever time I have left, I want to spend it with my friends, and maybe have a little quiet time for myself." Deborah wondered if she would be interested in motherhood after she graduated and got a job. "Time will tell," she mused.

Even after women decided, their decisions were not final, not writ in stone. Some women make their childbearing decision over and over. Each relationship, each sexual encounter, each day, women must negotiate, even wrestle with themselves about whether this is the time they may become pregnant.[4] Only as time has passed can they look at the sum of their choices and make sense of their decisions. Until that day comes, it is often easier to be swept along by life events or unconscious psychological motivations that make childlessness permanent.

Whether women actively or passively choose to remain childless has both social and psychological repercussions. Women such as Maggie who purposefully chose to remain childless felt more control over their lives than did women such as Veronica, who felt "hung out to dry" by her failed relationships, or Iris, who felt "cheated by my biology." Choice appears to have been a critically important factor in their mental and social well-being, and the importance of active decision making seems to have been a lifelong insulator against distress. "While I've never tested my ability to conceive, I believe I could. I've chosen to be childless. Unlike my friend who's infertile, I think it's easier for me because I believe I have choices. Our outcome may be the same—being women without children—but I'm in control of the situation and she feels she isn't," reflected Josi.

The capacity to choose, to sort through life alternatives and decide which course of action is best, impacts self-esteem. Those who were able to chose childlessness indicated that they were happier and more satisfied than were women who had childlessness imposed on them by physical problems, partner problems, or their biological clock.[5] Women who were childless by default or "circumstances beyond my control" experienced more sadness or remorse about not having children. Generally, they were "resentful" about situations that had made childbearing unlikely—a result that confirms the findings reported elsewhere in the literature, in which involuntarily childless women reported lower levels of life satisfaction and well-being, and rated life as less interesting, emptier, and less rewarding than did women with children.[6]

Whether women actively chose to be childless, passively allowed events or their subconscious to dictate their childbearing, or justified their childlessness as temporary, the physical outcome was the same— they all remained women without children. But the events that led up to their decisions were complicated. Family interactions, biological ability, psychological desire for a child, partnership decisions, work decisions, and other factors all played roles in the creation of their childlessness. Conversely, in this synergistic relationship, all these parts of a woman's life were influenced by her not having children.

CHAPTER 3   Impact of Body, Mind, and Family Interactions

Biology dictates that females are potential baby makers. Although most women will become pregnant at some point during their life, they spend most of their reproductive years trying to avoid pregnancy.[1] Assuming a woman reaches puberty at age fifteen and menopause at age forty-five, she will have thirty years of childbearing possibility. Multiply those years by thirteen menstrual cycles per year and a typical woman confronts at least 390 ovulation periods during which pregnancy could occur. If women began having babies soon after they began their menses and continued until they reached menopause, they could reach the average fecundity rate of twenty children each.[2] Most women, however, decide to limit their childbearing potential and are purposefully childless for large portions of their lives.

For women, the question of whether or not to have children cannot be easily dismissed because the potential for motherhood is not only in their bodies but also in their psyches.[3] Most women anticipate having children, want to, and do. But physical ability does not necessarily dictate emotional desire for a child. Certainly many females cannot wait to get pregnant; as Brenda stated: "All I ever wanted was to have kids. Even when I was just a little girl, I couldn't wait to have babies of my own." Yet other women, like Sylvia, "never really wanted kids—I don't know why, I just was never interested in them." The women I interviewed asked, "Is there such a thing as a maternal instinct that drives us to want children?" Both researchers and childless women agree—some are convinced there is a maternal instinct, some think there is not, and most just aren't sure.

Some women in the study were convinced that maternal instinct was real, because they had experienced a "burning drive to have children, to hold them, care for them, and love them more than I love myself," as Catherine said. Some described how their maternal instinct occurred slowly across time as hormones surged in their bodies. "I was a real tomboy," said Lucy. "I was better at most things than the boys. Then I hit puberty. Guys started looking at me, and I started to view myself differently too. I never thought about wanting kids, then Boom! Suddenly, I knew one day I had to have them." Others, like Brenda, reflected on how "I'd always wanted children. Ever since I was a little girl, I knew that being a mom was right for me." Women such as Mary talked about a desire for a child that was so great it seemed to "burn" inside. She said, "having a child is part of what it meant for me to be fulfilled. I desperately needed a child. It didn't matter how I got a child. I must have one. My husband didn't understand why I didn't feel we, as a couple, weren't a family." Betsy said, "I know there are social reasons for wanting kids. But what I felt was much more than social pressure to conform. I really wanted a child. It was gut level, a raw, animal instinct, primal feeling." Evie felt that the maternal instinct was a natural reaction not just within people but also within animals: "It's a natural instinct among all living things to want children. When I was a child, my cat Charlie, or Charlene, as we found out later, had a litter of kittens. My parents insisted we couldn't keep the kittens, so they found a woman who'd take them to the country to be farm cats. The day she came to get the kittens was terrible. As we talked with the farmer, Charlie kept trying to pick up the kittens by the neck to hide them, as if she knew what was going to happen." Evie continued: "Charlie sat on the back of the couch and watched out the window as the farmer drove down the street. She cried all night, and paced through the house, looking for her kittens. The next morning my dad went out to get the paper and saw Charlie lying in the middle of the road, dead. She got out of the house and ran in the direction of the car that carried away her kittens. She lay there on the yellow line of the road, the victim of a hit-and-run—or was she the victim of a broken heart from having her babies taken away? Who says there's no maternal, protective instinct?"

Other women such as Jennifer and Natalie argued that a desire for children is created from social expectation and that it is not an innate drive. Jennifer never desired a child: "I never had a time when I said, wow, I have to get pregnant, this is the right time. Perhaps I was too rational for that kind of thought, maybe I never really wanted kids enough, maybe I have low hormones or something." She reflected on "the expectation we'd all marry and have kids. It seemed natural—but I had no drive to do it." Natalie wondered if there was something genetic that prevented the women in her family from wanting to be mothers: "I don't think my mom really wanted kids, and none of my sisters or I had any. Maybe there's something in our biology that makes us not want kids. Maybe we don't have the right hormones for the mom stuff." The relationship between childbearing and hormones was frequently discussed by women as an explanation for why some wanted children and others did not. Maura believed that "while some women really get into this baby thing, I never wanted to get pregnant or go through all that baby stuff. I didn't like the idea of my body swelling up like a balloon, the notion of a baby sucking on me all the time was disgusting, and always having to be 'on duty' didn't ring any chimes for me. But my friend, Lou, loves that stuff." Nance never felt the drive for a child either: "I cannot imagine wanting to be a mom—even my own mom wasn't really into it. I think being a mother is a terribly important thing to do, but it doesn't mean we all should do it. There's a bunch of other things that are important too, you know." For some lesbian women, relationships—not motherhood—were often of paramount importance. Karen explained that "I've known ever since I was little that being married and having kids wasn't for me. Those things are great for women who want them. I don't. I want other things from life, and that's okay." But other lesbian women such as Martha felt that "I have strong maternal instincts. I really, really want kids."

Some scholars claim that there is no such phenomenon as maternal instinct.[4] Rather, they view it as a notion created and perpetuated to keep women powerless by being absorbed with childbearing and

child care. Women's desire for children is cultural, learned, and reinforced, not programmed into them on a cellular, instinctual level,
according to some theorists.[5] "Maternal instinct? We have no evidence
of it," says author Nancy Friday; "women want to become mothers for
lots of reasons; it's part of their biological condition, having the equipment for it, one of the things being a woman is about, but I would not
call this instinct. There are also social expectations. All her life a woman
has been expected to marry and have babies—it's been drummed into
her all along so that her whole orientation is geared toward these
expectations. But this is not 'maternal instinct.'"[6]

Others argue that the desire for a child is time related, having to do
with either hormonal balances or social timing. "My answer about
whether I want kids or not depends on the time of the month, or what
phase of life I'm going through," reflected Mica. "There are times I
want a baby so much I think I'll die, and other days I think I'd die if I
had one! I guess my hormones have calmed down because while I still
long for a child, it's no longer a cellular scream for one." Allison confessed, "I burned inside for kids. During ovulation I'd get extra hot. I
sizzled inside and knew the time was right to put a bun in the oven. Men
would tell me that they could look at me and tell when I was ovulating.
But for whatever reason, I didn't get pregnant. I ached inside for so long.
Then one day, I realized that I hadn't thought about having a baby in
ages. It was as if someone had turned down the fire. There are still
moments when I see babies and think, aw, wouldn't it be nice to have
one, but the period of absolute drive seems to be over. Now that my
clock has about run out, I don't yearn for a child much. I know now that
what I feel is emotional. But back then, ooooh, it was hormonal, biological. The urge was absolutely, positively real and intense." Whether
women found the desire for a child to be socially or hormonally
induced, they all talked about times when they really wanted children
and times when they didn't. Louis Davitz concluded from interviews
for his book *Baby Hunger* that all women, at one point in their lives,
experience an "instinctual, overpowering drive," a "baby hunger," to get
pregnant.[7] A businesswoman, Catherine, agreed; she had "had a true
physical ache, a sense of incompleteness, not necessarily to be pregnant,

but to have a child." But her husband did not want a child. "I felt like I let him down—when we married we'd agreed that we didn't want kids. I didn't then, but later I changed my mind. Being around people who had children was tough! All I wanted to do was sit and hold their babies. Friends with older children didn't bother me so much—older kids can be a real pain. It wasn't having kids that drove me wild—it was having babies." Iris also felt that the maternal instinct was real, but time limited: "It all feels so far away now that I'm too old to have kids, but back then it was so hard. I went crazy when I saw babies. The biological clock is real, and it hit me between the time I was thirty-five and forty. It hurt so bad, I contemplated how to steal a child. I know it was a primitive notion, to steal a baby. But I thought about it." This urge to have children may decline over time, but women such as Angela described how her interest in having children resurfaced during menopause. "I really wanted kids in my thirties, when the rest of my friends were having babies. By the time we got in our forties, I didn't seem to care since my friends were going through the adolescent rebellion phase. But when I became menopausal, I found this absolute crazy, nesting instinct. I wanted a baby so bad I thought I'd die. These feelings would fade in their intensity, then come sweeping over me again, and then subside. I believe in hormones and the maternal drive thing. I was there."

Yet other women were convinced that desire for a child was more psychological than biological. "Having a child is a symbol that conveys a certain status for woman. I realized I'm more in love with the idea of having a baby than actually having one," Sonya confessed. "I dream a lot about being pregnant. I think about shopping and wearing maternity clothes and having people come up and ask me about the baby that I'll have. I imagine what the nursery will look like. I fantasize moments with my husband looking adoringly at me. But I don't think about the baby crying and the demands and being sleepless and tired. I think about pregnancy and delivery and bringing the tyke home to roses and stuffed rabbits. After that, my fantasy ends," she said. The notion that pregnancy confers attention, encourages dreams, and provides social reward is not unusual.[8] "People open doors for my pregnant cousin, let her sit in their seats on the subway, and people she doesn't even know smile these knowing smiles at her. Me? I don't get that treatment," Heather, a deliberately childless woman, observed.

Although scholars have tried to disentangle the culturally conditioned desires for motherhood from biological desires, they have reached no concrete conclusions.[9] They have not proven that a maternal instinct exists, but neither have they found it to be a myth. There is no clear answer to this question among experts or among those women I interviewed. However, lack of definitive proof one way or the other has not swayed those who are sure it exists or those who are positive it is a social and mental construct.

What is certain is that the desire for a child is influenced by cultural considerations, psychological factors, and family relationships. Tashi and Julie talked about the importance their cultures placed on childbearing, which they identified as pressure that made it harder for them to remain childless. "In my black community, it's common for women to have children when they're young. Homes may be filled with generations of children, with grandchildren and nephews and cousins playing with each other. I've found it difficult not to have children, when the expectation is so high for that to be the norm," Tashi said. Julie, a Latina, explained that in her culture, children were adored, "which makes me feel extra sad that I don't have kids. Not having kids may be an issue for me, but my decision impacts the whole family, my whole culture." Rebecca, a Jewish woman who was childless because she could not find a mate, claimed that "so many of my people were exterminated in the Holocaust that I feel a sense of obligation to have children to carry on our wonderful heritage."

Cultural forces shape personalities, attitudes, and beliefs about childbearing and reproductive behaviors. "I was taught that girls were supposed to have kids when they grew up," said Sherri. Because the expectation of motherhood was ingrained in their experiences, women such as Iris, who were not deliberately childless, felt "a species apart, invisible and pitied among a cohort of women who all seem to have children except me. I feel totally outside of their experience. I've missed something about my own femininity, about my own personhood." Melinda said, "I feel like women who have kids have learned something about themselves that I'll never know. I can't know what it feels like—the physical and emotional sensations are beyond my comprehension. I do try to appreciate it, but I can't really understand their experience any more than they can understand mine."

Developmental psychologists point out that women's psyches are influenced by the motherhood messages they received as children. The psychoanalytic view holds that women model their mother's good (or poor) behaviors and incorporate them into their own personas. Rejection of having children could be a manifestation of women rejecting their mothers, who they perceive as having rejected them long ago. Author Nancy Chodorow alleges that the mother–daughter relationship shapes the female psyche and that women mother because of this psychological character formation.[10] Another model suggests that interaction with children can provide adults with a vehicle to heal unresolved issues of their own childhood. Pediatrician and child abuse expert Ray Helfer hypothesizes that children go through a series of key developmental stages and that if they are unable to pass through these stages successfully during childhood, as adults they have a second chance to do so through their children. He believes this is one reason why adults long to have children.[11]

The notion that women will have scarred psyches if they do not have children was not substantiated in my interviews with childless women. Although Melinda and Sherri were socialized into wanting children, Del was not: "When I was a child, my parents ran with the elites of the nation. My mother was a magazine fashion editor who was on the President's Council for the Arts. My father was an attorney. They traveled around the world. They enjoyed their work far more than they enjoyed parenthood. I became exactly what they groomed me to be—a strong, savvy, international professional." Maura, a deliberately childless woman who is a leader of her community, never cared about dolls and was always more interested in her father's work. "He'd take me with him and I learned how to make things with my hands and believed I had the power to do anything I wanted." Women such as Melinda and Del may have been exposed to the same cultural messages about the role of women, work, and motherhood, but their individual experiences were different. Their dreams for their futures and the meaning of children within their psyches varied. Why? They both attributed their interest in having children to messages they had learned years before from their families.

Scholars refer to this process as the reproduction of mothering. Experts studying mother–daughter relationships suggest that daughters learn attitudes, beliefs, and practices that are similar to those of their mothers and that an intergenerational transmission of gender attitudes occurs.[12] Among the women I interviewed, some were unable to articulate why they didn't want children, but on a subconscious level their childbearing decisions had been made years before. Ellie, a woman who never had children "because I was so ambivalent," recalled that "In subtle ways my mother passed on to me all of herself. She liked her job, but she also liked to be home, cooking and making things. I know she loved us, but sometimes I wonder if she wished she'd never had us. She'd lose her temper or closet herself away for long stretches of time. She knew she wasn't the world's best mother. It seemed like she found ways to be away from us when she could. Yet, I think she felt that being a good mother was the most important thing a woman could do. She would tell me over and over, 'Do as I say, don't do as I do.'"

Many of the women in my study believed that the childbearing messages they received as girls took on new meaning as they matured into women. Messages girls heard on television, read in newspapers and magazines, and learned from their peers and teachers were filtered through the lens of what they saw in their own homes. There, they learned firsthand about motherhood and domestic life. Although confronted with many possibilities to pursue in life, "it was what I learned at home that helped me interpret everything else I heard out there in the real world. At home, I saw how things were. I used my family's experiences as a barometer to compare everything else about becoming a woman. The things that jived, I kept. The things that didn't jive, or that made me feel uncomfortable, were things I decided I should change," said Mary.

Often women described mothers who were the interpreter for both social events and home situations. "My Dad shaped my reality some, but it was really my Mom who made me see the world in a particular way. She was with me more of the time, and in some bio-rhythmic way, what she experienced resonated inside me in a way that I truly cannot explain," said Stephanie. As they considered whether to become mothers themselves, women evaluated themselves, the way they were mothered, and their mothers as well.

Mothers, like Lucy's, who were satisfied with their lives wanted "us to join the motherhood club," Lucy said. Families put both direct and subtle pressure on women to have children. Direct pressure was described by Sherri, whose parents regularly asked, "Are you pregnant yet? When are you going quit fooling around and have a baby?" This type of direct confrontation was different from the more veiled attempts to manipulate daughters' behavior. Elise, a college professor, recalled her mother's subtle attempts to encourage her to have children: "My mother bought this lovely child's chair and gave it to me. She knew we weren't planning to have any, but she bought it anyway, as if she were sure that eventually I'd have kids." Women like Layne found that parents had difficulty accepting and respecting their choices about not having children: "They blamed my job, they blamed my husband, they blamed me for being irresponsible and selfish for not having children. It got so bad that I avoided seeing my folks. It was easier that way."

Mothers who were not satisfied with their own lives conveyed messages to their daughters that indicated they were burdens. "My parents made it very clear—they had better things to do than dote on kids," said Del. "They seldom played with me and did normal parent things, but then again, they weren't your normal parents." Heather said, "I know I picked up messages that said my life would be better off if I didn't have kids. But that seemed like such a taboo thing to think that I couldn't have admitted it to myself, any more than my mother could have admitted those secret feelings to herself."

Heather's experiences were not uncommon. In her classic book on mother–daughter relationships, *My Mother, Myself,* Nancy Friday states: "I have always lied to my mother. And she to me. Her denial of whatever she could not tell me, that her mother could not tell her, and about which society enjoined us both to keep silent, distorts our relationship still."[13] Friday's book explores the complex attitudes, behavior, and deepest, often unconscious feelings that mothers pass on to their daughters. "We want to believe that everything our mothers did for us and gave us was out of love," she alleges. Yet "often it is not love, but possessiveness, anxiety, and outright rejection that is expressed. We cannot afford to believe this on a cognitive level, but way down deep we feel it." In this reproduction of mothering view, women learn ways of intimacy and communication from mothers and automatically repeat the pattern with everyone else with whom they become close. Either women play out the role of the child and make other people into mother figures, or the reverse, playing mother to other children. All too often how women interact with others reflects old, unhealed hurts and rejections they experienced with their mothers.

Women such as Allison, who had abusive parents, "refuse to bring innocent little angels into the world to be hurt like I was." Among the women I studied, those who were daughters of cool and aloof parents were much less likely to want children than did women who had emotionally warm parents. Elise said that her mother "thought she was more nurturing than she actually was." "I never got hugged," Sue stated. "I don't remember ever being told 'I love you,'" said Meredith. "Yet I'm sure she loved me." Nance explained that "My mom was totally removed from her own feelings. She'd tell me 'don't cry,' 'don't be depressed.' These were signs of weakness. I called her Attila the Hun." Although Nance didn't want to become stoic like her mother, "I felt uncomfortable with the notion of becoming a mom." "I still feel uncomfortable showing others I care for them. I'm certain this is because of what I learned from my parents about how they felt toward us kids," said Samara. "We were not from that huggy-kissy crowd." Childless women told stories about how their mothers took care of basic needs—cooked hot dinners, sewed clothes, packed school lunches, and supervised them to assure safety—but they were mothers who were "unable to be enthusiastically physically or verbally loving" to their daughters. This "impacted my feelings about my competence to be a mom," Julie explained.

"Maybe my mom didn't know how to mother," Darlene observed. "Grandma died when Mom was nine, so she was deprived of the normal good mother role model. She wasn't well parented, so it's no surprise she couldn't give me the kind of parenting I now think I should have had." Olivia, who was in the middle of a six-sibling string, had been sent to boarding school and seldom saw her parents. "Mother was not an especially warm woman—she loved us but didn't spend much time parenting us in the traditional sense. But I try to explain this to myself by the fact that many parents of means during that time period thought they were doing their children a favor by sending them abroad to go to school." Valerie's mother was one of twelve Depression-era children in a family that found it difficult to make ends meet. As a result, "material comforts became critically important to Mom. Her desire for comfort even overrode the desire for her own family. I was an only child who always came second to Mom's painting the house, working in the yard, or having tea. I wasn't exactly a neglected child, but it was a foreign experience for me to see mothers drop everything to nurture their children. I never had the ideal mother figure to aspire toward. I can't relate to people who talk about their 'wonderful mom.' It's an alien thing to me."

It was also difficult for women to imagine living the same kind of gendered lives as their mothers. "Mom was a sales clerk and loved it, but when Dad came back from World War II, he made her quit. He felt that if she worked then he wasn't a good enough provider. When she wanted to nurse her kids and Dad was disgusted by it, she didn't. Over time, she lost her own sense of identity and became an extension of his. He was a nice guy and all—the issue is, she quit being her and turned into being who he wanted her to be," said Evie. "If becoming a wife and mother meant that, why would anyone want to become one?"

It is not surprising that women in the study reported that as daughters they had received from their mothers conflicted messages about motherhood. Mothers of the women born in the 1940s and 1950s were caught in the midst of social change, and they were confronted with contradictory messages about work and home life.[14] "So if my mom was confused by who she was supposed to be, think about what that did to my head," said Audrey. "She'd say one thing, and then a minute later say something that seemed totally contradictory—but to her, I guess it wasn't." Those confused messages impacted her as an adult "who has real mixed feelings about having kids." Contradictions about what women were supposed to be like were so prevalent that "we took them for granted without even thinking about them," Janice recalled. "My sister always assured me that I would be a mom, but you know, I never felt it. Even when we played dolls, we played Barbie dolls. I loved my Barbie and wanted to be like her, but Barbie never had kids! Look at her outfits, and the related Mattel dolls. Barbie could be a flight attendant or a cook or a babysitter or a doctor, but there was no 'Maternity Barbie.' She hung out with Ken and Midge and a bunch of other girls, and there were kid dolls now and then—but they were never Barbie's babies. I guess I did turn out like her, after all, eh?"

How mothers felt about having a career influenced their daughters' attitudes toward work. Maggie, who watched her mother assume the breadwinner role after her father died, chose career over children. So did Olivia, whose aunt "gave me a piece of advice when I was a young girl—she told me I should always be able to support a child by myself if I had one, because you never know what's going to happen. If you can't, you don't have any business having one at all." Sarah too experienced such contradictions—her mother was a nurse who quit her job to raise children. Her father had a Ph.D., and "it was a given that I'd go to college. But how to put the two together was confusing. I couldn't be a mom without being a nurse, because kids always have skinned knees, measles, and colds. Moms had to be nurses—but nurses who stayed home!" Jennifer's mom had a doctorate "but did nothing with it when we were little, and later had a part-time job—but never a career." Their experiences were unlike those of Mary Margaret, whose mother indicated "that motherhood was the most important role, since you could play God and mold the future," or of Jennifer, whose mother chose home over career.

Women "knew how I was supposed to answer the question, 'What will you be when you grow up?' We could say anything, but in that list we'd better have being a wife and mother," Audrey said. Their own mothers had minimal choices. Childless women grew up "envisioning ourselves as mothers, but as something else too," said Layne. Women like her, who felt pulled toward careers, had learned that "women were competent and should be treated as equals. There's no reason why we shouldn't be successful in the workforce." They learned that they should get equal pay for equal work. They learned this message at home, either directly by parents' words or indirectly through their treatment of their children. Consider how Elise's parents fostered her sense of competence and independence: "I am the oldest of three kids, and even though my parents didn't have explicit understanding of gender equality, my brothers and I were all treated equally. Mom was obsessed with equal treatment—for her it was not a gender issue, it one of fairness. This was born out of my mom's own experience. Material resources must be equal for all of us. We all had household responsibilities—vacuuming, dishes. Mom was really into cleanliness, and every day the house cleaning was done. We all learned to share responsibilities and to be self-sufficient. I was expected to do well in school and go to college. At an implicit level, this laid a foundation of equality. I never expected to be treated other than fairly. There was no pressure from my parents to get married and have kids," she recalled. When Catherine was young, she picked up the normal role prescription for females and "played dolls, had pets, and assumed I'd grow up to be married with children." Her mother worked full time as a secretary; she had four aunts who never married but who always worked, and "they were interesting women with fascinating lives as professionals—and they traveled. None of the mothers I knew did that."

A few women recalled mothers who weren't employed but who didn't enjoy being parents. "Mom didn't work, but she wasn't into being a mom, either," said Ramona. Ellie had "a stay-at-home mom while my dad was a corporate executive. The house was always spotless because the maid came in a couple of times a week. My mom didn't do much around the house, and yet she didn't do much in the community. I didn't realize at that time that she was an alcoholic. My dad did many more interesting things with his life, and he seemed like a happier person. So I always knew I would go to college and work." The message these women learned was that adult life consisted of motherhood or work, not motherhood and work.

"I grew up believing that women had choices about having kids, but not about working," Nance said. "We learned that work was what women did, whether they were paid or not." Success need not be found in the workplace—it could easily be recognized over the kitchen table. "My mom was always working," Nance continued. "She was up before I awoke and working after I went to sleep. She cooked, cleaned, sewed, did yard work, and helped my dad. I always learned that women worked." Maggie "had a wonderful childhood, full of love from powerful women. Both my mother and grandmother worked, and they gave me everything materially and emotionally I needed. It was the women in my family who held everything together." Maggie "saw how hard my mother worked to take care of us, and I respect her so much for it. I grew up knowing that I would do important work because that's what women do." Marilyn recalled how her mother, an administrator of a national corporation, "was admired for her work. Even when she wasn't home—which was most the time—I still had a sense that what she was doing was very important, and it was my job to understand that and do important things when I grew up." She observed that "my friends never felt that way about their moms or themselves. So if I had to pick one or the other, a career looked more appealing than having kids."

It was important for these women to have personal control over the trajectory of their lives. Studies indicate that children of working women do well in all aspects of life, mainly because of the positive influences associated with their mothers' working.[15] Women such as Karen who had learned to "take charge of my life and chart my own course" were more satisfied with their decision to be childless than were women such as Sonya, who "was never allowed to make decisions. My parents made them for me, I was always told what to do." When women were encouraged to make their own decisions, they developed a level of self-confidence in their choices that women who were more ambivalent about their childlessness did not have.

Women influenced by the 1950s images of motherhood were both critical and apologetic of their own mothers. "Sometimes I was so hurt by my mother that I think subconsciously I rejected the entire idea of being a mom. But then I had to stop myself and become more sympathetic to why she behaved as she did. She was caught, too. I don't want to throw out the good things about being a mom just because certain parts of it made me uncomfortable," said Mica. The split between what mothers said and did often left daughters unsure of themselves. Ramona confessed that "It was a bittersweet revelation when I came to the conclusion that on the one hand, I could take comfort in realizing that my ambivalent feelings about being a mother came from messages I picked up from my own mom. It was sort of a bonding moment. On the other hand, it was disconcerting to think that my mom may not have really wanted us." Lana is sure that "My mother loved me, but I don't think she liked being a mother, even though she made sure I had nice clothes, ballet lessons, rides home from school, sleepovers with friends, and the like. She always had a drink in a highball glass on the kitchen cabinet. I don't think I understood how unhappy she was until the day she was found dead. She committed suicide. I've never wanted kids and can't seem to hold together any sort of significant relationship. I'm cool and unemotional—a lot like my mother was." Belinda, a deliberately childless woman, explained that "while my mom said, 'why, you know that I love you,' her behavior said otherwise. She never held me, and never sat and really talked with me. Everything is so businesslike, and I always have to have a product she likes. She won't let me be me. Sometimes I think I must be just like her, and I can't stand it."

Desire for a child or desire to be childless, then, seems influenced by a complex series of factors that include biological influences, psychological predispositions, and messages learned from parents and society. Many women accepted messages to conform, such as "Our parents are our models. They married; we marry. They had children; we have children." Others did not accept those messages. They deliberately chose not to have children. But there are other factors as well, such as relationships, economics, and infertility, that affected whether or not the women in this study remained childless.

CHAPTER 4   **Consequences of Partnerships**

Most women I interviewed for this study said they were childless not by choice but by chance. This was particularly true for those who attributed their childlessness to dynamics in their relationships. Partners both directly and indirectly influenced women's childbearing decisions. They did so directly by their availability and willingness to become parents. Without an available, willing partner, "it's hard to get pregnant," as Deborah pointed out. Partners indirectly influenced women's childbearing decisions by sending subtle messages that bearing children together might be risky or problematic. Women such as Lucy described how these messages were often the determining factor in deciding whether to have kids: "It wasn't as much what he said as how he said it. It was the under-the-surface meanings that I felt but couldn't quite get a grasp on, that made me uncertain if I wanted to have kids with him." Karen had a similar experience with her female partner: "I think she'd go along with having kids if I pressed, but I don't think she really wants them, and if she doesn't, having kids together may be a source of trouble down the road instead of joy."

Deborah felt what demographers know to be fact: "There simply aren't enough men to go around for the numbers of us available women." Also, there has been a decline in marriage rates in recent decades—the percentage of people who never marry has grown, whereas those who do marry tend to marry at older ages.[1] As a result, more women remain single throughout their lives, making motherhood less likely.[2] For many, the demographics are frustrating. "I've looked for men I'd want to make a family with, and let me tell you, they're few and far between. The good ones already seem to be taken," lamented Jennifer. Ahanna, an African American woman in the study, explained that "It's even harder in my community to find a suitable mate. There's a shortage of economically stable men, which is especially detrimental to the marriage prospects of highly educated Black women like me."[3] Rebecca, another interviewee, wanted "to marry a nice Jewish man. As I get older, the odds of finding someone who I want to have a family with get worse," she sighed. Like the heterosexual women I talked with, lesbian women often had difficulty finding a partner who wanted kids, as Rose found out. Rose "came from a large, loving family and I always envisioned that I'd have kids. But it's not easy to find a partner who wants them as much as I do." This kind of experience, of being ready, willing, and able to build a family and not being able to find a suitable partner, was common among the women I interviewed. Desiring children could be a liability to finding a partner, as women such as Allison learned. Allison "used to have a list of qualifications for an ideal beau, what job he'd have, what he'd look like, what kinds of hobbies he'd do, and ultimately, what kind of daddy he'd be. Through the years, my list has gotten very short. I just want a nice, clean man who'll love me. I basically will take a breather," she said with chagrin. Indeed, these women wanted partners, but they had to be "more than a sperm bank. I want a 24–7 partner," Wendy asserted. She did not perceive "beer-swilling, couch potatoes who have the insight and sensitivity of a rock" as desirable partners. "What kind of father would he be? I'd rather be alone," she said flatly.

Many of the women in the study who did not want children either chose to live alone or with partners who also did not want children. "I'd decided long ago that my life plan did not include children," Monique said. "When I met Al, we were both busy with our careers. We had full lives outside of work—many friends and lots of things we enjoyed doing. There was no question about it. Each of us had made the decision to be childless. Perhaps that's why we were attracted to each other," she reflected. Maggie and her husband, like other couples, had carefully used contraceptives or had undergone sterilization to make sure she would not accidentally become pregnant. Couples such as Darlene and Freddie "felt closer" because they "didn't have rug rats." This was also the case with Martha, who felt her "wonderful twenty-five-year relationship with Gina wouldn't have lasted so long if we had kids." These partners had made thoughtful, proactive decisions not to have children.

"Our decisions were part of the times, you know," Laurel said, explaining how her high fertility moments coincided with a social movement that discouraged long-term relationships and commitments. "I was a baby boomer, and by the time I wanted a husband and kids, I'd missed my window of opportunity. Many of us said we didn't expect to tie one another down forever, that we'd stay only as long as love and faith in each other endured. In this context, having kids would have been unwise—and we knew it. We had the pill to safeguard us. We said we didn't want commitment, but I don't think we really meant it." Cultural and historical forces "clearly push us in our decisions," said Natalie. "My mom grew up at a time when she really had no choices. We did. Perhaps we went to an extreme, choosing freedom after a long history of women having no choice. Also, my guy liked the liberation from having to be a breadwinner dad. If we were to choose again, maybe we'd choose kids. Or maybe not. I'm a product of my time, and childlessness is part of that."

A mutual decision to be childless does not mean the couple won't think about parenthood from time to time. "Playing with the idea of parenthood" could be fun, even if a woman had decided she would never have children. Sharing the idea of parenthood together could be a bonding experience, even when a couple had decided against having kids. Josi reflected on a time when "A friend of ours had a baby and we went to see her in the hospital. She passed the baby over for me to hold. It was wonderful. They are so magical. As a female holding a day-old child in my arms, I was overwhelmed with the sensation that it could have been mine, that I could be holding our baby. As I turned and passed the child to my husband, there was such a preciousness at that moment." They could share this tender moment without compromising their desire to be childless. Couples who had decided to be childless were often quite matter-of-fact when they discussed it. Elise has been married for thirty-one years to Bill, a man she met when they were undergraduate students: "Neither of us had passionate times when we both wanted a child. Having passion for kids occurs at the same time as everything else—like having money and careers in place—was ready hard. We still check in with each other from time to time and wonder what it'd be like if we'd had one. We never had a firm 'we'll never have kids' stance. We just didn't."

Elise and Bill, Monique and Al, Martha and Gina, and Darlene and Freddie were all content with their relationship and attributed their high degree of relational satisfaction to their mutual decision not to have children. This finding is not unusual. Studies confirm that voluntarily childless couples experience higher levels of marital satisfaction. For example, studies comparing marriages both with and without children consistently report higher marital happiness in child-free unions. In particular, those couples value freedom from child care responsibilities; they also report greater opportunities for self-fulfillment and a more satisfactory marital relationship, and are more productive. Voluntarily childless couples have been found to express more concern about population growth and an apprehension about having kids, and sometimes they admit they don't understand the world of children. Lifestyle choices, early socialization experiences, doubts about parenting ability, and concern about physical aspects of childbirth and pregnancy were all factors that influenced couples to seriously consider childlessness.[4]

Voluntarily childless women in this study reported feeling that they had choices. Even if a part of themselves wanted children, most were committed to their decision to be childless. Women such as Barbara decided they were "more dedicated to the partner I have than the child I don't. Yes, I want kids and she doesn't—but in a loving relationship, you have to bend. Her need not to have a child is just as important as my need to have one." She actively decided to remain childless. Many, such as Ahanna, chose to give up dreams about motherhood because "I don't want to raise a child by myself." Although she could have become a mother through pregnancy or adoption, she did not. "All the ducks in my life needed to be lined up in order for me to become the kind of mother I thought I should be. They weren't. So I chose what I thought was best for me, and for the child of my dreams. And that was for me not to have that child," Ahanna disclosed. Barbara and Ahanna made decisions—hard decisions, loving decisions—that left them childless.

Most women I interviewed had believed that one day they would have children. Most had built a significant relationship with another person over the course of their lives. Some women had divorced before they had had an opportunity to have children with their spouses. Others found themselves in relationships without committed partners. Sometimes there was a lack of fit between the timing of a pregnancy and other things that were going on in the relationship. In short, I found that women reported a variety of reasons about why their relationships had caused them to remain involuntarily childless.

Many women in the study had anticipated being childless for only a short period of time while they, or their partners, got their lives ready for a family. Temporary childlessness all too frequently turned into permanent childlessness. Sometimes women pushed back the timing of a pregnancy until their husbands were through getting an education. Many women supported their husbands while the men completed degrees or training programs. Alicia and her husband had considered having kids, but "things got in the way. I had a job offer in California as a college English teacher, but I stayed in the Midwest so Tony could go to graduate school. The ironic thing was, he never completed his degree, and I never got a baby." Emma and her husband "didn't want to start having a family until we were in a better financial situation, and the timing was wrong and never got right. I guess you could say that inadvertently we made other plans besides kids." Samara worked and "put my life on hold so he could pursue his career. I expected to have children in the future and had plans to finish college myself. When you're young, the future seems huge, infinite. But it's not. He got what he wanted, but I didn't."

Some women explained how neither they nor their partner had explicitly decided that they would—or would not—have children. "We lived in limbo-land," Nicole said. "We were influenced by the Gestalt psychologist Fritz Perls's ideology of the day: 'You do your thing, and I do mine, and if we find one another, it's beautiful.' We were individuals together," she explained. "We were not a couple in a committed, forever way. Because we had no future beyond the here-and-now, having kids wasn't in the program." Some casually lived with a partner "more out of convenience than anything, I guess," Allison said. "We certainly had nothing close to a relationship that should sustain having a child."

Women sometimes learned the hard way that a partner wasn't as committed to the relationship as they had thought. This lack of commitment transferred into the women's not wanting to have children with the partner. For example, Evie "was practically engaged when my guy hopped in the sack with his old girlfriend. So would I feel safe having kids with him? I don't think so!" When Toots thought she was pregnant and her boyfriend told her to get an abortion, "I told him to hit the road. If this was his level of commitment, I didn't want this relationship." Ramona was married for about eight years before she divorced. "I assumed we'd have kids, but two years into the marriage I wondered if I'd made a mistake. We wanted different things, and the differences became greater, not less. I didn't consciously think 'I'm not going to have kids because I'm not sure if I'm going to stay.' My husband said he wanted kids, but I kept saying, not yet." Although being committed did not necessarily mean that a couple wanted children, lack of commitment usually transferred into childlessness.

Although some partners said they were willing to have children, they never exhibited other behaviors that made women believe them. This hidden agenda between men and women, "where he said he did but I thought he really didn't," was an important factor that influenced women's decisions about becoming pregnant. "There were always excuses" that men gave to postpone starting a family. "He said he wanted to wait until he was out of school," recalled Leanne. "Bob said when he got his career established we could start, but there was always some promotion or project in the wings that kept pushing back his willingness to have kids," reported Samara. Samara and Leanne, like other women who wanted children, were likely to interpret their partner's ambivalent or lukewarm reception to the idea of having kids as more positive than what their partners actually felt. "But maybe he was torn too," Samara mused. "Perhaps part of him did want kids and part of him didn't, and he gave me mixed messages because he didn't know how he really felt." Whatever the reasoning, Toni found that her husband "always had a justification for why 'not now.' There was too much of this thing going on, or not enough of that for him to consent to having a baby. He couldn't come out and say it—he really didn't want kids. It was only after a couple of years had gone by that he had the nerve to admit that he never, ever, wanted kids. He didn't tell me so because he didn't want to upset me. I'd rather been upset! Instead, he let this charade go on for years."

It was difficult for women to confront the illusion, to openly demand whether their partners "were in or out" when it came to having kids. "It was easier not to know for sure," Kris confessed. "If he never gave a definite 'no,' then there was always hope we might have kids. I was afraid that if I forced the issue, we'd never have them." Even when women did demand an open discussion about whether to have kids, there was no certain outcome. Toots went into her "second marriage with eyes wide open. I always wanted four kids—don't ask me why four, I don't know. I felt I did all the right things with this marriage. I was open and had no hidden agenda. We talked about my need for kids and his depression problems. Time passed, and when I felt we should start a family, he didn't want to talk about it. He became evasive, so I'd back off awhile and try again later. I kept hoping things would change, but they didn't," she said. "Each occasion I brought it up, I did so in more detail and I pressed harder, and it created a strain between us. His depression got worse and he went on lithium. God, I thought. I shouldn't push a kid on him if it was making him so depressed." Whether partners communicated their feelings about having children or not, Nicole summarized women's experiences this way: "His behavior spoke volumes more than the words he said about having a child."

Some of the women talked about how frustrating it was to be in a relationship they thought was committed, yet their partners were unwilling to "go the distance to have the children I needed," as Toots said. Many women I interviewed had hoped that their nonreceptive partner would agree eventually to become a parent.[5] Toni summed her feelings as "I just wish he would." Wanting a partner to desire children was discussed by many of the women. "We talked about it many times, but there was no changing his mind. I wanted children so badly that I left him while I was young enough to get involved with a man who would want kids. I fantasized about having children during my second marriage. But kids were my interest, not his," confided Kris. Men who had children from previous relationships believed they "had already done their parenting thing" and were less likely to want to start new families, according to women such as Kris. But this was difficult to accept for those women who had dreamed of one day being married and having children. Toots found that "their kids came first, and I found I couldn't compete—not that I wanted to. I'm willing to sacrifice, accommodate to others' needs, adjust my schedule, but I'm unable to compromise all of my needs all the time. I wanted kids, and they had enough." Women such as Lisa had dreamed of having children since she was old enough to play with dolls. "When I envisioned myself as a woman, it was always as a mother, first and foremost," she admitted. As she became older, "I found myself sorting through the men I'd dated, using as a primary consideration whether they'd be a good father and husband. After living with one man for three years, I decided I had to leave. We wanted different things. I quit talking myself into wanting what he did. There were other things that I wanted out of life. If I stayed with him, I knew I'd never get them. No matter how much I loved him, if I didn't have kids, sooner or later I'd resent him. Sometimes love is not reason enough to stay together. It was scary, but I left him. I don't know what I'll find, but the unknown is better than what seems to be writ in stone," she said.

In some cases, women told stories about partners who, while willing to have children, were not going to be available parents. Del described how "My husband and I were both workaholics. We both wanted kids, but we couldn't seem to agree on things. One Valentine's Day, when he went to Belgium, I suddenly found myself fearful of being stuck with a child and alone. I know that I was ready to have kids—I was thirty-three and it was the classic ticking time. He thought I didn't want kids, but I did! I just didn't want to have them and be alone. He had an affair shortly after that. It was messy and personal. We divorced, and I started my own company, which is now my family. Funny—I always intended to go back to my hometown where I figured I'd have a house, kids, and a working husband and a nice life. But life happens when you're not looking."

Although many women did not want to parent alone, they also weren't enthusiastic about being "an unwed mother. While I'd love a child, it'd be too hard to do alone," Kelly said. "It'd be too hard. Besides, what I wanted was the whole ball of wax—I wanted the baby, sure, but I also wanted the doting father, the pretty house, the picket fence and the golden retriever." Many, like Evie, desired "an equal opportunity partner to co-parent with." But what she found was that her partner "was like Peter Pan. He didn't want to grow up just then. Later, he said. But thirty years later, he's still Peter, and he still hasn't grown up! If I had a child with him, I'd be mothering two kids, instead of one!"

Evie and other women indicated that although in some cases partners were willing to parent, the women had not considered them acceptable parenting partners. "I don't trust his ability to parent," Jane said. Women learned to identify signs that told them when a man was not committed to the relationship, and these red flags warned that she could end up a single mother. Sometimes, women felt a general lack of fit with their partner. For example, Millie said, "Something told me that our relationship wasn't going to last, and I wasn't sure I wanted to become a single mom. I just knew that if we had a child, sooner or later he'd leave. Don't ask me how, I just knew. I think that's why when we got married I never took his name. Somehow, I figured I'd have to change it back, so why bother?" Evie, Jane, and Millie indicated that there were vague but omnipresent problems in their relationship with their partners, whereas other women pointed to clear patterns of dysfunction.

Women were less willing to compromise when they feared that their partner or their relationship was "fatally flawed." If a woman could not depend on her partner, "having a child with him wouldn't make sense." When Claire married Andy, they had a beautiful wedding in the woods, and she wore a wedding dress that she had made, on which she'd embroidered a colorful tree of life. "I thought that one day we'd have children." But her wedding-day dreams never came true. Her in-laws, who were living in Iran, sent his sixteen-year-old brother to live with them. Then his mother came to live with them. It was a very difficult time for Claire. "Sometimes we'd talk about having kids, but I dreaded the thought of it. The last thing I wanted to do was have a baby. . . . It was odd—when I thought about how I didn't want to have his child, I realized that I didn't want to be married to him at all. I was fed up with his parents, and I didn't want my child to even be exposed to them. It wasn't a good marriage, and so we separated." Helene recounted that her "husband was unfaithful. . . . But I was the other woman when he was married before, so why should I be surprised to learn that there's another woman when he's married to me? If we'd had kids, would he have been there for the child? I doubt it. He surely hasn't been there for anyone yet."

Although women found that some types of relationship dysfunctions were relatively "manageable," other types were more serious. Cynthia's "first serious man was a Vietnam vet, who had trouble dealing with things he'd experienced there—but I was head over heels in love with him. He got crazy, really crazy, and ended up hospitalized. Then came disappointment number two, the father of my aborted child. Disappointment number three came when I married a foreign man who was looking for a way to stay in this country, but it blew up when I found out he had abused my fourteen-year-old sister. This was the ultimate betrayal. I haven't had a man in my life over the last ten years." Mental illness, substance abuse, and domestic violence were common reasons why women had to leave relationships, or at least not have children in them. Allie's "main reason I didn't have kids was that I hooked up with Kim, and he was an alcoholic. I wouldn't bring kids up in that situation." Vicky married a man who was physically, verbally, and emotionally abusive to her. She was so afraid of him that she felt she couldn't leave, and she certainly didn't want to get pregnant with him. "I was embarrassed to be in this marriage. I felt like a failure.

Finally, it felt more like a failure to stay in the marriage than to leave it. We'd been living with my mother because I felt that if we had our own place the violence would escalate. He'd grab me by my hair, hit me, kick me so hard I couldn't walk. Finally, I told him he had to leave or that I'd go to prison for murder. For so long, I felt there was something wrong with me, but it was really that something was wrong with him."

Sometimes a husband or partner wanted children but the woman did not. A few women discussed feeling that they would not be a good mother and that it was the right decision for them not to have children. For some there was no physical reason not to conceive; rather, emotional reasons prevented women from choosing motherhood. "I felt awful that I could not offer him children. I think he thought I would not. But I felt I could not," said Penelope. "He wouldn't back off the topic. While he would let it lie dormant for a while, he must have been thinking about kids because he'd pop up and make a dig like, 'but you don't like kids, do you?' It wasn't that I didn't like kids. I just didn't want one of my own." The most common emotion experienced by this group of women was guilt. "I felt that I was letting him down because I didn't want kids. I felt that I wasn't a 'real woman,'" Tammy confessed. Women found that if they married men who already had children, this took the pressure off of them to produce. Randi mused that "I kept finding myself more attracted to men who did not have kids, or who'd been married before with families. It took me a while to figure out that this was because they were safe—they wouldn't want kids."[6]

Deciding whether to have children was not a one-time-only event. Women's stories described the serpentine routes of their lives that had resulted in childlessness. Their journeys described times when they wanted children and times they didn't, partners with whom they desperately wanted to have children, and partners with whom they absolutely did not. Catherine's tale of the vicissitudes of relationships conveys the difficulty a woman may experience in determining whether a particular partner is the right one with whom to parent. "Initially," she said, "we decided not to have children because it was in vogue."[7] She reflected how, at age eighteen, she'd allowed herself to be "talked into" not wanting kids by her husband, who "had gotten into this Ayn Rand group who thought it was selfishness that made people want kids. He didn't want to own property or have a family—these were things I didn't realize I wanted until later." They decided she should go to secretarial school to help out in his family's business and "to finish our silver pattern." At school, Catherine found "I loved working, I loved being needed. It was a small staff where I seemed to make a difference. My husband didn't treat me like he really needed me." They divorced when she was twenty-four. "I got everything—he only wanted the encyclopedia."

Catherine found herself in a "mating market." About that time, she met her second husband, who had been married four times before. "He was pitiful, and I married him because I felt sorry for him. Women are nurturing fools sometimes. This is where my nurturing plays out," Catherine said. She told him that she married him to have children, but he explained that "we should wait a while, until he was out of law school, before becoming pregnant. We were contraceptively safe during those years." Unexpectedly, Catherine lost both parents during a three-month period. "He was an S.O.B. to me then, and I decided I didn't want to have kids with him. But I stuck it out, hoping that maybe he'd change. I guess I displaced my nurturance after my parents died. I took in a stray kitten. Then I took in another cat and a stray dog. He didn't want me to work after he got his degree, so I played golf a lot and became a housewife. But this wasn't a life. I went back to college, but it wasn't enough. Work gave me satisfaction. My husband didn't want kids, and I didn't push getting pregnant, because deep down inside I knew it wouldn't be the right thing to do with him. My husband resented my working and that he couldn't be all things to me. He threatened divorce as soon as I'd mention working. He had an affair. Then we divorced. I went back to work again for my old company, but this time I was older and it was harder to fit in. My old friends had married, and I felt sad about things that should have happened for me but didn't. I was a recluse for a year. Then menopause hit." At forty-nine, Catherine is forever childless. She has pets and a live-in boyfriend who has three children. Although she doesn't feel maternal to them "because they have a mother who's wonderful," she does feel connected to them. "It used to bother me a lot that I didn't have kids. Maybe having them doesn't bother me so much now because most of my friends don't have little ones either—they all got big and grew up, so even my friends who had babies don't have them now." What Catherine's story conveys is the tale told by many childless women—that their mates did not want children and they did not either—at least, not with those mates. Although the statement "neither of us wanted children" sounds simple, often women's relationships were far from that. Instead, women renegotiated their childbearing status on a routine basis, until they become physically unable to negotiate it.

Yet as the women I interviewed reflected on their past, many admitted that although they had attributed their childlessness to some relationship issue, they had either consciously or unconsciously chosen not to have children. As they have matured and now approach the end of their childbearing years, most have examined the role of childless-ness in their lives. Although most of them have become comfortable with their relationship decisions, others are still waiting for their dreams of family to come true. As Nelly suggested, "It has been said that the better mothers are those who are older, more experienced, self-confident. I say, yeah, I hope that's true. I really want to have a baby. But things haven't fallen into place for that to happen. Maybe they still will. Or maybe things happen for a reason and I'll be living my life a different way, without kids. Who knows why things happen the way they do? Maybe one day I'll look back and figure it out."

A relationship, then, can be either a factor that pulls a woman into wanting something other than children or a factor that pushes a woman who had wanted children into childlessness. I found in this study that when a partner was supportive of a woman's desire to remain childless, the woman appeared more content than those women who had wanted children but attributed their childlessness to resistance or other problems with their partners.

CHAPTER 5   Lifestyle Choices

Although, among those I interviewed, relationships often influenced whether a woman would have a child, the decision was also influenced by what kind of lifestyle a woman wanted. Naomi, a deliberately childless woman, summed up her view of life this way: "We've only one chance to go through life. There are not necessarily tomorrows—only todays. If today is all I've got, I'm going to do the things I want in order to be happy. This means taking care of the people and things I love—including me. It doesn't mean gambling by adding a child with unknown qualities into an already full and enjoyable lifestyle."

Whereas childlessness was a subconscious decision for many women, it was a conscious choice for others. "We weighed our options, the pros and the cons. We tried to balance the many parts of who we are with what would be best for us. We made a leap of faith that we chose correctly," Penelope said about her experience of childlessness. Women who deliberately chose to be childless often felt pulled toward relationships with partners or friends, relationships they felt would grow best without children. They were attracted to jobs or careers, or by the passion of acquiring knowledge. Some were concerned that there wouldn't be enough money for the standard of living they wanted if they had children. Their desire to pursue recreational activities, hobbies, and civic activities was an important consideration. And women who wanted to have time to foster personal growth believed this process would be constrained if they had children. They are not alone. Despite pressures to become mothers, women choosing child-free lifestyles is a phenomenon that has become increasingly common over the last two decades.[1]

Although the presence or absence of children may actually have little to do with one's successes in life, deliberately childless women can regard the demands of motherhood as intrusive. Griffen, in "Childless by Choice," quotes a woman as saying, "There's no single thing I've opted to do instead of raising children. Mostly, being childless opens me to a sense of possibility; it gives me the feeling that my own path can take zigs and zags, that since I'm not responsible for another human being I can take risks and explore things that otherwise I wouldn't."[2] Stereotypes to the contrary, few of the women I interviewed disliked children. In fact, many felt that children were the "most important miracles ever," as Barbara called them. "I love kids and want what's best for them—and that may mean my not having them."

Many of the women in this study expressed positive attitudes about children in general, but they were less enthusiastic about embracing motherhood as a lifestyle choice. Voluntarily childless women viewed their decision as one based on quality of life. They believed they could live "a more comfortable and productive life" without children. They liked who they were and how they lived and "didn't want to jeopardize it by having a child" (Nance). Many women talked about how content they were with their life and how they were unwilling to risk change. From their observations of those women who had children, certain things seemed likely if one chose to become a mother: Children would be expensive. Children would take up a good deal of time. Children would have an impact on a woman's relationship with her partner and her friends. Children would likely affect a woman's career. And finally, all these factors would likely ensure that there would be little time, money, or energy left for oneself. "It all comes down to this," Mica observed: "To seize the dream of motherhood would mean sacrificing other dreams."

Major lifestyle factors that women attributed to their decision not to have children included employment, education, recreation, leisure time, health, appearance, and personal development. In particular,

"Work is satisfying for both the body and soul," Iris said. Creating and refining ideas and methods, and exceeding the bounds of what one thought possible are all important aspects of human growth and development. Work helps make dreams come true. Although women felt they needed to work for economic survival, they also needed to work for personal achievement. Elise described her experience of choosing what type of woman she wanted to be. "Choosing whether or not to have children was tied to my professional self. There's no way of knowing what would happen if I'd gone that route. I only know that I really wanted a career. I'd always seen myself as a teacher. Even as a child, I ran a school for younger children. I love children—I love teaching too. Yet I'd always seen myself, first and foremost, as a teacher. Perhaps if my husband had wanted a child I would have chosen to get pregnant, but he was ambivalent about it too. But I wanted to have my career, that I knew." Charlotte, a professional with at least three different lines of work in which she is involved simultaneously, always has a new idea for a business venture and is never bored. Del built her business into a $40 million operation in a decade. She built the business from the ground up, and it is now a contender in the international market. "The long hours, the travel, the meetings, the frustrations, and the celebrations are largely possible because I didn't have a child." Olivia found that not having children has allowed her to travel all over the world to fascinating places. As an anthropologist, she studies the lives of indigenous peoples. She pitches her tent wherever she wants and stays for as long as it takes to conduct her research. "The places I live are more beautiful than you can imagine. I'm always having adventures. While it's not a perfect life, I'm having a wonderful time," she said. Fern reflected how she "was bored by the thought of living a life that focused on the domestic life of babies and material objects and shopping. I was never the ruffles-and-silk stereotype." She was adamant that her life was better because she had not had children. "I'm so lucky, so blessed. If I'd had kids, I would have been deprived of this wonderful, enviable life."

For these women, work was a force that pulled them into wanting a career more than children. They were proud of the contributions they made in their careers. "I don't really mind the long hours; in fact, I love the challenges and benefits of my investment," Del confessed. Like most women, they worked not only because they had to but because they wanted to.[3] They described the advantages they gained from their professions and accomplishments as thrilling, fulfilling, exciting, and empowering. When women were employed in careers they enjoyed, they didn't want to inhibit their momentum by having babies. Feeling productive and successful, "I prioritized developing programs, products, and my professional life over having children. I didn't want kids when there were so many marvelous things to do and not enough time to do them all. If you're going to have kids, you ought to do it right. I had to choose," Heather said, "and I couldn't give up those critical years right then to have a child." Enjoying what you do "is a message, the same way dreading something is a message," said Tina, a deliberately childless woman who wants to own her own bookstore. She observed that "I work sixteen hours a day in a bookstore and just love it. It's nice to see all the new books first, and it's fun to get courted by publishers. But I baby-sit one night for my nieces and I'm exhausted. When you're doing things you love, you have energy—if you aren't, you don't," she said.

Many women, however, have worked not because a career was their first priority but because they had to work to survive economically.[4] A dual labor market still exists in which many fields and types of jobs are almost exclusively occupied by men whereas other fields and types of jobs (which typically are viewed as secondary) are almost exclusively occupied by women. Women are still located primarily in occupations that pay less, such as clerical and other support staff, sales, and health care.[5] Because they earn less, women, as Darlene observed, "have to work twice as hard as men just to make ends meet. I can't afford a child on my salary." Therefore, among the women I interviewed, work was a force that pushed many women into making lifestyle decisions that did not include children. Women who felt pushed into childlessness by their job often resented their job and their economic situation. Also, women found that "even though I wanted children, having them was not possible if I wanted to keep my job," Kris said. Some wanted children but feared loss of job security or reduced chances for promotion. "If I got pregnant when I first started my job, it would have knocked me off the career track and I'd have had difficulty coming back and being competitive. I love kids. But I saw what my mom-colleagues experienced—they were ridiculed when they were concerned about their kids, bosses watched their time more closely, sure they'd come in later or leave earlier than the rest of us. The best assignments entailed long hours and travel, which I felt I couldn't do if I had a family. Then, there would be juggling child care and work schedules. There were too many drawbacks for those of us who have to work," said Tanya. Women candidly discussed how their workplaces seemed to treat women differently from men, and mothers different from nonmothers. "Sometimes I wonder, when I look at how differently people get treated, if businesses try to weed out women with kids," Amanda observed. "I mean, look at it: for women with kids, there's no day care center where we work, and no child care subsidies. They frown when women take off work to take care of things like kids' dentist appointments or to attend school functions. Often I'll see mothers working with blue faces because they can't attend a game or something that's a big deal for their kids, because if they do they'll get in trouble with their bosses. When they use their sick days to take care of family business, bosses resent it. As a supervisor, I hear what other administrators say about the moms. To be honest, as hard as they will work, the cards are stacked against them getting ahead. They just don't know it. But it's true. Is it this way everywhere, I wonder?"

The corporate sector has sent a message that if women want to get ahead, they must be willing to put in long hours and make business their priority. "I put in sixty-five hours a week," Elizabeth explained. "When a woman at work got pregnant and cut back to forty-five or fifty hours—which is still more than an average person's work week, the male bosses acted as though she'd shirked her responsibilities and eventually forced her to resign. It was a clear message to the rest of us women who were considering working there and having a child." In some professions, if a woman seems to put her family before her job, studies indicate that she can expect to hit a glass ceiling that is considerably lower than that of men or their child-free female colleagues. The mommy track has been found to be filled with obstacles to advancement.[6] It is not surprising that many women thought it impossible to successfully balance both work and home. There is an illusion that the workplace is fair, just, and user-friendly for mothers. "They make it too hard to do both," Sue observed. "Do they really think that by making it so difficult to have kids and work that it will force women out of the workplace? Sometimes I wonder if it's a quiet conspiracy. Having kids as the 'right' thing is still pushed down women's throats. Yet you can't get ahead at work if you have them. So what's a girl to do? Seems to me that the system's forcing women either to decide to have kids and stay home, or to force women like me into not having kids. Those conservatives who reduce incomes and don't make child care available, who are trying to force women with kids to leave work to stay home, are into a rude surprise—women today have decided to forgo kids for work. Look at what's happening! Moms are outright frazzled, and I don't see the system helping to reduce the pressure on them. If businesses don't become more sympathetic to women who want both kids and careers, they'll end up with one or the other. It's a bad deal for women, for sure," said Sue.

A central concern expressed by the women I interviewed was the lack of high-quality, affordable child care. Their own mothers had put careers aside "for the sake of the children." "There's no care like a mother's care," this ideology held. Such a view made day care unnecessary and undesirable, and it implied that worldly success and achievements were less important than staying at home and raising a family. Leanne was convinced that mothers should stay at home with the children because "when I was a kid, friends would flock to my house after school because Mom was there, baking cookies with things for us to do. Their moms worked and they were on their own until their folks got home. My house was the neighborhood hub of activity." In contrast, working moms were often resented by their children. Layne remembered, "Mother was so busy with her work that she seldom had time to talk with us. I was alone much of the time, even when she was around. She may have been a success at work, but she could barely boil water and put my hair up in a ponytail." If an employed mother wasn't particularly good at managing domestic duties, a daughter often considered the mother's job to be the source of the problem. But some women I interviewed had mothers who had worked and done a great job taking care of their families. For instance, Maggie recalled a loving home in which her mother and grandmother worked but "always took excellent care of me." Jill's mother also worked, but Jill felt that her upbringing was "atypical because my mom worked and most of my friend's mothers did not. I hated that she worked, and I especially hated that she was a teacher in my school. For her, it was an ideal job because she had school vacation and hours, and she could pop in and check on me during the day. I wanted her to be like the moms who didn't work, so she could go on my field trips. I didn't want to have kids that felt like oddballs like me." It appears from these stories that it wasn't the fact that their mothers worked that caused them difficulty; instead, it appears that the daughters' resentments often stemmed from feeling like their mothers weren't adhering to the "good mother" norm, even though their mothers were making valuable contributions outside the home. It also appears that when mothers weren't emotionally or physically available to their daughters, it was easier for the daughters to blame their mothers' jobs for the problem instead of looking at deeper reasons for their mothers' unavailability.

Many women talked about how they pursued career paths instead of the domestic path because "employment wasn't an option, but motherhood was. Having a job was essential for survival whether I had a family or not. I couldn't afford kids without a job, and I couldn't get a good job without going to college. By the time I got both, my time to have kids had run out," said Kelly. Money was the driving force for their decisions. In this study, more than half of the women said that economic considerations were important reasons for not having a child. Their concern was not without merit. Even though children are often regarded as a font of love, hope for the future, and a continuation of one's bloodline, children do not come free. The issue of cost influenced women's childbearing decision in two ways. One way concerned "the actual cost associated with having children—it's really expensive to have a child!" Natalie observed. "It's really hard for most families to have enough available money to go around for everyone's needs." Although the issue of having enough money to adequately support children was an issue, so was the parents' willingness to spend their resources on childbearing expenditures: "My folks made a decent living, but they weren't willing to spend it on us kids," Cynthia recalled. "I resented it. They spent it on things they wanted, and my dad drank and gambled a lot of it away. I wore hand-me-downs and did odd jobs for a neighbor to earn extra money for things I needed," she said. "While I'm sure I'd be generous to a child, I sometimes wonder—if money was tight and I had to choose between me and them, then I might choose me, because I learned that's what adults do. By their behavior, I learned that kids shouldn't be given everything on a silver platter. Working for what you need is important. If I've worked hard to earn a decent living, then I have a right to use it for my enjoyment too," she said.

Today, raising a child in a middle-income family requires an investment of about $1.5 million.[7] Whether a couple has a child influences the size of the house they will buy, the amount of money they must have coming in on a monthly basis, and the amount they will be able to save for vacations, college tuition, or retirement. Added to the direct costs of parenting are opportunity costs—wage earning and investments that parents forgo when rearing children. There are costs associated with workdays missed during pregnancy and maternity leave as well as those associated with days missed for sick children, doctor visits, and other parental obligations. These costs are felt most acutely by women. There are also emotional costs associated with having children, such as added household tensions and restrictions on parental activity outside the home. Children require an efficiently organized residence and a daily routine—which can limit a parent's spontaneity and choice. Children also make for substantial work; not only is there physical care involved, but there is the work of parenting—such as teaching norms and guiding the child's social and emotional growth—as well as the anxiety that comes with being a parent. "It takes a lot of everything in order to take good care of a child," Kelly observed.

These trends were not lost on the women in this study. As Natalie said, "I don't mean to seem materialistic, but I want to get nice things and a pretty home. I'm not talking about a mansion or anything, just a comfortable home with tasteful furnishings. Growing up, we never had nice things, and I work hard and deserve them." Helene said, "We're just now looking at buying our first house; we're ten or twenty years behind people our age. We hope to be out of credit-card debt soon, if things go our way. So how in the world could we afford a child?" Audrey's dream is "to have a decent little house we can pay off in twenty years." She works with the elderly and wants to have "no debt and 401Ks with as much money as possible put away since there will be no government retirement help for us. I see the older folks, and they don't have many options, and it's going to be worse for us. That's one reason why we decided 'no kids.'" Another childless woman, Mica, said, "If we had kids we could never get ahead. I can't help thinking about retirement, because Social Security and the current insurance programs are not going to be like they are now—lots of managed care will hurt poor people, and I don't intend to be one of those who needs care and can't afford it." These women were aware of the costs of having children and wondered how on earth, if it was so hard to make ends meet now, they would support a couple of kids. Women such as Tina, who grew up in a home in which money was scarce and financial worries plagued the family, were determined "not to have kids unless I know I could earn the money to raise them right."

To get a good job, school was essential, and the women in this study indicated they needed a trade or a degree to survive. Education was also seen as an end in itself—pursued for knowledge and self-development. Natalie said, "When I was in school, it was my time. I was investing in me, in my mind, in learning. I was so excited about the whole new world of information that was at my fingertips. All I had to do was put forth the time and energy to learn it. What I didn't expect is that I'd never get tired of learning. The more I learn, the more I find there is to know!" Some women loved school so much they never left. Elise became a college professor because "I love the school environment. Unlike the corporate sector where money is the object, in schools everyone's obsessed with learning—which is a much better value, in my opinion." Although education was a means to the end—that is, getting a job—often education was seen as a desirable process in and of itself. As Lucy asserted, "I studied the humanities, in particular English literature and history, not to get a job but just because I wanted to know. My parents didn't send me to college to get a job—they sent me there so I could become wise, and so I could understand the world around me." Toni agreed. "I took up the arts because I saw the world as a beautiful place and I wanted to make my mark in it. I've done sculpture and worked with different mediums. Right now I'm working in photography. Sometimes I make money and sometimes my art costs me more than I bring in. But I'm pursuing what I love, refining my skill, training my eye, all the time."

Other women had wanted to become mothers but their schooling interfered, pushing childbearing to the perimeter. Deborah was in medical school when "I really got the burn for kids. But when I was in my residencies and internships, and then setting up my practice, when would I have had time for a child? I guess I could have had one, but I wouldn't have been able to provide it the time and support I think kids need." Mica also had "wanted kids, but at the time I thought it was too hard to have kids and do well in school. My course work was very demanding. By the time I went to class, worked, and spent hours on my homework and papers, how would I have had time for a child?"

"Just reading a good book" was regarded as an educational pursuit by some women but a form of leisure by others. Many women in the study valued the opportunity to spend their time however they wanted, whether it was at work, with their partner or a friend, or on recreation and volunteer activities. These women found that a child-free lifestyle gave them freedom to pursue both their personal and professional capabilities. Quiet time was an important lifestyle and recreational priority for the women who were interviewed. They treasured time to relax after busy workdays, enjoyed chatting with others, and appreciated the opportunity to curl up and read, or take long baths, or play music. Yet personal time was a rare commodity for many women. "Sometimes I just want to go home and not talk to a soul," confessed

Ahanna. "I'm with people all day long and when I come home, it's my time." Angela, a psychologist, admitted that "one reason I can give all day to others is because I have time to regenerate myself at night." But Amanda noted that "when a woman wants time for herself, she's seen as selfish. It's as if women are supposed to be on call twenty-four hours a day to take care of other people. That's nonsense. Everyone needs time for themselves."

When women are childless, their time is their own. Chi reflected that she needed time to think, to write, to paint, and to be. "When I watch videos of us as kids, sometimes I regret not having one of my own, but mostly it doesn't get to me. I'm curious about people who are devastated by not having kids. Last Friday night it was so pleasant to eat dinner in bed. There was a sense of freedom." Vicky agreed with this logic, saying, "I can sleep until noon or get up at 4:00 A.M. if I want to."

Quiet time today may be more important than ever before. According to author Esther Buchholz, "In the information age, finding solitude has become close to an impossible dream. Schedules are booked months in advance, faxes pile up, e-mails accumulate, and the phone keeps ringing. Our culture is not alarmed because it suggests that happiness can be found only by being with others, not by being alone. If anything, solitude has seemed the monopoly of artists, monks, and madmen."[8] Childless women, by demanding time for themselves, have joined that deviant group. Many have more discretionary time, whereas mothers' schedules are tightly regulated by their children's needs. Long Sunday mornings reading newspapers in bed, leisurely summer lunches, impulse trips, spontaneous visits to friends, and long, adventurous vacations are more common experiences among childless women—"my friends with kids never get to do those things," Ahanna observed.

Among the women I interviewed, parenthood often was seen as the ultimate sacrifice. The women talked about how much time it took to take proper care of children, and they felt that the care was more than what they were able, or willing, to provide. They were aware that their daily routines would become focused around the needs of their children. Living arrangements would have to change to provide space for another person in the household. Work schedules would have to be adjusted to allow them to be home more. Normal schedules of sleeping or dining would have to be drastically changed to accommodate the needs of children. Most of the women talked about friends who were mothers who could go nowhere without arranging child care or child schedules. Betsy felt "a loss of some sort because I don't have kids, but I like my life and can do what I want when I want. I enjoy traveling with my husband. I never had any 'really bad times' or major depressions over not having kids. I'm having much too good a time." Holly and her husband go to Disney World every year, and they often take their nephews. "It's like we're grandparents. Being with them is fun and we do things for them, but it's a responsibility and frankly, we're relieved to send them home after it's over."

Most women realized that even when mothers are not with their children, they spend hours organizing their care and activities. So the issue of childlessness is not just about physical freedom; it is also mental.[9] Audrey commented on how motherhood puts you psychologically on call. "My mom-friends always have first and foremost in their minds what their kids need, what they have to do for them later that night or tomorrow. Even when they're not with them, they're with them. They don't have mental free-space even when they're away from them. I guess it should be that way if you have kids and you're a good mom— but it looks like sheer mental exhaustion would set in, even if physical exhaustion didn't." Evie observed that "I love taking a book to the beach and letting my eyes close for a little sun-snooze. But when I went with my friend and her kids, my friend couldn't lie down or read—she had to sit up so she could keep her eyes on the kids. You dare not take your eyes off the kids, not even for a minute. So while we were both at the beach together, our experiences were entirely different."

Because being a mother was frequently associated with being tired, childlessness was a major consideration for women who were already tired. Many remembered how weary their own mothers had looked and how they wished to avoid becoming like their mothers. Tina noticed how "so many of my high school friends have kids. I looked at them and was so relieved I didn't. I'm not ready for that, they're too much responsibility. Most of my friends now don't have kids. Those who do seem tied down and they don't go anywhere or do anything or have any money. I watch my sister-in-law and all the time and effort it takes to bundle up my niece, put her in the car, only to have her scream. Having kids is too much effort, it is too limiting. My friends look at me and they're jealous. They want my life. So do I—I don't want to trade."

"Having kids makes women look and act old," Lucy observed. Women concerned with their physical appearance assumed that having a child might make them unattractive. "My mom said that every time you have a baby, you gain ten pounds that will never leave. She had four kids and constantly struggled with her weight. She was embarrassed by how she looked, yet she didn't have time to do exercise," said a trim Ellie. Tanya said, "I feel twenty-five even though I am in my late forties. Being a parent makes you mature more quickly. I have the same figure I did when I was twenty-five. This is good. How many women with children can say that?" Kris said, "For years, I felt like anyone who had a baby was older than me. I figured having kids was a stage that I hadn't gotten to yet. I'm still not there yet. At thirty-seven, I'm still younger than a twenty-seven-year-old with kids." Other women discussed feeling "healthier and more attractive" because their bodies had not "been forced to endure the stresses of pregnancy and staying up night after night."

Women without children had more time to engage in physical exercise and were involved with a wide range of recreational interests that ranged from sailing, skiing, and mountain climbing to gardening, traveling, and cooking. Most activities involved money, time, and relationships with others—things that were harder to obtain when one is in the midst of child rearing. Women enjoyed being a part of a group activity and felt they received both physical and social benefits from playing sports with others. Many women worked out regularly at a health club and engaged in swim programs, dance aerobics, racquetball games, and weightlifting. "Moms don't have time to do this," Missy observed. A few were involved with mountain climbing, kayaking, or rock climbing. More were involved in individual sports such as running, mountain biking, cross-country or downhill skiing, and ice-skating. "My sports program helps keep me fit. If I had kids, either they'd have to learn how to do it, or I'd have to stop. Unfortunately, most of my friends stopped" their physical recreation program after they had children, Rose observed.

Those who owned boats or racecars talked about how the vehicles required a lot of expensive equipment so they felt they should spend many weekends engaged in those activities. "There's nothing like being out on the boat, being lulled by the waves and listening to the wind in the sail," Valerie stated. "But if I had kids, I'd constantly have to worry about them falling overboard." "The smell of grease and oil is delicious to me," said Darlene, who spends each free weekend at car races. "Kids wouldn't appreciate it at all. I'd get mad at them after I spent all that money on my cars and then they didn't like them."

Gardening was another commonly cited recreational activity of childless women. "Some people raise kids, I raise orchids," Maura commented. Most grew flowers, although a few were also vegetable farmers. They chattered about the hours they spent in their yards, pruning, pulling weeds, and landscaping. The types of flowers varied, but the common themes were their "enjoyment of working in the dirt, making the world more beautiful, and having time to be in the sun, thinking. These are good things," Julie noted.

Cooking—especially gourmet cooking—was another popular activity. "My husband and I like to take our time cooking. We work together, sip wine, and talk as we cook up absolutely delightful dishes. We can nibble as we cook and feel no time pressure to eat at any particular hour. Many times it is nine o'clock before we sit down to eat, but we have had a nice evening together already, talking as we cook," Fern said. "We couldn't do this if we had kids. They'd want their mac-and-cheese at five o'clock!"

For all of these reasons—relationships, jobs, schooling, recreation, health—the child-free women I interviewed strategically decided that their lives would be better without children than with them. This is counter to the norm promoted by religious and political leaders. These women sought to understand and enhance their own identity. Some described their childless state as caused by "a general lack of interest in children" (Sylvia). Other women viewed their lack of desire for kids as "a by-product of hormonal imbalances" (Monique). Others viewed themselves as having a psychological orientation that did not predispose them toward motherhood. Instead of saying flatly, "I don't want kids," women in this category were inclined to take the "blame" for not wanting them: "The burn was never as strong for me as for other women. Perhaps that's because I'm the youngest in my family and never spent much time with kids. I'm not the type who automatically warmed up to babies and children. For me, having a child was just another part of being married. It was an assumption, like I would go to college and have a career. They went hand in hand, and one day I realized that I didn't have to," said Penelope. Darlene "didn't ever want kids. I was a spoiled brat, and hated baby-sitting. I was the original tomboy. I hung around with the boys, and especially around mechanics. I love the smell of gas and oil, not baby powder and Pablum." Valerie never expected to have children: "I don't think that having one would fulfill me. It wouldn't be a natural or comfortable thing to do, and I knew this from early on in life. Sometimes, intellectually, I think that having kids would be wonderful. But it's always intellectual—not emotional," she said. Robin never envisioned herself "doing the white wedding gown, getting married and having kids. I had three sisters and a brother, and I was the oddball. While my sisters were playing dolls, I was outside playing in the woods with the boys, doing the active, fun stuff. I'm glad that I was allowed freedom. It took a while to develop a feeling of comfort with being different—I was a late bloomer who took a long time to get into the boy-girl dating scene. Even in high school, I never really saw myself as traditional. I hated baby-sitting the younger children and had no patience with them when they were bad." Sylvia is "the extreme who doesn't regret it at all. Kids aren't in the cards for me. I don't feel any biological clocks ticking. I like my lifestyle and independence. It suits me better. I wondered if I was being selfish because I wanted all my time for myself, but figured no, it's who I am."

"But why don't I want one?" Sue asked. "I can't put my finger on it. Sure, there are pros and cons. Part of me really does want a child.

But I'm strategically choosing not to have one. Look at the men I've picked. Look at the career I've chosen. Look at my lifestyle. I may say I want kids, but deep down inside, I must not. I have chosen, not by my words, but by my actions. It took me a long time to figure that one out," she admitted. Some women confessed that they were uncomfortable with their feminine side, which made it hard for them to accept a motherhood role. Veronica noted that "while I always liked boy things more and didn't respect girls, I always had a feminine side. But I wasn't secure in it. I was more provocative, flirtatious, I think to distance myself. For a long time I wasn't much interested in women, and only later learned to like women. I don't think I was comfortable being a woman, in the traditional sense. Since motherhood is part of that traditional woman role, I've had to wonder—did I not want kids because I wasn't comfortable with my womanhood, or did I not feel comfortable with my womanhood because I didn't want kids?" Briana "knows that having kids is hard work, and I ask myself how moms do it. Even now, we end up being seated at restaurants next to a table of five people with three little kids and I wonder how they survive. At those moments there was no doubt that not having kids was the right thing for me."

Stark moments of revelation, when women realized that childbearing was not for them, were sometimes experienced when women learned they were pregnant. Of the almost 40 percent of the women in this study who had at one time been pregnant, approximately half of them had aborted the pregnancy. Some researchers have estimated that about half of all women who have ever been pregnant have experienced an abortion at some point in their lives.[10] It was clear from my interviews that women had received the specific message that unwed pregnancy was bad: "One of the cardinal laws was—don't get pregnant. Only bad girls screw around—or get caught at it, anyway," recalled Jessie. She laughed and continued, "We grew up in the sexual revolution and explored our sexuality like toys. It was fun to play with our bodies. But at my house, we learned to be careful and discreet in our behavior." Briana recalled that "during high school there were several girls who got pregnant, and they weren't the trashy girls. My mother acted like they were the scum of the earth and said I shouldn't even talk to them. There was no compassion for my friends who were pregnant." Toni's sister became pregnant right out of high school, and "this did a number on me; it was pretty embarrassing for this very Catholic family in a parochial school." Women also received messages that they should not have children unless they were fully prepared to have a child. "This meant a stable marriage, a good job, a nice house, and a happy heart. I found it pretty hard to get all those things at the same time," Natalie said. The major message Tashi received in her African American community was "do not get pregnant before marriage. Your life was over if you did."

Untimely pregnancies usually resulted in abortions, and few of the women who had them felt they had made a bad decision. "I did the right thing," Barbara said. "Nothing was right about the pregnancy. I wouldn't have done honor to the soul of the child if I'd had it at that point in my life." "It wasn't an easy decision," Evie recalled. "It was very complicated. I was surprised at becoming pregnant, because I'd been very careful not to be. I was afraid—afraid about my future, afraid about what people would think if I had it, afraid about what people would think if I didn't, afraid that I'd be a failure as a good parent if I did. I was so relieved when it was over. I know people want to hear me say I feel guilty about it, that I regret having the abortion. But I don't. I wasn't ready to be a mother. I thought that one day I'd have kids— only I didn't. Knowing I'd end up childless, would I have changed my decision? No. I did the right thing for the baby and me then and in the long run." These women's experiences are similar to those documented by scientific studies, which indicate that women who terminated pregnancies tended to have good mental health because they felt they had made the right decision.[11]

"Most women who get pregnant wonder, on some level, if they should have the baby," said Lisa. "The only difference is that some of us chose one path and some of us chose another. Our decision may have been different, but the internal debates we experienced were often the same," she observed. The stories of women in this chapter describe pull factors of childlessness, that is, factors in which the lifestyle decisions women made were not *against* children but *for* another type of life.[12] Careers, school, relationships, or other lifestyle choices were contributing causes of childlessness, as were activities into which women poured their time instead of pouring it into children. Some women made education, career, or relationships their priorities, and these interests left them little time or energy for children. Conversely, women who wanted children also "took the 'when life gives you lemons, make lemonade' approach," according to Angela. "I wanted kids, but since I couldn't have them, I decided to pour my attention and affection elsewhere. As one boy I work with told me, 'I'm glad you didn't have kids. If you did, you probably wouldn't have had time for me.' Maybe he was right, and maybe both of our lives have been better because I didn't have kids."

CHAPTER 6   Infertility, Miscarriage,
and Infant Death

Whereas some women in this study attributed their childlessness to personal choice, relationships, or family dysfunction, others remained childless because of physical problems. Many found themselves infertile or with health conditions that made it difficult for them to have a successful pregnancy. A few confronted life-threatening diseases such as cancer—diseases in which pregnancy had to take a backseat to survival. Some women miscarried. In a few cases, women had borne children who died soon after birth, leaving the women childless. These women experienced feelings of sadness, frustration, powerlessness, disappointment, and anger when they were forced to adjust to a condition—childlessness—they had not anticipated. No examination of childlessness would be thorough without a discussion of them.

Infertility

Women are considered infertile if they are unable to conceive after a year or more of regular sexual relations without contraception or if they are unable to carry a pregnancy to a live birth. Approximately 6.1 million women in the United States, or one in ten women of reproductive age, are infertile.[1] During a given year, more than three million persons will seek medical treatment for infertility, and approximately three-quarters of a million women will try some form of assisted reproductive technology. Most women, however, will try to conceive on their own, adopt, or resign themselves to childlessness.[2] Infertility has been described as a new epidemic, although the data do not substantiate a dramatic increase from past years.[3] Even so, increased public attention to the plight of some childless women makes childlessness and infertility seem to be on the increase.

There is no single cause of infertility. These days, people are older when they marry, and couples are waiting longer to start their families. This delayed childbearing is thought to be a contributing factor to infertility because women over age thirty have less chance of becoming pregnant.[4] Infertility, however, is not only a woman's problem. Men tend to have lower sperm counts today than they did twenty years ago, and some men have health problems that prevent them from impregnating women. Other common reasons for infertility among women include endometriosis, pelvic inflammatory diseases (including gonorrhea, syphilis, human papiloma virus [HPV], hepatitis B, chlamydia, and cervical infections), hormonal disorders, genetic anomalies, and tubal pregnancies. Infections, sexually transmitted diseases, environmental toxins, birth control measures such as the Dalkon shield IUD, drugs such as DES, and previous medical problems may inhibit conception. Some women are exposed to occupational hazards that also inhibit pregnancy. Stress, psychological problems, or situational and relationship factors are also thought to be sources of infertility.[5]

The women in this study sometimes discussed family medical histories that they thought might have contributed to their inability to get pregnant. It was common to learn that infertile women frequently had mothers who had had difficulties conceiving. Melinda's parents had wanted six children, "but it took ten years for them to have their only child—me. Mom had irregular periods and endometriosis, and I do too," she said. Sophie "should have gotten pregnant a zillion times. I never used contraception. Yet I didn't. My sisters all have problems getting pregnant. So did my cousins on my mom's side of the family. There's a pattern here that indicates we've got a problem." Sometimes genetic problems were the reason women decided not to have kids. Inez "was born with a chromosome that would give my offspring this bizarre metabolic or hormonal disease that runs in my family." As a result, she and her siblings "all decided that we'd stop the transfer of the disease here and now. There are times I'm so sorry that our wonderful family line will be gone when we are. Mother and Dad were just the most perfect, loving parents any kids could want. It's been a hard, but pragmatic, decision to stop the trait now." Rose is the youngest of nine children who always thought she'd have children. But she had a genetic disability, familial myelitis, which is similar to cerebral palsy, and a curvature of the spine. "The doctors told me that there was no way to know if I would pass on the gene if I had kids. So at age sixteen, I decided never to have kids. I went in for a hysterectomy. It was the only thing to do." Sometimes mental disorders discouraged women from becoming pregnant. Pat was "afraid to have children because depression seems a part of my family history. I know it's inherited, and it's been all I can do to manage myself—why would I inflict this on a child I love?"

Infertility was also attributed to diseases that were not necessarily genetic in origin. For example, Dawn's diabetes prohibited her from having children: "I've been a diabetic since age ten. During the 1960s in Maine, I was told I should never get pregnant so I never dreamed of getting married and having kids. Mom was diabetic and very sick. I knew I didn't want to give my kids a mother like I had. I feel like I'd been programmed not to have kids because of the diabetes. Now I know diabetes doesn't have to prevent pregnancy, but back then, we thought it did." Several women experienced cancer of the uterus and felt they could not bear children because of it. For instance, Grace, who first married in her forties, planned to have children "until I found out I had uterine cancer. We're trying everything for me just to stay alive. I don't know how long I can make it. So while I'd have loved to have a baby so that we can live on together through a child, it's not to be. I just want to make the most of the days that we have left together." Betsy was pregnant once, but "the pregnancy triggered cancer. Then I miscarried. Chemotherapy at Johns Hopkins saved me. If it had been two years before, I probably would have died. I never conceived again," she reported. Laura reflected on the difficulties created by her cancer and how she transformed her life as a result: "When we were thirty, my husband went to medical school and I was teaching. Life was very hectic.

There was no room or time for a child. In the last year of his medical school, I quit my teaching job and we moved. I got sick—either I had a tumor or I was pregnant. It was cancer. At times of illness, personal survival becomes the motivating factor in one's life—not pregnancy."

Women wondered if they had exposed themselves to toxins or diseases that prevented conception. "I smoked, I drank, I had multiple sexual partners, I worked in a factory where we were exposed to chemicals—did any of these things keep me from getting pregnant?" Sherri asked. Cigarette smoking has been tied to longer conception time, ovulatory and tubal disorders, as well as to fetal and early infant death. In addition, women whose mothers smoked during pregnancy were found to take longer to become pregnant themselves. Other behavioral factors are currently under investigation to clarify their suspicious relationship to infertility. They include caffeine consumption, alcohol use, drug use, and use of birth control pills and devices.[6] Sexually transmitted diseases and pelvic inflammatory diseases are both highly correlated with infertility.

One of the most frequently mentioned causes of infertility among the women I interviewed was endometriosis.[7] Sarah's experience was common: "Every month I had painful periods—I'd be sick three or four days with vomiting and cramps. It hurt so bad I'd scream and bite the pillows. The only other girl I knew who had bad periods was given codeine by her doctor and I was angry with my mom for not getting me codeine too. My periods got progressively worse as I got older. I wondered how I'd be able to stand the pain of childbirth if I couldn't stand menstrual cramps. In my thirties I wanted children but never met the right man. It kept getting worse, and it interfered with my relationships. I became careless with birth control and felt that if a baby came along, great. But I never got pregnant," she said. Sarah found that "no one in the medical profession linked my physical symptoms and my not getting pregnant. Having sex became painful, and some men were not understanding about it. I started to develop an aversion to sex because it hurt—not just during intercourse, but for several days afterward as well. Doctor after doctor told me I needed a psychiatrist, that it was all in my head. One told me my problem would be solved if I drank a couple glasses of wine before sex to relax!" Sarah never accepted the doctors' diagnosis of her problem as psychologically based. "It was a scary, lonely, frustrating time." In college she met other women who had bleeding and cramping problems. Then she learned about all the types of endometriosis. "I had the worst type." She traveled thousands of miles to see a leading surgeon, "who was outraged at how I'd been treated. It took a four-hour surgery for him to treat 'the worst case' he said he'd ever seen." However, the surgery was not successful, and Sarah ended up having a hysterectomy the next year. "It was a terrible ordeal. I feel as though I lost fourteen years of my life."

Some childless women interviewed attributed their infertility to "female problems." Mary Margaret's periods had been "wacky ever since I was a girl. I started periods at age ten, and they got very irregular." She would go months at a time without menstruating. She never went in for fertility tests because "I felt it was something God didn't want me to fool around with." Now she takes medicine in order to have periods, but "the medicine would cause birth defects if I did get pregnant," she said. Other women talked about physical problems they thought made getting pregnant difficult. Allie was overweight and did not want to have a child when she was heavy. She waited until "the time was right, but by then I was past forty. Sometimes I still think about having a kid, but the likelihood of getting pregnant is low—the eggs are old, as they say." Other women had "body parts that don't work right." Elizabeth had a "fallen uterus" that resulted in her having a hysterectomy. Ruth learned that her infertility was due to a thick-skinned uterus—which was common in daughters of women who took the drug DES. Kate sustained an injury to her pelvic area when she was in first grade and "now I cannot get pregnant. While I always dreamed of getting married and having kids, I've known for most of my life that I can't. Maybe this is why I never really dated anyone seriously. What's the use?" she asked. Having a body that "let them down" was difficult for women who had thought that someday they would have children but then could not.

Like many women who spent the early part of their childbearing years going to college and building careers, Sherri was infertile by the time she got around to trying to get pregnant. She had postponed having children. "I was a professional with a sense of urgency to build my career. It was not that I didn't want children. I was absorbed with getting my education and career under way. But around age thirty-five, I really wanted a baby. I needed a baby to feel complete. I tried and tried to get pregnant, but nothing happened. So I went in for tests. There were fertility programs for 'women who are getting older,' like age thirty-four! I began heavy-duty tests for a cost of $5,000 and spent $40,000 on a treatment program—but we knew there was no guarantee. Nothing happened, and then they wanted me to have more treatments. But I felt I couldn't get pregnant, so I didn't. Today, it's still an issue for me to get pregnant."

There is a great deal of controversy in general about the appropriateness of fertility treatments, especially their use in older women. Studies among women ages forty and older indicate that they experienced more medical complications and interventions during delivery than had been expected. First-time mothers who gave birth in their forties were twice as likely to have a Caesarean section than were those in their twenties. The older group also experienced a substantially higher rate of pregnancy-related diabetes and high blood pressure than did the younger women. Overall, the potential risks to the mother and fetus seem to increase as the mother's age increases; however, experts assert that such results should not deter older women who want to become pregnant.[8]

How do women feel about being infertile? According to Mardy Ireland's findings, the inability to bear children makes women feel defective and increasingly vulnerable every time they answer, "No, I do not have children."[9] Women grieve the loss of their physical integrity, the loss of their anticipated child, and the loss of their imagined identities as mothers. An infertile woman does not become childless overnight; instead, she must undergo a process of perceiving herself to be childless over a period of time as she experiences ever more signs that she will not get pregnant. The longer a woman pursues pregnancy unsuccessfully, the longer it may take for the mourning to be resolved. For many women, it is as if each new fertility treatment, each failed attempt to conceive, is a new experience of loss. Infertile women have been found to be twice as likely to be depressed as those who are fertile; they have the same levels of depression as those with life-threatening conditions such as cancer, heart disease, or AIDS.[10] In its severity as a stressor, the inability to fulfill the culturally prescribed life goal of bearing children has been compared with death and divorce. Some women reported that infertility was the hardest thing they had to face in life.[11] "It was awful when I wanted a baby so much and couldn't have one. I was depressed and angry. I blame myself. I didn't feel feminine; I didn't want sex any-more; I felt I let my husband down; I felt I was ending our family line. It's frustrating—I had so much to offer and it'll be lost because my body let me down," said Kate. It appears that some infertile women have lower levels of psychological well-being. They rated life as less interesting, emptier, and more disappointing. They were also less satisfied than other women with how much success and fulfillment they had in their lives.[12] "I blamed myself," Iris confessed. "I couldn't understand why my body wouldn't be like other women's bodies."

For some women, infertility is more than a life crisis—it is a spiritual crisis. Many of the women interviewed turned to a spiritual or philosophic framework to explain their infertility. "I guess that God has a greater plan for me, one that doesn't include children," Lana said. "My job is to handle the emotions and wait to find out what that plan is." Supernatural explanations for infertility are based on a long history. In the Bible, infertility was regarded as a punishment meted out to those who lost favor with a vengeful God. Sarah, Rachel, Leah, Hannah, and Elisabeth conceived only after finding favor with God.[13] Medical science has replaced this notion with biological explanations. However, biological facts do not necessarily conflict with a woman's spiritual understanding of her condition. "I thought there was something wrong with me, not just my body, but wrong with me," Sophie confessed. "In an odd sort of way, I wondered whether I was being tested or punished for something." Iris shrugged and talked about her self-doubt that she just cannot shake: "I tried and tried to get pregnant, but couldn't. There's no big medical reason—I just couldn't get pregnant. My best friend, a social worker, asked me why it was that I didn't want a child. I told her that I desperately wanted a child! To her, my inability to conceive was due to my psychological rejection of pregnancy. Even though I knew she was wrong, I still process the issue—Did I really not want a child even though I thought I did?" Joanna, who became pregnant, wondered "if I subconsciously caused the miscarriage. I read about a study about women with multiple miscarriages and I fit their profile. They alleged it was a control issue, where people stuff their anger and expel their feelings that result in a miscarriage. It's too bad to learn these lessons so late. Part of me believes that the miscarriages were caused by psychological, not physical, reasons." Was Joanna's infertility caused by psychological or physical problems? She may never know—but she has attributed at least part of the cause to her own failure as a woman.

As author Barbara Menning, a nurse specialist in maternal and child health, related, she was devastated to learn of her infertility. Her inability to have a child dashed her girlhood dreams of becoming a mother and forced her to process what she'd experienced: "I did not understand what was happening to me, in spite of an advanced degree in maternal-child health and nursing. I did not understand my feelings, in spite of the fact that I had counseled others extensively. I did not understand why my husband could not understand my pain, in spite of a marriage blessed with good communication. Most of all I could not understand why infertility hurt so much. After all, I had a career. I was born of a generation who's doing things like cohabiting instead of marrying, having open marriages, and choosing not to have children at all. They key word here is choice. I had chosen to marry; I had chosen a traditional relationship; I had chosen to have children. Infertility robbed me of my right to choose to have my own genetic children."[14]

Although some experts have alleged that infertile women tend to experience greater emotional distress than do most other women, others have challenged this assumption and declared that the overall psychological state of infertile women is mostly on a par with that of mothers and the voluntarily childless. Personality profiles of fertile and infertile women look fairly similar, with no significant differences in the reported levels of self-esteem, sexual functioning, and life satisfaction or in expected levels of success, fulfillment, and achievement among both groups of women.[15] "I'm not a sick individual, but rather heart-sick. Wouldn't you be too? Wouldn't this be a normal response to what I've gone through?" Sherri asked. "I've had to experience emotional distress from my infertility, but distress is not equivalent to psychological impairment."

Despite the stress that infertility can place on a relationship, studies indicate that childless couples experience greater marital satisfaction and happiness than do couples with children. In fact, infertility patients have reported being happier with their relationships and perceived their partners as happier than did couples with children. Researchers have proposed that partners who were supportive of their infertile wives and willing to seek infertility treatment were more committed, communicative partners.[16] "We were partners in the process," Nora explained. "He went with me to appointments, gave me the shots, and was there every step of the way. We talked about what the whole process meant to each of us. When I couldn't get pregnant, he felt just as sad. He never blamed me, or him, for our not being able to have kids. He gave me perspective, he gave me hope, and let me know that everything would be okay, even if we didn't have a baby," she said.

Infertile women also discussed how their experience isolated them in social situations. "My extended family and friends didn't see my moment-to-moment struggle with infertility. They didn't know what it felt like to be in a family of Fertile Myrtles and not be able to get pregnant, or how it feels to go to baby showers that are never for you. They really didn't want to hear about how sad I felt—they preferred me to put on a happy face and pray for a miracle to occur," said Jennifer. Women who went through expensive and time-consuming infertility treatments like Melissa did "found that my family was great during the procedures, and they grieved with me every time an attempt failed. The support I got from my friends was tremendous. But over time, my distress was forgotten by people who assumed that I should be done processing my infertility. I'm not a light switch. It takes time to get over not having kids," she said. Jennifer finds that her sisters use her as a "convenient dumping ground for taking care of their kids when they want to go out, since they think that my having their kids around will make me forget about not having my own, or make me feel needed or something." She resents that her infertility is a too-common topic of conversation within her family. Non-Caucasian women such as Ahanna indicated that in her subculture, "childbearing is a woman's pathway to identity." In a national survey of families and households, men and women were asked to respond to the statement "It's better for a person to have a child than to go through life childless." Almost no one felt that childlessness was desirable; most regarded having children as very important. Among those surveyed, Hispanics and African Americans were more likely to agree that having a child is very important.[17]

Many of those who were unwilling to accept their infertility invested a great deal of money and emotion into reproductive therapies that were not successful. Medical innovations in the area of reproduction "could have been a god-send for people like me—but they weren't," asserted Kate. Thanks to a host of reproductive therapies, however, single women, lesbian women, infertile women, and menopausal women have some reproductive options, and the medical community proudly advertises these options. Meanwhile, the media dish out tales of reproductive perversity, such as the Baby M case, postmenopausal pregnancies, and surrogacy cases, with relish. Success stories, such as the "seven-with-one-blow"—the brave little Iowa woman who asked for one child and got many—make the front pages of the *New York Times*.[18] Although such success stories are the exception, they kindle the hopes of the would-be mother. But not all those who use one of the technologies available on the menu of reproductive options—now known collectively as assisted reproductive technology—will end up with a child. Although today more women are seeking treatment for infertility, and one out of six couples has an infertility problem, most never use some sort of assisted reproductive technology. Even so, more than three million women use some form of therapy to become pregnant.[19]

Sometimes infertility treatments work and women have children. Yet among the women I interviewed, the treatments were not successful. Women such as Sherri "spent thousands of dollars and endured emotional and physical distress to experience failed attempts at pregnancy. I traveled over an hour every day at 6:00 A.M. for a month for pergonal and ultrasound treatments. It was hard on me and my husband, but the treatments brought us closer together. I must admit that I resented that it was my body that would not get pregnant that I had to go through artificial insemination and all the treatments. Still, I chose. I was not a victim. I chose that this was what I wanted to do." For all women who seek alternate pregnancy techniques, there are costs. The emotions of loss and frustration associated with infertility are one thing; those that come with the treatment are quite another.[20] "We were really surprised when the doctor said I'm infertile. We couldn't accept that diagnosis. There were too many other reasons why it couldn't be correct. We talked to all our friends, went to other doctors, read scads of books and articles, and used all kinds of herbs and potions and positions and everything you can imagine to have a child. We were willing to undergo expensive treatments that made me feel like Hell. I was willing to make the long drives and make my body into a pincushion, an object that doctors could do all kinds of things to. I think I ceased to exist as me—I existed only as a thing, a vehicle to carry eggs and sperms. My emotions were wild because of all the drugs, and because of all the hopes and frustrations. I didn't talk about anything else, I didn't think about anything else. While I worked and went through my daily routines, I was like a zombie where nothing else mattered," Melissa said.

Women such as Kate have undergone more than twenty-one in vitro fertilizations, so far without success. Yet, she believes she may get pregnant one day, so "I'm going to exhaust all efforts emotionally, physically, and financially until I'm convinced that I can't." Why do women keep pursuing reproductive therapy options when they are so costly, so emotionally difficult, so physically draining, and so unlikely to end in a pregnancy? The answer seems simple—they hope against all odds that Lady Luck will be on their side. "Going through the therapy is like playing the lottery—I know it's unlikely, but I hope I'll win," Sherri said. According to professionals who work with infertility patients, many who have tried just about everything keep coming back to try again, despite their decreasing chances of success. Scientific data are not convincing to those who are hopeful. One physician said, "I have patients whom I tell, point blank, you should stop, and they say to me, Well, I want to give it one more try, and I say, Here, look at the data. Your chance is 1 percent. And they say, I'm going to be that one, Doc."[21] The women I interviewed seemed more likely to undergo ongoing infertility treatments when they liked their physician and had faith in the treatments. "They were so nice to us. When we started to believe that we might not be successful in having a child, they always had stories of other couples who had succeeded. Going gave us hope— and hope was what we needed," said Melissa. Although reproductive therapies gave such women as Melissa "peace of mind, knowing at least I tried," sometimes she and others viewed the treatments as a form of exploitation. "They call pumping my ovaries full of drugs, time after time, the Ovarian Olympics," said Melissa, whose fertility tests, treatments, surgeries, drugs, and frustration over ten years cost $6,000. She had in vitro fertilization twice. "It was hard. They used huge needles, and my husband had to give me daily shots. It was a group effort. It's been almost as hard on my husband, who would have made a sensitive, wonderful father."

The women in this study indicated that often the focus of treat- ments—creating a successful pregnancy—was so intense that the emo- tional, economic, and physical risks associated with the treatments were downplayed. "The infertility treatments turned our dream of hav- ing a child into a nightmare." The treatments can be "the most stress- ful thing you can go through as a woman. I can't even describe it. You become a scientific experiment and your body becomes a laboratory that isn't even yours anymore. Strangers look inside you, give you tests and shots and examinations of all sorts. Every time they do I hope we're one step closer to getting a baby. But here we are, still trying. It's a real roller coaster, all the way," said Iris.

Women who did not receive physician support during the time they were undergoing infertility treatment found that deciding against further treatment was easier. "The technicians weren't particularly sympathetic about our physical and emotional distress. It's a baby mill. They hustle women in, poke them with this or that, and take your money. Do they really care how it feels, or what our failure means? I don't think so," observed Melissa. Some, such as Jennifer, talked about how they went to the doctor for assistance with reproduction and found themselves "so angry over the way we were treated that we quit going, even though they could have ultimately helped us to have the child we wanted."

Are the therapies worth it? "Maybe they are if you come out of it with a child. But enduring any amount of pain and inconvenience to have a child makes you stop and reassess whether this is healthy or sick behavior," said Angela, a psychotherapist. Iris wondered, "Are these treatments really good for you? Are they good for society? I mean, wouldn't the money be better spent solving existing problems, like disease or improving the lives of kids who are already here? Also, it doesn't seem quite fair that only rich women can afford these expensive procedures."

An increasing body of research links certain infertility treatments with cancer.[22] Hannah argued that "I think these therapies can kill you. When I went to the doctor to check out my reproductive options and she said, 'I'm sorry, at thirty-eight you're too old. The only thing I can do is put you on pergonal, but your chances of getting pregnant will be about 2 percent,' I went home and talked with my husband about what to do. As we talked, we came up with a startling conclusion. We realized that three of our friends who used fertility drugs had come down with uterine cancer. One died a few months ago, one's in the process of dying, and another thinks she can beat it. Sure, some of our friends did get pregnant and had babies after using the drugs. But the ones who got cancer—the drugs were the only thing that they had in common. These were women who took good care of themselves, who ate right and had lifestyles that didn't expose them to chemicals. My husband told me that he couldn't bear for me to risk my life to have a child. Having a child and not having me wasn't worth it."

Miscarriage

Approximately one-third of the women I interviewed had been pregnant at some time in their lives. Of those, about half had chosen abortions, about 8 percent had given birth to children who had died soon after, and the remainder had miscarried, many of them several times. Miscarriages were, according to Melinda, "children we never got to see or hold, but our children, nonetheless." Grieving for an unborn child is a lonely experience. When a woman miscarries, there is no baby to look upon, no hands to caress. There are no funerals, no pictures or memories to give voice to the grief. A woman is left with only dreams and plans of what might have been. The grief is often compounded by the lack of a logical explanation for why the miscarriage occurred.

The women in this study who had miscarried talked about feeling alienated and receiving little social support. "People really don't understand about what it's like to miss," Betts said. Many talked about how they had not gotten the help they needed from their doctors or medical staff, as Betts found out: "I was at home when I started bleeding. By the time I got to the hospital, it was too late. They made me have a D & C [a surgical procedure called dilation and curettage used to remove fetal material from the womb]. The hospital staff regarded it as a routine procedure, but it was anything but routine for me. They weren't even going to allow my husband in the room, and acted like they just wanted to get it over with. They didn't tell me what to expect afterward, like pain and bleeding, and I was scared."

Many women also received little support from their friends or family to help them through the physical and emotional ordeal that followed their miscarriage. "But people didn't know what to say, so they said nothing. They could have told me they were sorry; they could have held me, they could have asked me if I needed to talk, but they didn't know what to say. Just listening would have been enough," Joanna said. "Then there are the ones who say all the wrong things, like 'it was for the best,' or 'at least you know you can get pregnant,' or 'it wasn't really a baby.' They made my grief worse, instead of better." Other women such as Christina found that "People think that it's no big deal if you miscarry. They dismissed my feelings with the old, 'well, get busy and pop another one and you'll have better luck next time' talk. It hurts so badly. Don't they know? Can't they imagine what it must feel like to be me?"

When confronted with infertility, miscarriage, the loss of anticipated children, or the realization that they would never be mothers, women sometimes perceived these challenges as tests from God or spiritual obstacles to be overcome. Toots said, "I feel I have failed one of the most central acts of life by not having a child. I feel sorry for myself because no matter which way I turn, it hits me in the face. I try to dwell on the good things I have and I tell myself that God has a path for me that I'm supposed to be following. I don't think God would punish me and that's what gets me by. It just didn't turn out—my having a baby wasn't in the cards. While I tell myself these things, I can't even talk to my mom about it without crying and getting upset," she said.

Women also discussed the support, or lack of it, that they received from their clergy. "I thought the minister would be able to help me through this. I guess he tried, but he was used to burying old people who'd lived out their lives. He didn't know how to help me deal with the loss of a child that never existed in a tangible way to anyone except me," said Brenda. "He didn't have prayers in his book for situations like this, and he wasn't a warm, creative kind of guy who could automatically say and do the right things to comfort me. Ministers are supposed to make you feel better in times of crisis, right?" Other women had talked about the failure of their clergy to address the emotional and spiritual crises that accompanied their inability to bear children. But other women such as Anne found strength through her religious convictions. Although organized religion has been slow to address the needs of women who have miscarried or lost infants, Anne found that they are "slowly rising to the occasion. This is out of the need to find other ways to impart God's love."

Because friends and relatives are uncomfortable discussing the topic, they often minimize the woman's loss, withdraw their support after a month or two, and expect the grieving parents to "pull out of it" and recover quickly.[23] However, "It takes longer to get over it than others think it should," admitted Betts. Although women who experience miscarriages today may have more resources than did the women of their mothers' generation, and although the subject is talked about more openly, still women may feel just as alone.

Presumably, women who have experienced several miscarriages might accept them more easily, yet among the women I interviewed, just the opposite seemed to be true. "After the second, I wondered if I could ever have a child," Brenda, a professional woman, said. "The only people I felt understood were the people who had more than one miscarriage." It was difficult to get support from others, Joanna and her husband found, because people denied the importance of the miscarriages the couple had endured. "We've lost children, and most people don't honor that. One has to wonder if it is harder or easier to have a miscarriage or lose a baby." It may be "harder to miscarry, because there is no name, face, or personality that you would have had if you had lost a baby," said Martina. "People didn't know what to say when I had the first miscarriage, which was hard. But after my third, people acted as though nothing had happened at all. They were real matter-of-fact about it, and I guess they expected me to take everything in stride. But for me, having more miscarriages didn't make it easier. It made things harder—I had lost three babies."

Although sadness over the loss of their anticipated child was great, so was guilt and self-blame. Some women wondered if they had somehow caused the miscarriage. "Maybe I didn't take good enough care of myself," Martina wondered, whereas Brenda blamed "my stupid body that doesn't work right." Others, such as Veronica, wondered if they had lost the child "because I had conflicted feelings about being pregnant," because she knew that her husband "didn't want a child." Betts's pregnancy proceeded normally until her sister, who was also pregnant, lost her baby. "I think that part of me couldn't have stood to have a baby when my sister lost hers. It would have been too hard for us. I never wanted to miscarry, but I wonder if subconsciously I sent a message to my body not to have it?" Guilt and self-blame "may not do any good, but they whisper in your ear when you're not expecting it," Martina observed. "This makes it hard to move forward."

Women learned that often their husbands or partners didn't share the extent of their grief, "which made me feel so alone," Martina admitted. A study by Ruth Carroll and Carol Shaefer found that women who have lost a child often reflect and express sadness, whereas men tend to be more stoic and emotion-suppressing.[24] They also found that a person's level of education, income, and age had little to do with the amount of grief suffered when a child was lost through miscarriage. Fathers were more likely to see getting pregnant again as a solution to their grief, whereas mothers were likely to mourn the lost child forever. As Joanna insisted, "One child is not a replacement for the other." Dr. Joseph Hill, director of reproductive medicine at Brigham and Women's Hospital in Boston and a specialist in recurrent miscarriages, is reported as saying that couples "might have a lovely daughter and son at home, but it [a miscarriage] is still a loss. It's a mistake to say bonding occurs when you hold a baby. Bonding occurs when you see an ultrasound, when you miss a period."[25] Melinda agreed: "As soon as I learned I was pregnant, I went out and bought some baby toys and little socks. I began to dream immediately about what he or she would look like, and how I'd walk around with a big belly that everyone would smile at. I was a mom from that moment on. Only once I miscarried, it was over. No one could look at me and ever tell that once I was a mom, even though it was for a short time and even though I never got to hold my child."

Depression may also occur when the once-pregnant woman finds that her name has not been omitted from a list of expectant mothers. Receiving notices for childbirth education classes, hospital admission packages, coupons from baby food, diaper, and formula companies, or magazines for new parents may be painful reminders that they are no longer pregnant. "I thought I was getting over it; then that material came in the mail, and I lost it. I had to start grieving all over," Martina said.

Joanna's story is one of trial but with some resolution. Joanna had miscarried once, and it took her four years and therapy before she was willing to try to get pregnant again: "I got pregnant right away. This pregnancy felt normal. I had morning sickness and my gut feeling was that everything was OK. You don't know how happy I was to be morning sick—it was a sign that everything was developing normally. I was so surprised and upset when I started bleeding. Then I miscarried." When she told her child-free friend about what had happened, "I was dumbfounded when she said, 'But everything is OK.' I had to sort this comment out. She felt that everything was right in the world and things were as they were meant to be. I'm still not sure I agree with that," Joanna said. Unlike the other miscarriages, "at least this time I had tissue to discard. I was more spiritual at this point in my life. A friend had given me a pretty marble box. When she did, I hadn't known why or what I was going to do with it. Then, after the miscarriage, I knew. I took the box and put a little of the tissue in it, a picture of my husband and me, and a mother's journal that I'd been keeping. We had a little ceremony, and I read part of the journal during it. Having the service, and reading aloud my private words was a hard thing to do, but in many ways it was the healthiest pregnancy of all because I was able to resolve it in this way." But this was not the end of her saga. She became pregnant shortly afterward. "We watched it carefully. From the beginning, the pregnancy didn't proceed right. The heartbeat was slow, the sac was smaller, the hormones decreased instead of doubling. It took four weeks after no heartbeat before I was willing to terminate the pregnancy. It was so hard—I kept wondering if there was a mistake, that I could still be pregnant with a live fetus. Yet I wanted it to be over, because I knew deep down inside that the fetus wasn't alive," she said. The doctors believed her problems might have been the result of chromosomal problems and age, "but we decided not to do any more detailed tests, because blame would be assigned and it wouldn't change things anyway. This pregnancy was hard because there was a greater sense of incompletion and no resolution, except to think that I'm never going to able to have a child. So I'm going back to school."

Infant Death

It is common to believe that, with today's advanced medical technology, babies seldom die. "But that's not true. There are all kinds of people out there who've lost children. They've learned not to talk about it with others usually, so the rest of us think it doesn't happen—until it happens to us," Harriet said. "It was the worst thing that ever happened to me, to lose our baby. I wrapped all my hopes and dreams into him. When he died, part of me died too. I go on each day, and I guess if you didn't know you wouldn't know. I mask it very well. This is great for everyone else—my acting normal makes them forget what I cannot. Although there are good days and hard days, he's inside of me all the time," Harriet confessed.

The women I interviewed gave various reasons for the death of their babies. Some died soon after birth because of undiagnosed or untreatable infections, some were unable to overcome genetic or physical malformations, whereas others died from sudden infant death syndrome (SIDS). Whatever the reason, the outcome was the same—women who thought they were going to be mothers were left without children to care for.

After trying so hard to become pregnant, experiencing elation over the pregnancy, and then losing the child at some point during the pregnancy or delivery process, a woman will likely experience tremendous grief. Sometimes a woman's milk comes in after the birth (or even after a miscarriage), which is a painful shock for the childless mother. "There I was in my hospital bed, and my breasts leaked milk and there was no baby for me to nurse. Of course, they gave me pills to dry up my milk, but the trauma of losing my baby was inflicted over and over, in countless ways," Ina said. Some women I interviewed were afraid to get pregnant again for fear that the new baby would die. Ina confessed that "sometimes I avoid having sex, for fear I'll get pregnant. This creates problems with my husband, who just doesn't understand—that I need and love him, that I desperately want us to have a baby, yet I'm terrified to get pregnant again because I just don't think I could go through losing another child."

It was difficult to stop grieving because grief was the only tie left to the child, as Harriet said. "Part of me doesn't want to let go. I don't want the pain, but the pain of remembering that I once had a child is better than the reality of being without. That may sound crazy, but in my grief there is solace, and unity in my aloneness. I don't want to give them up." After Ina's miscarriages and the death of her infant, "I became depressed, fat, and divorced. Sometimes I hear my babies calling me from heaven and I want to be with them. I've thought about suicide so I could be there to take care of them. When I die, I'll be buried right beside them so I can finally be with them. You may think this is morbid, but it's hard to have part of you in this world and part of you somewhere else." Parents have much to lose emotionally when they cut themselves free from the children they hoped they would raise. According to author Dennis Klass, "When a child dies, a part of the self is cut off. Many parents find the metaphor of amputation useful. . . . Like amputation, parental bereavement is a permanent condition. The hopes, dreams, and expectations incarnate in the child are now gone. Bereaved parents do find resolution to their grief in the sense that they learn to live in their new world. They resolve the matters of how to be themselves in a family and community in a way that makes life meaningful. They learn to invest themselves in other tasks and other relationships. Yet for parents who have lost children, a part of them is missing and their world is forever changed. It is that part of the self which seeks consolation."[26]

Friends and family may not know how to act or console a couple when their baby dies at birth. "People are not comforted by the statements, your baby is an angel in heaven, or there is a purpose, or God wanted that baby. They are angry, and want that baby with them, and empty arms hurt. Lots of women have empty arms that physically hurt when they go home from the hospital without a child," Harriet said. She found that silence could be comforting, when people who loved her sat with her, supporting her. But used as a tool of avoidance, silence can be "like a knife in the heart." It is difficult to talk about losing a child with people who have never experienced such a loss. Those who are sought out for help may find they are uncomfortable with the topic, so the grieving woman fails to get the support she needs. For most women, the denial and rejection of loved ones hurt the most. May and her husband had a baby that "was born dead. It was awful, being there in the hospital, and all these people coming to see my empty arms. My belly was big like the other moms, but I had no baby to take home." Afterward, May had to grieve not just the loss of her baby but also the loss of her marriage and the loss of her dreams about how life was going to turn out for her.

May's experience was not unique. Marital deterioration and break-up is a common outcome for couples who lose a child.[27] "You never really get over it," May said. Women I interviewed talked about how, at these times of gut-wrenching emotional distress, their husbands and partners were often emotionally unavailable to comfort them.

When Ina's son was born with a rare genetic disorder, she recounted, "My husband blamed me for it, although he could have been the transmitter of the gene as easily as I. He said he would leave me as soon as the baby died, and he did. He made me feel responsible for both the baby dying and our divorce." Anne wondered if the hospital was to blame for the problems she encountered during the delivery that resulted in her child's death. "If only I'd gone somewhere else, if only I'd had a different doctor, or there had been other staff members attending to me. If only I'd been more assertive about what I felt we needed, maybe then he would be alive." Vanessa found one of her twins dead in the crib a few months after she brought them home. "They said he died of SIDS. Other people said that SIDS is related to the parent's treatment of the baby, that maybe I had done something wrong. I loved him! How could they think I would hurt my child?" she said with painful outrage. Anne's "entire soul and body was consumed with grief after our baby died. I couldn't move, it all hurt so bad. I took my son's ashes and spread them in Colorado. But the grief is still in my heart and I carry it inside. I feel responsible, guilty, like I did something wrong that caused the deaths of my children. I know I didn't, but sometimes I can't help but feel that way."

Finally reconciling a child's death is one of the greatest challenges women can face. When they do, it is inspiring, as in Demi's case: "I was losing amniotic fluid and the baby didn't have fluid to grow in. It doesn't happen often—they say once in a million. We kept thinking that it was going to seal, but it didn't. I couldn't take a bath, I couldn't laugh because I could feel the fluid leaving me. The last specialist told us that the baby would be terribly deformed if it survived, and it would probably die from lung damage. They wanted to do a therapeutic abortion. I had a few days to think about it. This was the hardest decision I had to make. The rational part of me knew that bringing a terribly deformed child into the world was cruel, but my heart was carrying this little knot of life. I am so grateful that the decision was made for me, when suddenly I went into labor and he didn't survive. It took me a long time to get over it. It was a no-win situation. Nothing could make it better. Whatever the decision, the outcome would have been the same. There was a while when I couldn't talk about it. It hurt; I felt a loss. I needed to talk it out, to know I reasoned it through correctly. People who love you enough to have honest dialogue will help you to rethink the issues. I've put it in perspective. It's helped me to understand. For instance, when I was in the business world, I didn't have a lot of patience with pregnant women. I felt they should eat well, exercise, do their job—and give me a break! In my logic box, I didn't have a lot of patience with them, and I didn't understand why their goals weren't the same as mine. After going through what we did, boy, did my attitudes change! With postpartum depression, and all, I have an insight that I would never have had otherwise. I'm now a better person, a much better manager. As tragic and awful as it was, I learned from it."

According to those women who lost children, it takes time to learn the lessons death has to teach. Many didn't cope well even when they received support. Vanessa "transformed my entire personality. I became a workaholic, and I guess a sexaholic. I drank and changed my wardrobe and became somebody else. I developed problems at work and was fired. I got divorced. I find that I can't get close to kids now. I love them, but I can't stand being with them. I now work in medicine and donate time to work holidays so that other mothers can be at home with their children." Others found that they could not talk with others about the loss of their child. "I can't go to support groups. I think they're good for some people, but not me. There are other women like me. Some write letters to the newspapers, or to causes or politicians, to encourage them to take the right stand for kids. Others will develop bicycle safety programs, or plant memorial gardens, or hold celebrations of some sort to commemorate the betterment of the world. Remember the child in the Oklahoma City bombing who was carried out by the firefighter? Her parents held a party for the community, to bring people together, not to mourn her death, but to celebrate her life. Everybody has to find their own way to grieve and make sense of such senseless things," said May.

Adjustment to the loss of a child is a lifelong process. Women such as Harriet found that when they look at other children who are the same age as their child would have been, a new set of adjustments is prompted. "After I first lost my baby, I couldn't stand to be around new babies, because it hurt so bad. Then, when I saw kids going off to elementary school, and selling Girl Scout cookies, and going to dance recitals, I'd fall apart, thinking how mine should be there. High school graduation time posed an unexpected opening of the wound, and as my friends are having weddings and anticipating grandchildren, I find I continue to mourn the loss of my baby," she said.

For the women I interviewed, their stories of lost children were painful to tell, and painful to hear, but as Harriet said, "women need to near the truth, that women do lose babies." In one especially poignant interview, Anne talked about the loss she endured when not just one child but two died. She had been diagnosed with a uterine abnormality. "Doctors assume that I was a DES baby, but there's no record of it. I always knew I could have troubles conceiving and having a baby as a result. Doctors encouraged me to get pregnant when I was young. They found two cavities and cervixes in my uterus. The doctors told me, 'you'll just have a few miscarriages,' as if it were no big deal. It was such a medicalized view of such a personal event. I got pregnant, and at twenty-nine weeks I had to be put to bed. My son was born normal at thirty weeks, but he was tiny and they put him on machines to help him survive. But four days later, he had a brain hemorrhage. The first time I got to hold him was when he was taken off the machines. You think about all the times mothers hold their babies and rock them to sleep. The first time I got to hold my baby was when I got to rock him to death."

Anne continued her story: "We didn't really know that babies die. There is this conspiracy of silence that women don't share. They don't share miscarriage and infant death stories. As a result, we don't know about pre-term babies that die. It wouldn't lessen the pain, but perhaps it would lessen the shock." Anne explained that the doctors never found a cause for her son's death. "After that, we went through all kinds of genetics tests. We did not want to go through another situation like this." The doctors encouraged her to try again. "It took two years to work through the emotion of it." She did have a few miscarriages. One pregnancy she terminated because it was clear that it would not go anywhere. "It was difficult for me to consider the abortion, but the pregnancy couldn't have gone to term, the baby couldn't be born normal. It was the only reasonable thing to do," Anne, a minister, explained. Finally, Anne became pregnant with what seemed to be a viable fetus. "We had ultrasounds to look for four chambers of the heart, we talked to surgeons about the baby's treatment, and ultimately decided to continue with the pregnancy." At thirty-two weeks her second son was born. "I weighed about 190 pounds because the bigger the baby, the better the chance he had to survive," Anne said. "I was in the hospital, and I woke up and couldn't feel him kick. They threw me into the delivery room and conducted an emergency C-section. I saw them rip him out fast! They found that the baby couldn't oxygenate his own blood. The put him on a machine to help. They thought it may be due to an undiagnosed infection. The doctors told me that night that our son had made a turn and was getting better. I was so happy. Then boom! The next morning the baby died. The medicines they used to save him killed him." Doctors encouraged the couple to try again, but Anne was "in utter shock. We couldn't believe that it had happened a second time." After that, the couple refused to get pregnant again. "Before we became pregnant, we had both wanted work and family, but we weren't obsessed. But having the second child drew out of us love we didn't even know we had. It was one of the greatest gifts we ever had—we were given the wonderful gift of two boys, even if it was only for a short time. We now know something about love that we couldn't have known before."

When birth and death occur on the same day, it is generally too much for most people to bear. There needs to be a way for people in this situation to grieve, for other people to help them mourn their loss. Without a ritual, the loss seems unreal to some parents and others who are familiar with the death. When there is a funeral or wake, people know what to say and do. There is support in these situations.

According to chaplains who have worked with grieving parents, parents go through certain stages as they recover emotionally from the loss of a child—stages that are similar to those outlined by Elizabeth Kubler-Ross.[28] These stages of coping with grief include shock, denial, anger, bargaining, depression, and disorganization, and ultimately reorganization of life and acceptance of the death of the child. In the first stage, when women first lose a child, they tend to experience shock and numbness. They had not anticipated losing the child; even those women who suspected that the pregnancy was not proceeding normally still felt surprised and upset over the death of their infant. According to those I interviewed who had lost children, they had a hard time hearing consoling words, and there really are few words people can say that can soothe the pain. Several clergy members who were interviewed for this study said that they used a "ministry of presence," where they tried just to be with the parents in their moment of grief. They found that they had to make repeated visits to help parents hear the message.

In the second stage of coping with death—anger—women may be angry at God, at their bodies, at their partner, at the child for dying, at friends and family, and at professionals who say and do things that only increase pain instead of healing. Women may feel as though they are failures; many in this study wondered what they had done to cause their child's death. Sometimes women who have experienced repeated losses may get angry with other pregnant women and women who do not take care of their bodies—such as smokers or drinking moms who end up with healthy babies. It was common to find that women blamed themselves for the death of their child. Many went through a host of "if only" scenarios—although even if they had done everything perfectly, the outcome may well have been the same.

After the loss of an infant, depression inevitably follows. It is natural to be depressed when one carries not a chubby, giggling child but shattered dreams and broken hearts. While they were pregnant, women had fixed up nurseries and visualized children playing in the house. Now they mourned holidays and celebrations that they would miss with their dream-children. Women I interviewed indicated that their depression comes and goes. They may think they are doing well, and then something may trigger memory and the loss comes painfully back again. Over time—and it does take a long time—women said that they had experienced some resolution of their child's death. Yet some grieving parents do not want to hear about resolution when they first lose their child. They cannot seem to move on with their lives. Deep down inside, many in this study feared that if they lived as though they had forgotten the child, the child would cease to matter. There was psychological danger, therefore, in emotionally releasing their deceased child.

Women talked about the need to process the death of their babies. Anne spoke of her process of reckoning. "It is okay to question God. I think God feels the pain you feel, and doesn't want this to happen to you, and God weeps with you." Jan, a hospital chaplain, has had to find ways to help parents of full-term babies who have died. "What I hear from women who have lost babies is to please allow them to spend as much time as possible with their baby before taking it away to prepare it for burial. They want the options of dressing their babies. One woman went forty-one weeks and unexpectedly had a stillbirth. It was shocking to her, and to the doctor. She and her husband spent two and a half days in the hospital with their daughter before she could leave her. The mother needed time to examine its fingers and toes, and see the perfection of it, and how wonderful it was. She needed time to hold her little girl. During her pregnancy, this mom had knitted a sweater and ended up burying the baby in it. She dressed her for the funeral and invited family into their room to baptize their baby. Because the parents knew people would ask them what happened when they realized that the pregnancy was over and yet there was no child, the parents sent out announcements with a red bird on it. After the burial, a month or so later, a red bird began appearing at their house—similar to the one on their announcement. The mother was sure that this was a message from her daughter—that she is still with her parents in a special way," the chaplain reflected.

Clergy talked about the importance of a rite of passage so that parents could end that part of their lives and be free to move forward. Some people wear a piece of jewelry, such as a bracelet, pin, or necklace that helps remind them of the child they lost. Others planted a tree or flowering bush so that the memory of the child could continue to grow. A few parents lit a candle each day to remind them of the child that did not live. Others preferred a naming or baptism service. As a result of this demonstrated need, more hospitals and chaplains routinely offer infant death services to parents of a dead child. I found in interviews with women who had lost children that naming the child was very important; even women who had never been pregnant but who knew the spirit of the child they felt they would have had, had sometimes named the child. Calina said, "If I had had a child, it would have been a daughter named Samantha." "Mine would have been Sebastian," said Janice. Some women named their babies for relatives, but more often they selected names that had spiritual connotations for themselves.

While physically burying the dead or miscarried children, women also had to bury them emotionally in order for the healing process to continue. But there is no protocol about how to go about this—especially after a miscarriage. If parents want to mourn an early miscarriage, there is no identifiable fetus; it appears as tissue. Yet they may still feel a connection to it and want to give their "child" a proper burial. Sometimes memorial services are created by the couple. Parents have written a poem or letter to the child, explained the significance of the name selected, and used the moment as an opportunity to say what they would have if the child had lived. A ritual service helps the parents find closure, because in their hearts they feel that the children can hear them. Parents and chaplains explained that in these ceremonies, parents often emphasized how much they had wanted the baby. One couple who had experienced an early miscarriage sought to bury the placenta: "From the moment of conception, even if it was not recognizable, it was our baby." Parents gave much thought to the type of container or box selected for this purpose. Harriet talked about how her husband had built a special wooden "coffin" and carved the child's name on the top. They had put letters and items inside that represented their relationship with their unborn child. "I had been collecting things for the baby, and there were some things that I had when I was little that I always planned to give to my child one day. I needed to put some of them in the box. We both wrote letters to our baby and put them inside. We held each other, and after we were done, then we could move on." After she miscarried, May said her husband began talking about wanting to adopt a child. "I didn't want to do it, and I didn't know why. I mean, I wanted a child so much, and I was happy to adopt, but I was dragging my feet about it. One day, he asked, 'Why are you doing this?' and I had to stop and think about it. What I realized was that I had never had any closure to our miscarriages. Without being able to really cry and say good-bye, I couldn't move forward. So we talked about it and decided what we would do. It was just the two of us. But we played certain songs and had prayers and words. We lit a candle and drank some wine and really did a communion with each other. After that ceremony, then I felt I could go on and adopt."

Some experts believe that the focus on mourning dead or pre-term babies can be unhealthy. For example, some have suggested that those who over-mourn the loss of a pregnancy may be transferring their pain over other issues, such as the reality of their infertility.[29] But for the women interviewed in this study, having time to experience the totality of their loss was essential for moving forward. Even when parents have a funeral, however, the emotional loss of the child continues. In a unique interview, Anne discussed her experiences conducting funerals for babies and older children: "It is terrible Hell for me to officiate at children's funerals. There is no good in the deaths of children. There is only good in their lives. My sons taught me how much I love and wanted children. I have learned to never take life, or those I love, for granted. I cherish [my adopted daughter] more. I do overprotect her; I know I fear immunizations, since my son died because of the medicine they gave him. Doctors seem only to give bad news, not good news. I cry when I'm in hospitals. I know I overreact sometimes. I refuse to accept any notion that God caused the death of my children. People create toxins that kill us, not God. God may send earthquakes, but it is our will to build on a fault line. I have struggled with the will of God and had a true spiritual crisis through the death of my children. I wondered where God was in this. After lots of talking, screaming, and praying to God, I still don't know why my boys died. But God gave me the strength, power, and courage to survive their deaths. They moved from my arms into the embrace of God. Probably the knowledge that they were going to God was the only way I let them take my babies out of my arms."

Officiating at funerals for other children was extremely difficult for Anne, but ultimately this forced her to deal with the loss of her own children. As she sought to comfort other parents, she came to grips with her own spiritual beliefs and was able to resolve her sons' deaths. Here is an excerpt from a sermon she gave:

> When I am asked why I continue to believe in God when God chose, intended, willed, whatever words you want to use, for my sons to die as infants, I have one very strong response. I am able to keep the faith because I do not, in any way, shape, or form, believe that God made such a choice. For God to choose or will the death of an innocent, sweet baby could only be described as sadistic and cruel. And I believe, in no uncertain terms, that God intends, wills, chooses, only good for us, for all humanity. God wants the children to be happy, healthy, and whole. This assertion about God's will or intentions is based on my most fundamental beliefs about God. I believe that God is love. And I believe that God is good. God will not abandon us. God is with us for the long haul, abiding with us. God who is good and loving will restore us to wholeness despite bitter grief, disappointments, frustrations, and tragedy. How many of us have wondered, "I don't know if I have the strength to carry on." That's a miracle of God. God can heal our grief. In Jesus' day, it was customary for each person to have a tear cup. This is one my parents gave me on the anniversary of my son's birth (which was also the anniversary of his death). The tradition was for each individual, when shedding tears of grief, to let a few run off his or her cheek into the tear cup. So the tear cup literally held within it the tears of sorrow from a person's life. It was a tangible reminder of what a person had endured and of the loved ones a person had lost. . . . I have offered my tears to God. I have and continue to experience the miracle of healing. My hurt and grieving soul is being resorted. Where is God? The God of love and goodness is right here, ready to heal. Just pour out your tears.

Many of the experiences of these different women—infertile women, women who had miscarried, and women who lost full-term babies—were similar. Their emotions of hope and devastation were intensely experienced. Emotionally resolving their childlessness required support, insight, and time. Their reactions to their childlessness were very different from the reactions of those who had chosen to remain childless. They felt less control over their bodies and lives than did the other women in the study. Their childlessness was a more painful emotional experience for them than it was for the others in the study. They had expected to become mothers and were emotionally, financially, and physically heavily invested in making that dream come true. Although most of them, like Harriet, adjusted to remaining childless, "it was nothing I ever wanted to be, nothing I ever wanted to experience. I just wanted the same thing that most women take for granted—to be able to have a healthy baby."

CHAPTER 7   Choosing to End
            Family Dysfunction

Family dysfunction—a catchphrase of the era—refers to families in which poor communication or nonfunctional interactions, interpersonal violence, substance abuse, illness, or other problems are regular occurrences. The underlying assumption is that these kinds of problems create problematic family dynamics that can have long-term consequences for those who grow up in such families. One of the main reasons some of the women I interviewed deliberately chose to remain childless was to end a cycle of dysfunction that they perceived to be perpetuated by their family. Certainly many of the women in this study had felt loved and well cared for by nurturing and devoted parents, and not every woman who chose to be childless felt rejected by her mother. Some, like Maggie and Laura, felt they "had the most wonderful, loving mom in the world." Ellie's mother "hugs me hello, hugs me good-bye, and gives me hugs for no special reason in between, all the time even today, just as she always has." Veronica adores her father and his nurturing ways. But many deliberately childless women, as well as those who were ambivalent about having children, indicated that the parenting they had received left something to be desired. Many felt their own home life had not perfect, and as a result they seemed to long for the ideal family—a happy home in which both mother and father were emotionally stable and healthy.[1] Whether these women's family life had actually been more dysfunctional than that of others is irrelevant; the point is that some of the women decided against having children because they felt they had grown up in pathological homes and didn't want to transfer their problems to a new generation of children. Some voluntarily childless women, because they had not received what they felt they needed from their own parents, were unsure if they could provide good parenting for children.

Social dysfunction was another major reason for choosing childlessness. Many of the women I interviewed felt that in good conscience they could not bring a child into this world. Some, such as Lucy, began their explanations about why they had no kids by looking at global dysfunction: "Just look around you—why would anybody in her right mind have a child today?" Indeed, children are regularly confronted with a host of problems that inhibit their ability to grow up well—or to grow up at all. Child abuse, youth homicide, street violence, and youth suicide have increased dramatically, ending children's lives before they reach adulthood.[2] Iris, a psychotherapist who specializes in domestic violence, recalled that she was once asked if she never had children because she was afraid that no female child could be safe. "I don't think children are safe—I don't know if I could let them go out into the world the way it is." Sue said, "I will not bring my precious miracle into a world where I think it will be harmed. If you love children, you have to think twice about whether or not you can do a good job so they will end up healthy, safe, and productive." Audrey agreed: "I don't want to bring a child into the world to be hurt by gangs or terrorists or druggies. And if my kid isn't 100 percent perfect, well, I don't necessarily want to be blamed for that, either."

But women quickly turned their attention from social problems to their own family environments. They were concerned about children who all too frequently live in homes in which poverty, substance abuse, illness, emotional distress, and exploitation are common experiences.[3] Some women knew even as young girls that they didn't want to have children, because, as Tina said, they "didn't want to perpetuate the problems we experienced at home growing up." For other women, such as Laurel, "it took a while to sink in why I was so hesitant about having kids. As I've gotten older, moved away from home, and had some time to distance myself emotionally from my family, I now realize that I don't want add another member to our family constellation. It wasn't a very pretty one," she confessed.

The kinds of problems experienced in the childhood homes of the women who remained deliberately childless ranged in seriousness from brutal physical abuse, to hushed sexual abuse, to hidden emotional mal-treatment. The most commonly shared problem among these childless women was that of not feeling well loved, especially by their mothers. This feeling of rejection and being a burden influenced their self-perceptions about being a competent, nurturing mother. "I can't give what I didn't get," Samara stated. "My parents would be horrified to hear me say we had a dysfunctional home," said Belinda. "But we did. It wasn't for a lack of things—we had plenty of things. But I didn't feel much emotion, no passionate parent love. Dad yelled and growled all the time. There was no gentleness coming from him. Mom carped and nagged—'Don't do this,' 'Why won't you do that?' or 'What are you doing?' Dad just told me outright that I was stupid. And they'd both pull away emotionally every time I screwed up. So yeah, I had the canopy bed and the pool and the pony. From the outside it all looked great. But inside me, I'm empty, I'm lonely, I'm not whole." Not feeling loved created emotional scars for women like Belinda and Yvonne, who would "watch TV shows and see the perfect, loving families where the mom always hugged their kids hello and kissed them good-bye," said Yvonne. "I don't remember ever being hugged or kissed like that. I don't remember even being told 'I love you,' although I am sure that my folks must have loved me. They just never showed it." Judy said, "We had what we needed materially, but we missed something other kids seemed to get—that huggy-kissy stuff." She "never felt a sense of unconditional love. Isn't that what moms are supposed to feel toward their kids?" Rather, these mothers cared for their daughters in a detached, instrumental way. Mothers were likely to "do the right thing, but not say the right thing or do it in the most loving way," Yvonne con-tinued. "She'd pack my school lunch or make me a dress, and once she made chicken soup when I was sick. But there's more to being a good mother than that," she said. This group of childless women talked about how they wanted to be held, kissed, touched, and told "I love you"—but these were things they seldom experienced. If they did, the signs of affection were few and done in stiff ways, "as if Mom felt she was supposed to do them but really felt uncomfortable with it." Deliberately childless women who felt they could become dysfunctional parents often demonstrated "cooler," more reserved, and less overtly nurturing interaction styles than did other women in the study, "probably because my own mom was one cool cookie," Veronica recalled. "When my mom dropped me off for college and asked for a hug, I about fainted! She'd never hugged me in my entire life!" The women assumed that mothers were supposed to be warm and demonstrative in showing their love. When theirs were not, women perceived that either their mother had a problem or that they themselves were unlovable.

Being inadequately parented resulted in some women deciding "not to parent at all if I can't do it right" (Laurel). Minnie recalled that "Mother tried very hard, I think, to be a good mother. It's just that she failed miserably at it." Many, like Evie, talked about how they were "so much like my mom it scares me." They were aware of the "reproduction of mothering" outcomes, even when they were unaware of scholarly research on mother–daughter relationships.[4] Women's stories reinforced the notion that "for every definition of mother which contains connotations of love, respect and reverence, there seems to be another connoting fear, hatred or disrespect."[5] Even though some childless women such as Minnie were willing to forgive their mother for "all the times she failed me," others were not. "After all she's done, she's not getting off the hook that easily," said Jessica. The women had learned from their own mothers not only that motherhood was often difficult but that mothers were not necessarily fond of their own children. "I believe my mom loved me, but I don't think she liked us kids very much," said Barbara. Victoria alleged that "the only reason I was adopted was that my dad wanted a child. It wasn't my mom who wanted me, and she let me know it in a thousand different ways as I grew up. She just agreed to have me because it was the thing for women to do, and my dad wanted me so much." Toots realized, after doing "some self-analysis on the family and kid issue," that "subconsciously I really didn't want to have kids. Mom raised her own brothers and sisters because her own mom died, and she took care of her father too. Us kids were born close together, and there had been a lot going on. I think Mom wanted my twin brother, but an unexpected twin was more than she could handle. She wanted a boy, not another girl. She didn't want me. As I got older, Mom was always too busy doing things for other people to bond with me. We never went shopping together or did things that most girls do with their moms. When my sister and I got old enough to have our own lives, Mom had little to do with us unless we came to her. It's like I owe her for something, but I'm not sure what." The kinds of family experiences women had when they were young influenced what they anticipated their own futures would be like. "I simply don't want to re-create my experiences in another generation," Lana said.

Some women viewed their mothers harshly, using words such as "cold," "mean," and "calculating." They had difficulty identifying any positive maternal characteristics. "My mom was cruel in some ways," said Jessica. "She'd smack us for no good reason, deny us things we really wanted, and embarrass me at points in time that absolutely were critical ones for me. It was as if she was a shark, and as soon as I was vulnerable and she smelled blood, she'd come in for the kill." Her mother was emotionally abusive to her, and she felt that "I couldn't have stood to have a child and let my mother near it. She's an awful person, and I'd never want her near something so precious as a baby." Jessica "can't get pregnant, and there's no good reason why," she said, "except to think that on some level I'm afraid to have kids." Emma asserted that "the thought of having a baby with my mother near makes me sick to my stomach." Emma described her mother as so dysfunctional that she was fearful for the child, and fearful to expose herself to a new round of her mother's pathology. "And I'm sure that has a lot to do with why I sub-consciously won't let myself get pregnant," she said.

Although two-thirds of the women did not say they were abused, those who felt they had been were often unwilling to become parents themselves. But women could feel that they were poorly parented even if they had not been abused. Those women who were not abused were sometimes parented in ways that made it less likely that they would want children. "Maybe we were abused and didn't know it. Back then, I don't even think we knew what abuse was. All kids complain about their parents, and the really bad stuff no one shared, so how were we supposed to know if our parents were better or worse than other kids'?" Nelly commented.

Insufficient parental warmth and recalled unhappiness of early family life can be important factors leading women to select careers instead of motherhood.[6] Some of the women I interviewed perceived that their mothers did not really like children, but they had them because "motherhood was the natural outcome of marriage in those days" (Janice). Women often painted a picture of mothers who were emotionally absent or who wished they had done something else with their lives. "Oh, Mom would cook meals for us and sew and do the things most moms did back then. But it always seemed like drudgery to her. Her head was somewhere else, and when we asked too much of her, she let us know it. I don't think we asked that much—most of what we wanted was attention and affection," said Bess. Sally felt that "Mom married men who would do for her, but I don't think she ever really loved any of them. I don't think she enjoyed us at all, and I learned that mothers can deep down inside hate their kids. I don't know how to be a mother. I think kids are neat, so why would I want to screw up a kid the way my mom did me?" Briana got her "nurturing from my sister and from my Dad's mother, not from my parents. By the time I was six, both parents worked every day. Mom would take off a day from work now and then to go on field trips, but she wasn't like any of my friends' mothers. I could talk to my friend's mom for hours, but I could never talk to my own. Then Mom started helping our family doctor in the evening, so she was never really there. My sister and I never got along well when I was small, but as I got older and had a problem, I called on her and she helped me. My mom didn't know how to mother. Her idea of showing love was buying me things because there was enough money, but emotionally I didn't get what I needed." Briana found out later that her mother "had serious prescription drug abuse problems, and she drank on top of it. She could be awful to be around. No one outside the family knew. It was our family's secret." Samara felt that "women should not be victimized by having kids like my martyr mother. None of my sisters have kids—you can see why not. There's too much abuse of kids by women who gave up their lives for kids." Judith's mother was cool, controlling, and emotionally unavailable. "Neither my brother nor I want to have kids. We both got as far away from her as possible. I don't think that mom would begin to understand why we don't want any part of her. It wasn't that she abused us. She never hit us or molested us. We always had nice clothes, enough to eat, and a nice house. The trouble was her. She was just mean. I have all kinds of issues related to her that I can't begin to go into. Trust me—my not having kids is the right thing for me."

Viewing motherhood as negative helped the women in this study to become more committed to the advantages of the child-free life-style.[7] The fewer the expectations women had for motherhood and the less nurturing they had received from their parents, the greater their fear of being dysfunctional parents. Especially important was the relationship between mother and daughter. Often a poor relationship with a mother was transformed into a daughter's fear of becoming a dysfunctional mother. But the relationship that girls had with their fathers was also important. According to most of the deliberately childless women I interviewed, fathers were typically absent from the home, fulfilling the social mandate of breadwinner. When they were home, most were emotionally absent, but some were alcoholic or violent men whose behavior physically or emotionally harmed their daughters. "When he would come home after work, especially after a hard day, he'd drink," Minnie recalled. "When he drank, he became verbally aggressive and say mean things. We were expected to hop to his irrational demands. If we didn't hop just right, he'd get crazy, violent, screaming and throwing things, and sometimes grabbing us and hurting us. We got to the point we hated to see him come in the drive." In cases of domestic violence, daughters found that their mothers were also victimized by their husbands. "Dad would hit her, but Mom wouldn't file charges. Instead, she'd make up things to explain her black eye, like she 'ran into the cabinet.' He'd feel bad about it later and be all mushy to her, and she'd forgive him. Until the next time, and there was always a next time," Kelly recalled. Mothers who were powerless were often unable to protect their daughters, and the girls grew up resenting them.

Women such as Mary, who had been sexually abused by her father for years, found that her mother, "who was also emotionally abused by him, did little to stop his abuse of me, even though she knew about it. Mom was a good Greek wife whose strong personality was subdued by my father. In the old country, women had to do what the husband said. My father had a prestigious job in the community, and I guess she doubted if people would believe her if she made public how awful he was in the privacy of our home. Even though she couldn't protect me from my father, she was wonderful and did lots for me. She was a counter to my father's inflexible, discouraging manner. Greeks are nurturing people," she said proudly. "But it was awful for me. My father gave me a sexually transmitted disease when I was a child and I developed adhesions as a result. The adhesions were the reason I could not bear children." She cried during the interview but pointed out that "bringing it up doesn't make it hurt any more or any less now. When I became an adult, I sued my father in civil court for what he had done to me." As a result of a legal case against her father, Mary experienced some emotional release as well as financial compensation when he was ordered to pay damages. "Because I couldn't have children, we have adopted a beautiful baby, and I used the settlement money to essentially pay for all the adoption costs. I am so angry and hurt at my father, and angry at my body for all its medical problems. But taking him to court for what he did helped. I now provide sexual assault prevention services, and good touch–bad touch classes. I have transformed my awful childhood into something good that can help others."

In reflecting on her childhood, Toni wondered, "Why do we women stay in bad marriages just to keep the family together?" "How could parents hurt their beautiful, innocent children?" When her father acted inappropriately, "I needed my mom all the more and wondered why she would tolerate it. I was her little girl! I've forgiven her, I understand it now, thanks to therapy, but I'll never have kids of my own. Instead, I've become a psychologist to protect little ones from the abuse that my mother failed to protect me from," she said. Among the women I interviewed, approximately one-third had experienced physical, sexual, or emotional abuse in their homes when they were children. Many women recalled their fathers as alcoholic, intimidating, and passive-aggressive. Others had fathers who beat their mothers or emotionally abused them. Childhood physical, sexual, and emotional abuse were common themes in stories told by these deliberately childless women. Mothers were much less likely to be physically abusive but were more inclined to be emotionally abusive or neglectful. If the women I interviewed felt they had been abused, I found that often they did not want to marry, and they especially did not want to have children with men like their fathers. Sixty percent of these women were afraid that they wouldn't be a "good enough" parent.

Some of the abused women felt they had the potential to be dysfunctional mothers as a result of what they witnessed and experienced when they were small. Ramona "never saw my parents in a friendly relationship. I always wanted them to get divorced and couldn't figure out why my mom married my dad. He was violent, abusive, screaming. He didn't provide emotionally or materially for us kids, even though he earned a good living. Yet I still thought I'd marry and have kids one day. But I haven't yet, and know deep-down inside that I never will." Iris feels that she's lucky to be in a stable marriage. "I never wanted to have kids in the same passionate way as my friends did. My home life was dysfunctional, and I'm sure that's got lots to do with it. Mother was always gone, and my brother never saw her much. He still harbors extreme resentment toward her, and he's never married." Tiffany felt she had learned no reliable relationship guidelines. "I have no measuring stick, no role models, to determine what is normal or abnormal, or how people should relate. I went into psychology in college because I never got the role messages at home. Even at age forty-three, I still read voraciously about relationships and how to build them. My parents weren't nurturing, and they gave me unhealthy messages. Instead of repeating the pattern, I asked myself, how can I learn to be different? How can I change, and change my relationships with kids? I have sought out assistance from all kinds of organizations, groups, readings, meetings, and so on to learn more about issues of parenting and alcoholism. I look at what will lead to patterns of behavior and how I can do the right things." Lisa recalled the toll it took on her psyche when her uncle and brother sexually abused her "for years. I didn't dare tell anyone. When I tried to tell my mom, she slapped me and told me never to lie again. I must have carried the abuse like a scarlet letter on my chest, for even strange men I'd never seen before would come up and proposition me. I married an abusive man who treated me terrible. I love kids, but I have no business having them. Even though I fight to empower myself, I don't think I have it in me to really empower a child. I couldn't stand to have my child victimized like I was."

Jane's unhappy childhood made her afraid that she was "doomed to re-create the pathology" she "abhorred. My parents fought a lot and home was so uncomfortable—the tension was unbelievable. I've had to struggle with depression, even though I understand the dynamics now. My dad was sexually abused by his father, and it was a problem for him to relate to us kids. My mom's mom was emotionally abusive. My parents were never emotionally available. Mom had lots of anger and took it out on my brother and was physically vicious to him. I was afraid that I could be violent to children and that I wouldn't be a good parent. Child abuse is part of my own past, and I wouldn't want it inflicted on any other children. I am not patient. So I decided not to have kids. I didn't want to raise a child to have the same feelings I had as a child." Patty's parents were "so dysfunctional you can't imagine. I'm so scarred by them it's unbelievable. Yet I've been able to put together a functional life. Dad was an alcoholic, and both of them were so cold and mean. My sister had kids, but they're all screwed up. I'd adopt them if I could. But my marriage didn't work out, and my lifestyle is so erratic that no court would probably give the kids to me. But I love those kids more than anything, and I do all I can for them. They're my kids."

These stories describe the sorts of family dynamics that women attributed to their decision to remain childless. Yet it is important to recall that two-thirds of the women who were interviewed for this book did not think that they had been abused in any way. Women who had received less than stellar parenting showed some apprehension about having children—but so did women who were well parented. Although family dysfunction may be a contributing factor to some women's decision not to procreate, their childlessness should not be directly attributed to it. Almost always there were other mitigating factors that seemed to push women into their desire to become mothers or to remain childless. According to some women I interviewed, abuse could be an impetus for better parenting. Consider the experience of Mary, who talked at length about how she hoped to use her own experience of abuse to improve the lives of children she cared for. "I've tried to transform the abuse that I experienced into something positive. For me, I'm trying to protect other children so that bad things never happen to them. In this way, the abuse didn't win. Something good has come out of the bad I endured. I have a choice about how to live my life, and whether I'll allow past events to influence my current and future life," she said.

Whether women were abused or not, it was common that most were concerned about whether they would be "good enough" parents. According to Evie, "Everyone ends up on the shrink's couch for something. If you take it as a given that there are no 'perfect' families, there's some liberation in it. Most of us, I suspect, didn't have families that were any wackier than anyone else's. But whatever kind we had, and however we perceived what they did to, and for, us, it helped shape who we are," she said. "We were just families, struggling to get by like everyone else," Rose said. Sometimes "it was hard to know if we were a normal, American family or if we were pathological. Everybody has some things at home that aren't ideal, right?" Natalie observed. Mica was reminded that "we were the first generation to watch TV shows like *Leave It to Beaver* and *Father Knows Best*. These shows taught us about how real families were supposed to live. Really, who ever lived that way? They were so nice! While we knew it was fantasy, we couldn't help but compare our own reality to them." Indeed, families may have looked warm and healthy to people outside the home, but the behind-closed-doors family life sometimes conflicted with appearances, according to women such as Briana: "My friends would say, 'gosh, your parents are so neat, they're so much fun,' but they didn't see how they really were. When we were alone, the screaming, the hits, their drinking, the chaos of it all—they never saw that."[8]

It was common for women to recall part of their home life as normal and part of it as problematic. Darcy was one of the deliberately childless women who described her childhood home as dysfunctional, even though it may have looked to the world like it was normal: "As a kid, I came from a real dysfunctional family. I was so glad when the word 'dysfunctional' became popular. Before then, the only term I could use was that they were fucked-up. Dad was a professional and quiet man. Mom assumed all responsibilities of rearing children and housekeeping, and Dad was content to let her do it. A woman came every morning to get us kids up and out, giving us breakfast, getting us dressed. It didn't matter if Mom was at work or if she wanted to sleep in, the woman always came," she recalled. She continued: "Mom and Dad had problems, and I had to help the younger kids with homework. I had lots of responsibility that I assumed willingly at a young age—I took charge of things because I didn't want my brothers and sisters to feel neglected, and I didn't want Mom to deal with things that she emotionally couldn't. My parents divorced, then remarried each other, then divorced again. They brought out the worst in each other. It wasn't always bad—I got anything materially I wanted, probably as a payback for what I did. I got a party dress, a car, extended curfew—I got all I could ask for—except a normal home life."

Whereas Darcy described her family as dysfunctional, Tina painted a picture of hers as repressive but reflective of the community in which she lived. She had "a meat-and-potatoes kind of mother who never traveled and lived her whole life in [a little town in a rural state]. She worked in a shoe factory town that had one bowling alley, one movie theater, and is a redneck place where all the kids hang out at the laundromat. They always seemed to be working to earn extra money to raise us," she said. But "even though they worked, we were never latchkey kids. Mom juggled her work hours to be home soon after we got home from school. My mom was nurturing, never pushy, and easy to talk to. She'd stand back and let me make my own decisions, let me travel around, and let me be independent. My dad was an alcoholic who always had a beer in his hand. It got worse and worse, and my mom divorced him. But she just found herself another alcoholic boyfriend. I feel like I'm coaching Mom about how to live a happier, better life. My mom would call me all the time to talk, and I heard all about her troubles." Tina was "so glad I moved to another state. Life is easier now; it's more fun and calmer with my friends. My sister ended up as the caregiver to Dad. I'm so glad I wasn't trapped into taking care of him. I don't want to repeat the cycle."

When one compares Darcy's and Tina's stories, it becomes clear that some parts of their childhood lives were very "normal," even healthy and loving, whereas other parts were disruptive, abnormal, or dysfunctional. Sometimes, dysfunction in the family had unexpected benefits. Tina's home experience "influenced my choice about no marriage and about not having kids. I don't consider how I grew up to be all that bad. It was more sad than bad with my alcoholic dad in that boring, redneck town. As a child, I spent all my time reading to escape, but this turned out to be the best thing that ever happened for me. I got accepted to one of the best schools in the country because I was smart. It was totally outside the realm of experience for my parents. Going to college exposed me to music, art, and culture. I'm a professional now and going places, not staying put in that awful place." Stephanie, whose parents pushed her "too hard to succeed as a professional ice skater," found that the rigidity and cold attitudes of her mother resulted in her becoming a psychotherapist for children "so they can live better lives than I had."

A "normal," socially expected behavior that sometimes had later consequences in the lives of deliberately childless women was taking care of family members when they were younger. Rose remembered taking her little brother and sister everywhere she went—"to the library, to the movies, on dates—because there was no one at home able to take care of them. They were like my second skin. In my backpack I had their bottles and toys to keep them busy, right beside my schoolbooks. Sometimes I wonder how I ever made it through school. I don't have any desire to continue doing this for the rest of my life. I've done my time. I sort of missed out on being parented because I was so busy being the parent, taking care of everyone else. If I've already done the mother thing, why do I have to do it again?" Women such as Julie explained that there were seven children in her family, and she had been emotionally neglected and isolated. "No one took care of me, except me. My parents simply didn't know how to nurture me, and maybe they did the best they could. I've forgiven them, but they were ill equipped for being parents." Large sibling units also contributed to older girls feeling that they had missed their own childhood because they had been responsible for taking care of younger children. Elizabeth was the oldest child who "took care of all the other kids. Mother was so busy doing other things that somebody had to watch over them, and it was regarded as my responsibility. To this day, I continue to be the one they call on for advice and help."

Children often assume that parents are invincible, always strong and never sick. Yet women talked about how parental illnesses had influenced their lives. Dawn's mother had a heart condition. "Mama was so sick she was unable to get out of bed many days, and I had to bring her things and help clean and cook. She had a heart attack when I was in first grade and became paralyzed. It was so frightening." Dawn was not nurtured "like kids are supposed to be. I'd never want to put a child through what I went through." Wendy helped care for her father, "who was disabled with a chronic disease and couldn't work. I lived with tension, not knowing how long he was going to live. He lived lots longer than anyone expected him to, which was great, but we all lived day to day, always thinking that death was just around the corner. This was hard on us, and we probably would have lived our lives more normally had we known he had a certain period of time left." Brianna's mother "was frequently in an alcohol- or prescription drug–induced stupor, and I ended up taking care of Mother, instead of the reverse." Carole was the primary breadwinner in the household at certain points during her teenage years because her father was an alcoholic and her mother had a mental illness. "She was really crazy. It was all on my shoulders to keep everything together. You can't imagine what that was like as a child, never knowing what she was going to do. It was a bizarre, schizophrenic upbringing. I love kids and want to protect them, but I don't think that I'm a good person to have some of my own." Having to take care of family members either made the women unwilling to sacrifice their lives to take care of others or made them doubt their ability to be a good parent.

Alcoholism, suicide, domestic violence, control—these are issues consigned not just to childless women. All women may experience such relational problems. However, as the women in this study sought to understand why their family problems had occurred and to ascribe meaning to them in their adult lives, they consciously, or subconsciously, decided to forgo childbearing. "Am I a coward for not overcoming my past and having a future that I direct myself? Maybe. But I'd prefer to think of myself as having learned from my experiences and trying to make the best out of a bad situation," said Dawn. "If I had a child and it wasn't perfect, then I'd blame myself forever," Melissa said. "There's regret if you don't have kids, but there can also be regret that you do. Mothers get blamed for every bad thing that happens to kids. When kids get hurt or in trouble, it's the, 'you didn't love them enough,' or 'you loved them too much,' or 'you didn't give them enough,' or 'you gave them too much,' 'you didn't watch them enough,' 'you didn't scrutinize their friends enough'—no matter what happens, it's the mother's fault. I can't live with that."[9]

Many women felt that therapy had helped them understand what had happened to them, but "therapy alone wasn't enough to bridge the gap into convincing me that I should have kids," Lisa said. As Valerie summarized her experience: "I'm a big girl now. I've done my personal work with counselors and friends, and I understand why I am the way I am. Could I have a child and be a good mother? Probably. Knowing what I know about myself, I'd be on guard to monitor my behavior so I'd do the right things. But it would be unfair. In vulnerable moments, I could see home taking precedence over a child. I am my mom—and it scares the hell out of me. It wouldn't be fair to my child to have me for a mother."

CHAPTER 8 **P**rocessing Childlessness

As women age, their needs, relationships, resources, and self-perceptions change. Some of a woman's reactions to being childless may be physiological, and so as she moves from puberty through adulthood and into menopause, her desire for children may change as her hormone levels change. A woman's desire for children may change across time because of social and psychological factors as well. A girl's ideas about having children are largely learned through gender role formation, imitation, and social reinforcement. Women are rewarded for having children at certain points in their life and penalized for doing so at other times. A woman must weigh the benefits of motherhood against career, relationship, and lifestyle demands while at the same time dealing with pro- or anti-child messages and a ticking biological clock. Whether a woman's realization that she will never have children is conscious or unconscious, it poses a developmental task that must be resolved as her personal issues and social roles and expectations change.[1] Societal pressures, personal needs for fulfillment, psychological rites of passage, genetic continuity, proof of femininity, and the need to rework issues from the past all may be evoked during this period when women process whether or not to have children—and if not, what the short- and long-term implications may be.

A woman's definition of childlessness changes in predictable patterns, and it takes a lifetime to process its meaning.[2] One after another, the women I interviewed described similar patterns of behavior as they attempted to resolve the meaning of their childlessness. Childlessness is not a singular event, nor is it the result of a single decision made at one point in time. It is the product of accumulated events that interact over decades of life. Women described how different pushes and pulls toward childlessness influenced their initial decisions about whether to have a child: "I both wanted children and didn't. There were so many reasons why I felt I should have kids and so many why I shouldn't," said Ramona. As girls, they were bombarded with role prescriptions about motherhood, independence, and career that created expectations for their own adulthood. But life situations influenced whether those expectations were met. Some women chose to remain childless whereas others did not. Those who anticipated becoming mothers found their lives affected by a host of different factors. For instance, the desire for a child was influenced by physical factors ("I couldn't get pregnant," said Mary Margaret), emotional factors ("I didn't feel I'd be a good enough mom," according to Valerie), relationship factors ("He didn't want a child," said Catherine), or situational factors ("We were both involved in our careers, and there wasn't time when it was time," said Del). The result was that none of these women had children. Over time, women who subconsciously decided not to have a child, or who let life situations dictate their choices, often redefined their passive reaction of becoming childless into one of active decision making in which they elected to be childless. In short, they transformed their interpretation from "situations or relationships prevented me from having a child" into "I chose not to have a child." Although women in their post-childbearing years may have defined their choice to be child-less as deliberate, the statement "I chose not to have a child" does not convey the long process by which that "choice" came to be made. For most of the women in this study, the decisions were made gradually over time. After women realized they were never going to become mothers, they all experienced periods of processing and adjustment that affected them on emotional, familial, social, and occupational levels. These adjustments are the focus of this chapter.

The emotional processing of their childlessness appeared more intense and lengthy for involuntarily childless women than for those who deliberately chose to be childless. Women who proactively decided not to have children, such as Janice, indicated that "I'm fine with not having kids. It's not been a big deal or a life crisis for me. I knew who I was and what I wanted. I know there are women who go through this long, convoluted process to resolve not having kids, but lots of us haven't. Sure, I get snagged from time to time, but I can't honestly say that I've experienced grief or really regretted not having them. But I chose, you see. Maybe women who felt they had no choice have more unfinished business to process." Martha also felt comfortable with her decision not to have children: "Life isn't always perfect, and I'm certainly not, but I don't think I've ever been sorry that I didn't have kids. While there have been times in my life when I thought seeing a counselor might be helpful, it was never over kid issues. I'm perfectly resolved with my lifestyle. If other people have problems with it, that's their problem, not mine, so don't inflict me with it," she said. However, although involuntarily childless women may have had to do the most processing, it appears that most women—even those who deliberately chose to remain childless—went through predictable stages of emotional adjustment in a world in which motherhood is still the norm.[3]

Women experience the meaning of childlessness differently across time as they confront new social situations and relationships. As Betsy reported, "When I was in my early twenties and all my friends were having kids and I didn't, I felt so sad that I didn't. Later, when their kids became adolescents, I was so glad I didn't have any to put up with. There were some years I didn't even think about kids, I was so busy. Then, when I hit menopause, I mourned all over again because it was clear that my childbearing chances were over." Women such as Betsy responded that they "felt differently about not having kids" as they "matured throughout life from young adulthood to middle age to older age—not that I'm old yet." Yet their "emotions could also fluctuate on a moment-to-moment basis. Day by day, my view changes," she said. "There are some days, even though I normally don't miss having kids, that I ache inside for one. It hurts so bad on those days that I don't think I can stand it. It eats at me, and everywhere I look, it's all baby, baby,

baby! Yet, other mornings when I get out of bed, having kids simply is not an issue. I've got plenty of other things—important things—to think about and do, so sitting around getting weepy over a child I never had seems like a pretty dumb thing to do." Women were not consistently glad or sad that they did not have children: The answer "depends on when you see me. Wednesday I might be glad, Thursday maybe not."[4]

"There's no way around it—you have to live through it to get past it," said Barbara. "Realizing that you're never going to have kids when you really want them is a life crisis. You've got to go into the pain, experience all the emotions that go with it, and come out on the other side in order to grow through it." A life crisis is a threat, loss, or challenge of a life goal that may seem insoluble and beyond one's usual coping mechanisms. Women's behaviors and feelings fluctuated as a normal part of a healthy coping process.[5] The first stage in this process of adjustment experienced by involuntarily childless women was shock: "I was just so shocked when I realized I couldn't have kids. I never dreamed I'd be infertile," Iris confessed. Kate said, "I went to the doctor thinking that he could do something to help me get pregnant, and instead I walked out hearing that I'd never be able to have children. I was devastated and didn't know what to do with it." For women like them, the moment they realized they'd never have children was one based on physiology. These physiological portals of entry included learning that one was in menopause, having reproductive problems that were clearly not going to be resolved, or being diagnosed as infertile or as having a serious or even life-threatening condition that made pregnancy unlikely. Laura "never predicted I'd have cancer instead of babies." Deborah was "so surprised that my childbearing years were over. I went to the doctor for my physical. I knew my periods weren't normal, but I never imagined that I was in menopause. Until the moment he dropped that bombshell on me, I still believed I had options," she said. "I'd believed I could get pregnant if I'd wanted to. I guess I needed some expert to tell me what I already knew deep down inside—that my time to become a mom had passed."

But infertile women weren't the only ones who experienced surprise at learning they were destined to be childless. Even deliberately childless women found that there were times of reckoning when they had to process exactly how and why they didn't have children. Nicole reflected how "startled I was to realize that all through my life I'd picked partners who didn't want kids. I said I wanted kids, yet I'd lived my life in a decision to be childless. I wasn't consciously aware that was what I was doing until my friend confronted me with my pattern. I was shocked with how far apart my behavior was from what I'd always said I'd wanted."

Usually the realization that they were never going to have children occurred at an exact moment that women could pinpoint. Sometimes the moment was physical, as it was for Anne or Deborah, or it could be social, as it was for Nicole or Louise. Louise said that "While I guess I'd known for a long time that I'd never have kids, it didn't hit me until I was at the beach watching babies play with their moms that I was too old—that I looked more like their grandmothers than their mothers. It was at that moment when I knew it was over." Women with relationship problems or other issues did not seem to experience as much shock as infertile women when they realized they could not have children. More often, the following kind of experience was common: "For me, it was a slow accumulation of the reality that I probably would never have kids. I always thought I would have kids, and yet nothing ever seemed in place for that to happen. I just kept pushing that time back and back, until I woke up one day, and said, 'wow, I guess I'll never have them.' Maybe I had been denying it for a long time, since obviously I had not gotten pregnant or done anything to help it along," said Missy.

Denial that they were destined to be childless was common among the women who were interviewed. "No, this can't be true. I figured my doctor must be wrong. I still have my periods," Lucy insisted. "Today women my age have first babies, so I'm still young enough to have kids." Others, especially those who were confronted with infertility, "went to get second, third, and even fourth opinions from doctors. I wouldn't believe I couldn't have kids—until each doctor said pretty much the same thing," Elizabeth said. Hannah "pleaded with my doctor to find some way that I could get pregnant. She told me how low my odds were and suggested that I pray, since 'miracles still happen sometimes.'" Hannah was "horrified" by her doctor's response. "In this day and age of medical technology, for her to resort to telling me that my only chances to get pregnant were to pray for a miracle, well, you can imagine how angry and hopeless I felt. I demeaned her professional opinion because I disagreed with it. I wondered why I should pay $250 to her for that sterling piece of advice, when I felt she must be wrong."

With time, the initial shock diminished, but women found new ways to deny the reality of the situation, uttering canned statements such as 'Oh, I chose not to have kids,' or 'Life without kids is better than being strapped down,' when they had wanted children and couldn't have them. Denial is a common experience among grieving people and serves positive functions in the process of "saving face" as one strives to adapt to the reality of the condition. Denial of infertility may be a part of our national heritage. George Washington, for example, reportedly denied that he was infertile and blamed his not having children on his wife, Martha—despite the fact that she had borne children from a previous marriage.[6] The main function of denial is to provide the grieving person with a temporary safe place from the unpleasant realities of loneliness and pain. Denial also provides individuals with a rationalization, or excuse, for why they were unable to live up to normal social prescriptions for procreation. Inevitably, denial was one stepping stone along the path toward acceptance.

As women realized they were going to be childless, many described how "disorganization ruled my life. I didn't fit in anywhere. Even though I didn't have kids, I always viewed myself as a 'one-day' mother. With that taken away from me, everything seemed different. My interactions with others changed. I avoided talking to mothers about their kids—it was too painful. I didn't want to be touched by my husband— I no longer felt sexy or desirable. I poured myself into my work. I hated my body. The world hadn't changed—but I had," Hannah recalled. "I had to re-find my place in it." Disorganization is the stage of grieving in which one may feel out of touch with reality. Nothing makes sense, and a woman may feel that her life has no meaning. She may be confused, and her psychological disequilibrium may be associated with periods of high anxiety. Unresolved issues may be awakened from the near or distant past. "It's like I went through a period when I didn't know who I was supposed to be. When you believe for your whole life that you're going to be a mom, then you realize you won't be, it's hard, it takes time to fit your old image of yourself with the new one. I played in different social groups for a while, trying to see how each would feel, to help me decide who I wanted to become for the next couple decades of my life," said Mica.

Inevitably, involuntarily childless women—and even some deliberately childless ones—experienced a range of volatile emotions, including depression, grief, and regret. Women indicated that it was common for them to feel a lack of control when they were unable to have the child they wanted. Reactions of depression, terror, hatred, resentment, and jealousy are often experienced as emotional manifestations of feeling cheated. A woman may direct her grief at objects or people, and common recipients of her wrath may include God, medical personnel, other family members, in-laws, friends, or even strangers who triggered a sensitive emotional issue.

Even women who had chosen to be childless also experienced occasional emotional distress. "I was simply caught by surprise by the moments when I found myself angry—angry at my body, angry at relationships that had gone awry, and angry at women who had kids who didn't do a good job mothering them. I wanted to rip their children away from them, saying, 'well, if you don't love them, give them to me—I'd do a better job than you!'" said Josi. She continued: "I chose not to have kids, but sometimes I mourn that I don't have little ones crawling over me, pawing my face, smothering me with kisses. It's natural to wonder what life would have been like if I had, and to have moments when I regret that I didn't." Emotions were clearly the most intense when women talked about having babies. The idea of being pregnant and caring for an infant seemed to touch an especially sentimental place. "Teenagers can be a pain," said Greta. "They're rebelling to find themselves, and in doing so they drive their parents crazy. But who can't help but fall in love with a sweet, cooing, sleeping infant?" Melinda, however, felt "adolescents are really neat as they gain independence and become adults. I like older kids—you can reason with them and get into real conversations. Even so, when someone asks, 'Do you have kids?' I always get a mental picture of a happy, healthy baby. It's this baby thing. It gets you right here," she said, pointing to her heart.

One of the most common emotions described by the women in this study was depression. When experiencing "a wallop to your dreams and about who you thought you were going to become," as Josi said, depression can be a normal, understandable, and even healthy response. But some women turned their anger and resentment inward, which led to self-deprecation and depression. "For a while, I think I hated myself because I couldn't have kids," Hannah confessed. "I felt like a failure, which made me feel unlovable, which made me pull away from people and become as unattractive to them as I felt inside. It took me a while to grow out of that awful phase," she said. Although the range of responses varied in intensity, depression usually occurred and "helped because it provided me with information about feelings I was denying that I had to address in order to move on," Josi said. "Even if you aren't sure if you want to have kids, it's nice to know that could be an option for you. To realize that it's never going to happen for you is hard to manage," said Sue. As Louise stated, "There's this void when you have no kids, and I found myself wondering how I'd fill my nurturing needs. I'll never have grandchildren. Nieces and nephews are just not the same. There is this sense of melancholy, depression, a deep sadness that's too strong for words. I'm aware of not experiencing motherhood. That's an area of my life that never was fulfilled. I have wondered if I made the right decision. But one person cannot experience all things," she mused. Other women such as Maggie confessed that "I get depressed around the holidays. We try to plan our vacations and visits around holiday times. Can you imagine sitting alone on Christmas or Easter?" Rose agreed: "I try to surround myself with my nieces and nephews during those days as a way to keep me from getting depressed."

The most intense emotion discussed by the women in this study, especially by infertile women and women who had lost children, was grief. "I thought I'd die during those days. I'd sit and stare at nothing, and would weep uncontrollably. It was so awful. The only thing that got me through was faith and hope," Anne recalled. Although intense when it occurred, few women felt consumed by grief all of the time. Grief was more likely to be experienced periodically, and it was usually the result of a triggering event. These triggering events could be a doctor's diagnosis of infertility, the onset of menopause, a reaction to something someone said, or a response to realizing that they would "never have one of my own." Jennifer recalled, "After my baby died, I had a couple of days at a time when I'd locked myself away from others, because I just couldn't deal with trying to explain or justify my sorrow. People who had kids, or who didn't want them, couldn't fathom how heartbroken I felt. After a while, I came out of my shell, but from time to time would have to excuse myself from a conversation because it was just too much to bear." Grief could be triggered by conversations with others in which childless women felt their experiences were not understood or valued by others.[7] "People can say such heartless, mean things without even knowing it," said Rose. "In a flash, they can say something and waltz on, while I'm left holding my heart in my hands."

Women I interviewed often indicated that it is difficult to find a socially acceptable way to grieve childlessness. Childlessness may be unrecognized by others—when suffering the loss of the dream of motherhood or a cellular growth that might have developed into a child, there is no obvious object to mourn. Subsequently, women found that they received little support from others, which made resolution of grief more difficult. "When my dad died, there was a wake, a funeral, and an opportunity for an outpouring of support for our family. We were expected to grieve," Hannah said. "But when you're grieving over a baby you never really had, people look at you like you're crazy. They don't understand your loss." Because childlessness is not a visible loss, it is not openly acknowledged, socially sanctioned, or publicly shared. Known as disenfranchised grief, the loss is not acknowledged by others as genuine. "They'd say, 'Come on, try again, it wasn't really a baby,'" recalled Joanna. "Because few people ever knew that we were trying to have a child," Sarah said, "they didn't know about the emotional angst we went through, the physical distress, and the relationship pressures." Most people do not know when a woman has experienced an abortion or miscarriage; if they do, the importance of that mother–child relationship is often ignored or deemed insignificant: "Not many people knew I was pregnant, since I'd miscarried early on. When I mentioned it, so often people dismissed it, and dismissed me. I'd been brave enough to tell them sometime intimate, and I guess they had problems dealing with the fact that they blew me off. That made me feel worse than if I'd said anything. Now I have two things to grieve—the miscarriage and the insensitivity of people I thought cared," said Sherri. People may assume that in the case of abortion or adoption that a child was unwanted, so grieving is unnecessary, "but that's the view of narrow-minded people who don't understand how hard it is to make such a decision, how complex all the factors are that I had to take into consideration," said Jane.

It is common for women who are childless to have occasional pangs of longing for a child.[8] "My biggest regret in life is not being able to have kids. But at least I tried. I'll always have a sadness about it, like a piece of me is missing," Joanna stated. Women identified several different aspects of regret—they regretted missing the physiological experience of being pregnant; they regretted being unable to participate in child rearing, planning, and celebrations in the same way as do mothers; they missed the opportunity for personal growth that accompanies parenthood; and they regretted not having the interaction and social opportunities provided to parents. "I'm left out of a big part of what it is to be a woman, just because I don't have kids. I miss nobody ever calling me Mom. I don't know what it is to give birth. I'll never plan for a wedding or birthday parties or graduation or anything for a child. I cannot go to school for a meeting and be with the other mothers. There are simply things that most women experience that I'll never know," Amanda said. Lucy confessed, "Even knowing all the benefits I've had because I haven't had kids, and all the difficulties there would have been if I'd had a child, I must admit that deep down inside, I still wish I'd had one." When a woman wants a child and cannot have one, the world seems full of reminders that other people are having children, according to Betts: "Babies, children, pregnant women, toys, Little

Golden Books, advertisements for baby products—they're everywhere! If I don't see them, I don't think about what I'm missing. But when I do, I feel intense longing. I don't know what to say when people at work proudly show off pictures of their kids, or when they take off to go to soccer games or piano recitals. I'm envious, yes. Sometimes I act angry as a defense, to protect this vulnerable part of myself."

When women lost babies through miscarriage, death, or abortion or gave up babies for adoption, they found that regret or other emotional distress could hit them from out of the blue, when they least expected it. Darcy described "how I saw this handsome young man who would be about the same age as my boy would have been. Somewhere out there is a young man walking around who looks like me. I gave him up for adoption when I was young, unmarried, and nothing in my life was in order. I gave him up for the right reasons, and I don't want to go looking for him, and I hope to God that he doesn't come looking for me. But I hope he's all right. I can't help but wonder what he's like," she said. Karen confessed that "I had two abortions when I was younger, when my life was not well suited to have children. It was the right thing to do at the time. They would be fourteen and sixteen years old now. Sometimes I look at kids that age, and wonder what my kids would be like, what I would be like, if I'd had them." She does not regret having the abortions, "but I do have a sense of wonder, regret, and loss about never having had a child. There's a big difference, you know," she said. Joanne said she would "never be the same after having lost my baby" to a congenital birth problem. "I dreamed for nine months what it would be like when I had her. Then she was born ill. I dreamed that somehow she'd get well. But she couldn't. So now all I'm left with are dreams about what was, and what could have been."

Jealousy was another commonly experienced feeling: "Am I jealous? Yes, absolutely! If I meet another friend who is pregnant I'll just scream! I'm the one who wants kids—and yet I'm the one that can't have them," said Rebecca. Toni agreed: "Three babies are due in my network. It's hard—I hate hearing their news. I feel like it should be me." Although children evoked pangs of longing for some women, others, like Mica, wondered: "Am I jealous over them having kids and I don't, or is it that

I'm jealous about their lifestyle? Moms have little people to think about, plan for, and who are waiting for you when you come home. They wear 'I'm a Mom' like a badge on their chest, and I can't." Lucy said, "Sometimes I wonder if I regard kids as a play toy. I imagine myself buying things for a baby, dressing it up, taking it places and doing things that I think would be fun to do. I wonder if my wanting to have a child is not for the child, but for me, for all the things having a child would mean I could do and be. I always dreamed I would have done all of those womanly things like getting pregnant, nursing, buying white walker shoes, being a schoolroom mother. When I didn't, I had to wonder—did I really miss not being pregnant and doing all that goes with it, or did I miss being left out of what I thought I was supposed to do? I have a real fear of exploiting kids and wouldn't want to do it."

The women I interviewed for this study conscientiously evaluated the meanings behind the intense emotions they experienced. Deborah confessed that "I think I feel sorry for myself sometimes, which in turn makes me mad at myself after I have a chance to think about it. I'm a whole person. I like who I am. But there's this nagging little part of me that's envious over what those women take for granted." She admitted that "I was pretty hard on a secretary I worked with because I found her too much into her kids and not enough into her work. In retrospect, she was a nice gal who adored her kids and put them first. Wouldn't I be the same way? Weren't her priorities in the right place? I'd want to be the kind of person who worked to take care of her kids, not one who put her kids on the back burner for her work. I think I was harder on her because I resented she had something that I didn't— kids." Pregnancy stories can be especially alienating to childless women. According to Mary, an infertile woman, "It's hard going to showers where women tell labor and pregnancy stories. It alienates me. As women, we're expected to know what childbirth is all about, yet I don't have firsthand experience with pregnancy, labor, and delivery. Part of me is excited to hear about their stories and share their experiences vicariously. I'm happy for them. But part of me cringes when they start talking about the details of their pregnancy—I'll never feel those butterfly wings inside as the baby stretches and moves, I can't relate to having my breasts full with milk, and so on. It's so weird to have their joy and my sadness being all jumbled up together, and sometimes I just don't handle it well."

Not having children can create feelings of alienation. Women in this study talked about how children bring people together, and "if you don't have a child, you can't enter into certain types of conversations, do certain things, or attend certain kinds of social events," added Rebecca. "Kids bring women together," observed Betsy. "I see women hanging out in the schoolyard waiting for the dismissal bell to ring, or pass the park and see soccer moms shouting instructions to their kids from the sidelines. When I went to a friend's daughter's school play, all the moms either sat together or nearby, chatting it up. Through kid events, parents get to know each other. Because I don't have kids, I don't have an easy way to enter into the normal world of women my age," she said. In general, the more negative the messages women received about being childless and the greater their alienation from routine "female" roles, the angrier or more depressed they felt.

Fighting off "nonmaternal guilt" can be difficult, according to some women. Fern said, "I'm told that I'm selfish and stingy because I don't want kids. My parents have used subtle—and even dramatic—pressures on me to give them grandkids. For instance, I have six ducks and my mother calls them her grandducks. Why do you think she does that?" Elise's mother-in-law talks about other people's grandchildren with longing because "we don't have grandchildren in *our* family." She told Elise, "My mother would have liked to become a great-grandmother, and she keeps asking me when you're going to have a baby." Her mother-in-law, knowing that Elise would not be having children, continued, "Grandma gave me two darling children's chairs for when you have a baby." Elise said, "She really used to get under my skin. Now I try to stay away and not let her bother me." Mary Margaret, who was infertile, felt sad when "even people who were supposed to care about you go out of their way" to say or do things that hurt her feelings: "I resent my husband's mother always pulling out the photos of her grandchildren. It's as if she's flaunting it in my face that I can't have kids and she's intentionally trying to hurt me."

Guilt and self-blame were common emotions experienced by the involuntarily childless women in this study. Laura blamed her body for getting cancer; Anne blamed her body for not being able to bear healthy babies; Deborah blamed herself for not being able to find a suitable partner. "When you wanted a baby and couldn't have one, you naturally look for someone to blame," Ellie observed. "Sometimes we blame others, and sometimes we blame ourselves. Either way, we feel guilty because part of us feels like we should have known better, that we should have made better decisions." Even normally quiet, passive women such as Catherine described how "I'd rant and rave, weep and wail and fall apart" at certain points as each attempted to resolve feelings associated with childlessness. "I felt so responsible for everything, mostly for the way things ended up, since they were so different from what I'd always dreamed I'd be." Iris recounted how her emotional upset usually occurred after a social interaction "that made me feel guilty or attacked." The "attacks" were not physical; rather, they impacted her self-esteem and anticipated social role. "I naturally felt angry, frustrated, helpless, and hurt by people who I let make me feel sad and bad because I couldn't have kids," Iris said. "The trick has been for me to not get hooked by them," said Janice. "You've got to keep your head screwed on straight. There's so many messages out there that'll make you feel guilty if you don't have kids. But really, there's so many wonderful things to do! Having kids may be wonderful, but what I'm doing with my life is also quite wonderful."

Often, woman can transform feelings of guilt and blame into feelings of loss and loneliness, which can then be transformed into depression and sadness—especially when fed by feelings of pity.[9] "One nurse asked me why I didn't want the baby [that I had miscarried]. She was blaming me for my baby's death! Even though there were medical reasons for why I lost him, I still hear her words sometimes—usually when I'm feeling vulnerable," said Ina. Anne's story was retold in slightly different ways by many women, with essentially the same message each time: "I used to dream about what my baby's room would look like— what kind of wallpaper I'd put up, the toys I wanted my child to have, the types of clothes and little shoes I'd buy. I thought about having baby showers and all the cute little things people would bring me. I used to play with names in my mind, combining first, middle, and last names for boys and girls to figure out what fit best. But most of all, I dreamed about what it would be like for my husband and me. I dreamed about how wonderful it would be for us to go to the doctor together and feel the baby kick. I dreamed about going into labor and rushing to the hospital and about what it would be like to have the baby. I dreamed—and he dreamed with me—about what it would be like to first hold our child. And I dreamed about all the parenting things we'd do, the first steps, all the lost teeth, and how we would become a real family. It all sounds embarrassing when I say it out loud, like I had all the fine details of my life planned out. But I loved dreaming about how wonderful it would be, of having it all."

Children provide company, even when they are in utero. "Before I was pregnant," said Melinda, "I'd never dream of going into a restaurant by myself and eating. I'd grab fast food and eat it in the car. But when I was pregnant, I'd go into the restaurant, eat well, and never felt alone. I'd think to myself, 'I am eating here with my baby.' Since I miscarried, I find that I'm back to eating fast food in the car. It's too lonesome to go in and sit down by myself to eat." Children are also emotional company, and even when mothers aren't with their children, they "think about what their kids need for their science project, or if the baby sitter picked them up on time, or stopping off at the grocery on the way home to pick up milk and Fruit Roll-ups," said Mica. "My friends with kids are never alone," said Toni. "They're always with one or another of the kids, rushing here and there. Even when they have a few minutes to themselves, they are constantly thinking of others and what's next. But for me, the bulk of my life I spend alone. Oh sure, I see people at work, and I do things for friends and family, but I have this sense of my life being just me. I have choices of what to do with my time. That's great, but I sometimes miss the fact that nobody counts on me, the way kids seem to count on my mom-friends." Children insulate women from the physical and emotional sense of being alone.

"When you're young, attractive, and alone, you don't get invited to couples' houses for dinner, parties or socials. I get together with my single friends, but not my couple friends. There is a dividing line between families, couples, and singles. I felt socially isolated, as if I was ostracized by them," said Mary Margaret. Women who are not employed or actively involved in some community group reported more loneliness, as did women whose husbands work out of town. Joanna said, "My husband has a new job. We have moved to a town where I don't know anybody yet. He's always busy, and I'm often alone. I feel like a little girl who is rejected and neglected. I wait for him to come home, and when he does he's got so much on his mind that he does not really listen to what's going on inside me. I get angry and resentful. I wish I had a child to fuss with. If I had kids, I wouldn't feel so dog-gone alone, and I wouldn't drive him so crazy."

When Alicia came home from work and found her husband dead on the floor from a heart attack, she realized a new sense of loneliness: "I feel his loss so deeply. It would be nice to have had kids with him. They would have helped to move me out of my grief. Kids would be someone else for me to love and care for. They would be extensions of us. While I never felt unfilled because I didn't have kids, I have worried about what it would mean to me not to have them. Everybody always thought I'd have kids. But maybe it's better we did not. He would have been a tough dad. His father hit him, and he was troubled. I'm an independent person, and I figure that we're meant to be born and to die alone." Alicia found herself grieving not just the loss of her husband but also the loss of the child she never had, and the loss of what she expected her life would be like.

Sometimes grieving women in this study looked for ways to retain relationships that had been lost. Sometimes women would decide to keep the memory of a loss alive, and then they would organize at least part of their lives around retaining that memory and relationship. This was most clearly seen among women who had experienced miscarriages or infant deaths. Harriet planted a tree outside of her office at work in memory of her infant son who died, and it grows sweet blossoms and provides shade to others. May formed a support group of women who lost babies, "so they won't have to be as alone as I was through my child's death." Keeping the memory need not be unhealthy, provided one recognizes the reality of the loss, allows for continued individual growth, and does not inhibit the development of new relationships.

Confrontations with babies and the past are inevitable. Melinda said, "I think it's the babies that do it to me. I look at those little miracles, with those perfect little fingers and velvet skin, and I just fall apart. A dear friend I knew had a baby, and we had to go see it. I wanted to, and I didn't. When we got there, I simultaneously wanted to rip the baby out of her arms and take it home, and the other part of me didn't want to even look at it. It made me remember the baby I lost." Her loss reemerges when "I have worked with clients who want children but who have fertility problems. Their stories are so similar to my own! This is sometimes hard. I have to remember to be objective. I have pangs, yes, when I want kids, but pain is too strong a word. But there's still an emotion there, nonetheless. Maybe this is what they mean by a sense of loss."

Childlessness and sexuality are intimately linked, and the women I interviewed consistently reported feeling they would never know the feminine nature of their bodies as intimately as would women who have had children. Tashi said, "I really wanted to be pregnant. I wanted to feel my belly move with the baby inside, I wanted to breast feed, I wanted to do the whole experience." Kris agreed: "They say you know at the moment of conception that you are pregnant. I wanted to know that feeling. I wanted to see my belly swell, and watch the baby swim across it. I wanted to go shopping for maternity pants with those funny fronts. I wanted to go through labor and relish the pain. I wanted to deliver my own baby, and cut its cord and hold its bloody, wriggling body against mine. I wanted to nurse my baby and watch milk flow from my breasts. What does that milk even taste like, anyway? I wanted it all. And I got none of it. Except from friends. And books. And dreams." Jennifer confessed that "I want to know the excitement at the moment when you look at the pregnancy test and see it's positive. I want to see my belly getting big and feel life moving inside of me. I want to know the agony and ecstasy of labor and then holding my new, wet child in my arms. But I won't. I can only imagine what it would be like. This sense of loss, of being cheated, is sometimes too much to bear." Joanna also felt "so cheated. For my whole life I believed I'd be a mom and now I can't. I'm sad, I'm mad, and I'm frustrated because I can't do a thing about it—we tried everything and nothing took."

Knowing the physical sensations of pregnancy and childbirth yet being unable to share the emotional experience that their own mothers knew and felt was a consistently difficult part of not having children. Iris sighed, "Every birthday I think I should try to get pregnant again—but I don't. Even though I don't have the same baby lust as I did years ago, I still have it. Menopause will be really hard for me. I dread it." Deborah said sadly, "I've heard men say things about how their wives looked prettiest when they were pregnant. I won't ever know if a husband would see me as prettier if I was pregnant." Jennifer admitted that "I found myself thumbing through a maternity clothes catalog some woman brought into work. I saw the long, baggy tops and thought, 'gee, they look comfortable' and the women look so pretty wearing them. So I ordered a couple. I liked wearing them. But then, I felt odd when this gal asked me where I got them. I avoided the answer. Another gal asked me if I was pregnant. That was hard. I must have been put on some mailing list, because I started getting other maternity catalogs, and then baby catalogs. That was pretty weird. It hurt. I let them come for a couple of months, then got a grip and called them up and told them not to send them again."

Holidays may pose special problems when a woman feels that she should have a child to celebrate with and for. The general consensus among the women in this study was that "Holidays are especially painful. Holidays are for kids," said Greta. Holidays, particularly Mother's Day, Father's Day, Easter, Passover, Halloween, Hanukkah, and Christmas, can be particularly difficult for women who want kids but don't have them, so many women "borrow" kids for the holidays. Christmas caused the most distress for the women in this study. "Can you imagine getting up Christmas morning and not having little voices squealing with delight? I've done Christmas with and without kids, and let me tell you, I'll travel hundreds of miles just to be with the kids in our family for that moment," said Laura. Maggie and her husband "go to my sister's house for most holidays. Christmas is so much fun when you have kids. The people at work couldn't believe I took a week off of work to go stay with them while my sister and her husband went away on vacation. Sure, there are lots of exciting places to go on vacation. But I so enjoy spending time with my nieces!" Mary Margaret and her husband stayed up until 4:00 A.M. one Christmas, putting together a dollhouse, train set, and other toys for the children of a friend who was a single mother. Rebecca described how hard it was for her during Passover, "when there are no children to tell the stories to, no children to search for the afikoman," or at weekly Shabbat rituals when "I have no children to bless, like the other parents." Women's birthdays often prompt reckoning with the reality of being single and without children. As Allie said, "Another year has clicked by without my getting any closer to having a husband and a child. Each year, I hope that the next one will result in my being married and pregnant. Most of the time it does not bother me, but at my birthday, it is a time for reflection, and it can get damn depressing!"

For a woman who wants to have a child race to her arms shouting "Mama," Mother's Day is also cause for reflection and distress. Some women talked about how the holiday gnawed at them because they would not receive a card or gift, although "it seemed like every other woman I know did," said Evie. Hannah "hated to go to church on Mother's Day—all these women are there with corsages and I sit there alone, unadorned, and feeling as if I'm naked, with my childlessness painfully apparent for the world to see." For women who have miscarried or lost a child, the day cannot help but evoke a strong emotional response. As Joanna said, "Mother's Day is a day for celebrating that, at least for a little while, I was a mother. But mostly, it's a day when I grieve. I don't want to go anywhere that day because everywhere you go there are kids and moms, and I just can't stand it."

Although some women talked about borrowing children for holidays or special events, not every woman finds comfort being around other people's children—especially if she wants a child of her own. Veronica said, "There have been times when I felt left out of situations because of not having children. But I can never fully share in my friends' lives who have kids. Sometimes getting together makes me feel more lonely, not better, even though I think my friends think that I'll feel happier by sharing holidays with them."

Only after women went through the various stages of adjustment were they able to understand the full impact of childlessness on their lives. "When you're in the thick of it, it's too hard to see what's really going on," observed Angela. Only later were women able to look at their own role in their childlessness and move toward acceptance of it. However, even when they thought they had resolved their childlessness, a normal interaction could trigger intense, and sometimes volatile, emotions. Even though a woman had passed through a stage once didn't mean she wouldn't return to it again.

As women in this study went through different stages, new issues of childlessness emerged, coupled with a new wave of emotional processing. It was common for a woman to feel she was "doing well" one day and be "devastated" the next. Nance said, "Just when you think you've got it all under control, you realize you don't. At the time I had the hysterectomy, I was okay with it. I accepted that I couldn't have kids and didn't let it get me down." But later she found that her acceptance was not as complete as she had thought." There are plenty of times when I see families and little kids and I feel very sad. Sometimes I just feel odd at the time—sometimes I want to run away, sometimes I feel hostile, and sometimes I want to join them. It's only later when I'm quiet that I figure out that I'm not as resolved about the whole thing as I thought I was. I may feel sad for a moment, then I pick up and go on." Yet there were other deliberately childless women such as Rhonda who felt "society seems to have a need to assume that I've felt terrible about not having kids, when really, it's not been terrible at all. I think others have a hard time handling the fact that for me, having kids simply hasn't been an issue. Me and Jimmy Stewart—we're having a wonderful life."

It was not unusual to find women in this study who had once denounced childbearing but later admitted that they had wanted children. "When I was young, things in my life weren't fitting together for the baby and family scenario. It was much easier to say to myself that I really didn't want kids, they were really too much work and expense and bother. But now that those chances are over, I can admit to my more quiet self that part of me really would have liked one. I gained a lot by not having kids, but I also missed out on a lot of sweet moments that other women get. It is not exactly sorrow that I feel, but resigned regret," said Heather. Chi said, "I was never pregnant, but if I had been I don't know what I would have done. Back then, I thought that women who wanted kids were having kids without thinking, or for the wrong reasons. Now I think it's not neurotic to have children—there are lots of healthy reasons to have them." What made her change her view? "I always felt intuitively it was very beneficial to have relationships with children. It was not just my needing the children's loving energy because of my own lack of it, but it was truly mutually rewarding. Children and I complement each other's loving energy." Layne admitted that "now that my [childbearing] decisions have been made, it's easier to go back and couch my behavior the way I want people to view me now—like I had chosen to be childless all along, that I had been totally in control of my life. This wasn't exactly true at the time—but I guess it's not totally untrue either, since my choices led me to where I am now. At this point in my life I can talk about how it may have been good if I'd had a child, since now there's no chance of that happening. It's always easier to make definitive statements about something when you're safe that it can't happen. Maybe this is all part of the process of building a life without kids."

After many of the involuntarily childless women I interviewed "made it through my journey into confirmed childlessness," they experienced relief, according to women such as Betsy. "I'm comfortable with myself. I'm ultimately pleased with the decisions I've made, even though I've had times of second-guessing them. Perhaps I'm luckier than women who've never been forced to deal with their secret motivations for why they do what they do." Iris and Angela, Maggie and Barbara, and other women were glad to tell their stories of how they had grown into "wonderful, warm, giving women who have made a difference in the world." They attributed the contributions they had made to the fact that they had not had children. Did their childlessness create difficult times for them? No, not necessarily. Many women felt comfortable and satisfied, even glad, for their decisions not to have children. Yet most women confessed that there were some moments in their lives when their childlessness "smacked me in the face and forced me to deal," as Evie put it. But Heather quipped, "No pain, no gain!" Then she went on to say, "Honestly, I've been able to turn what could have been a crisis [childlessness] into an opportunity. It took me a while to figure out that I never really wanted to have kids. But since I felt I should, I felt enormously sad and guilty that I didn't. So my problems came more from the outside pressures than internal distress. All our emotions and the agendas of what we're supposed to be get all mixed up, and it takes a while to sort it all out."

CHAPTER 9 Child Haves
and Have-Nots

Speaking frankly about the experience of childlessness has been a social taboo. Those who believe that parenting is desirable often assume that women who have no children must feel terrible about it. Indeed, many of the women I interviewed did experience emotional distress because of their childlessness. But the assumption that all childless women feel distressed is not accurate. This assumption sometimes made it difficult for the women in this study—especially those women who enjoy their child-free existence—to talk honestly about their feelings with women who have children. Sylvia observed that "my friend Susan is so into her kids that she can't see the world from any other point of view. It's hard to have an adult conversation with her. She's convinced that somehow I really long for kids, and frankly, I don't. To talk with her, her lifestyle is the best way, the only way. Maybe for her, but not for me. It's gotten so awkward that we don't see each other much anymore." Conversely, women who have yearned for children sometimes found it difficult to talk openly with women who believed that life without children was a wonderful and liberating experience, as shown in Betsy's statement: "I'd really liked to have had kids, but I'm hesitant to talk with them about it because they'll think I'm too old-fashioned, or that they'll make fun of me. They can't relate to my sadness, and when I try to explain it, I feel goofy. So most of the time I keep my mouth shut about wanting kids."

The childless women in this study reported that often they kept their emotions private. As Maggie pointed out, "People interpret what you say according to what they want to hear." A good example of this can be found in readers' responses to an Ann Landers advice column in which Landers had responded to a childless woman, "Childless and Happy in PA," that she might someday change her mind and want children.[1] Reader reactions to Ann's response ranged from support to outrage. She received letters from women who were delighted not to have children, from women who were sad or frustrated because they could not bear children, and from women who felt it was a private issue about which others should mind their own business. The subject of childlessness is by no means one around which women can instantaneously bond. When it is unclear why women are childless, and more unclear how they feel about it, it is understandable that others may not know what to say.[2]

Although women in this study may have felt sad about childlessness at certain times, these emotions were not necessarily a dominant force in their lives. Grief, anger, loss, and other emotions were more likely to surface when childless women encountered the attitude that "You don't know what it's like to be a mom!" Although most of the women in the study seemed to have stable self-concepts, they talked about obstacles to being an emotionally healthy childless woman in a world devoted to motherhood historically as well as today in many parts of the world. Many of the women believed their choices reflected poorly on them as women. "In many ways, my worth seems associated with my ability to bear children," Ramona said. "I'm somehow seen as a better person if I'm a mother than if I 'just' have a job." Greta agreed: "There are these cultural assumptions that somehow you're lacking, you made a mistake, or there's something wrong with you if you don't have a child—that you're somehow less because you don't 'bear fruit.'" However, when confronted with people who "made me feel bad about not having kids," women such as Betsy had options—they could accept them, ignore them, confront them, or change people's attitudes when possible.

But women found it hard to ignore when "kids seem to be a universal topic. Our neighbors assume that we'll have kids one day. They're so innocent it's hard to be mad at them. They say things like 'when you have children ' with joyous anticipation for us. This is the normal course of events," said Sarah. Childless women often resented people prying into their private lives. Ahanna said, "Sooner or later, a woman with kids will get around to asking you 'Do you have kids?' When you say no, either she'll get nosy about 'what's wrong' with me, she'll start talking about her own, or she'll start talking about some other mindless thing that neither one of us really cares about. Then she wants to avoid the topic because she doesn't know what to say to me."

Women in the study reported that it was common to be asked if they were, or had even been, pregnant. Fertility is regarded as a public, not necessarily a private, experience among women. "Somehow, whether or not I've ever had kids seems to be something that other women, total strangers, feel comfortable coming up and asking me," Tina said. "Other women will be talking to me while we're washing our hands in the restroom, or sitting by each other on the subway, and just up and ask, 'You ever been pregnant?' as if they were asking if I'd ever bought a lottery ticket or flew on a plane." Women were surprised at the "people you don't even know come up and stick their nose into your private business, like they feel they have the right to interrogate you, or berate you just because you don't have kids," said Rachael. "People are so rude, coming up and asking why I don't have kids. It's none of their business," Greta said. It was the casual nature of handling an intimate topic that bothered many childless women. Randi agreed: "I'll be having a pleasant conversation with women and then after they figure out I have no kids, the conversation will dwindle, and they'll start talking to someone else in the group. It feels like a subtle form of rejection of me as a woman. If we're talking business, it works okay, then people can relate to me as a business machine. But if we're relating to each other as women, then I pick up they think I'm not a 'real one.'"

When childless women assumed that mothers thought they had little in common, "their rejection of you because you don't have kids still bothers you," Ellie asserted. Veronica agreed: "There have been times when I felt left out of situations because of not having children. I feel I can't fully share in my friends' lives who have children. Their experiences are foreign to me and that makes me feel rejected." Children seem to provide women with an opportunity to talk about "very natural, base, human, things," Julie observed. "You can talk about normal stuff with moms, where at work all my conversations with other women seem to put me on call, to be talking about professional stuff. Sometimes, I just want to talk with women my own age about things that women my age go through." But that includes the world of children, as Monique observed: "Whether you're out to eat or shopping or flipping through a magazine or watching TV, kids seem to be everywhere. Yet my friends, who have kids, say that they have to search high and low to find good kid stuff. Perhaps I notice kid things more because it's an issue for me." Because women have to live in the real world, "we have to adjust accordingly," she said. Fern noticed that "In the community in which we live, there are many parents who are active in their kids' school and who socialize as part of the 'parents' community.' We don't have the same things to talk about, and sometimes I feel left out of the main group of people who are my age. I cannot talk about the things they do, and I don't really want to."

Janice resented that she was treated differently by women friends with children. She was left out of conversations because her friends thought she couldn't relate to their experiences. Through remarriage, she acquired a stepdaughter. "Now I'm having the experience of bonding with my friends as a mother. I get invited to events that they never invited me to before; we do more family-type things. I'm more acceptable now to them, not that they were never unacceptable to me. It's such a rapid, noticeable thing. I never changed—only their view of me did." The world need not be compartmentalized into women with children and women without. Rhonda observed that "sometimes I think I've become hypersensitive to the kid issue. I mean, the whole world isn't out to get me because I don't have kids. Some gal at church was complaining that they have groups and events for singles or gays or marrieds-with-children, but none for us who don't have kids. It's true. They don't. Maybe they don't know exactly what to do with us. But I'm not sure if I'd want to be in a group in which that was its focus," she said. "I know I've never felt left out because I didn't have kids. Perhaps if I lived in a small town it would be different. Maybe if I'd been the only one it would have been difficult. But I cannot remember anyone ever asking me why I don't have kids. I have a pretty decent sense of myself so even if I was asked, I wouldn't take it as a sense of failure. I would have assumed they were curious about me as a person, that's all."

The issue of how to communicate with women who had children was consistently a tender spot among women in this study. When it comes to children, mothers are attributed legitimate expertise—irrespective of how much they know about children, child development, or human relations. "Mothers assume that experience is the best teacher in this arena, and they know more," Maggie alleged. "I've got a degree in child development and worked for years with kids. Moms may know their own kids, but I know hundreds." Another woman, a physician, Deborah, found that her professional training mattered in the examination room "but at dinner parties or barbeques, the mama crowd bonded together and I was left like a fish out of water. They'd ask me medical or professional questions, but nothing personal, like I was a real person." Other childless women questioned why people assumed they didn't understand children: "How many mothers do you know who don't know what the hell they're doing? They act like I couldn't possibly understand what it's like to have a child. But I do, because of my stepdaughter. Working with kids is my line of work! What audacity they have! I'd like to punch them, because they don't know what I know, or what I feel, or what relationships I have with others," said Greta. "I've got a degree in psychology," said Angela, "and most of my caseload consists of children. I've got great rapport with them, and I think they'd say I understand them better than their own parents do." Yet the issue of experience leading to understanding has some legitimacy, according to Tina: "I don't understand what mothers feel. I can guess, but there's no way that I can tell them with absolute certainty that 'I know how you feel.'" But Janice asked, "How can you know everything about every human experience?" Women felt they were able to understand children's needs even though they may not have had children of their own. Pregnancy does not necessarily create insight; delivery does not necessarily develop understanding; biology does not necessarily make a person concerned about others. As Evie observed, "My neighbor sold recreational vehicles for years and never so much as even spent a night in one. Yet he knew everything about them and could help people who wanted to buy one or who were having trouble with the one they had. He knew what they should buy and how to fix things. If he could know all this about RVs and be the town expert even though he never stayed in one, then why can't it be possible for me to know a little something about raising kids, even though I never had one?"

Being pregnant is different from any other human experience, but being able to talk openly about what it's like not to have children can be equally as unique. Talking about childlessness can be an important part of healing the raw spots in one's psyche. "I need to talk with other women about their feelings, their experiences about not having kids in order to understand my own," Lucy said. "Otherwise, I don't know when I'm normal or when my experiences aren't." Stephanie found that "there are sometimes when I'm down and other periods when I'm upbeat—pretty normal, eh? I do get depressed. It helps when I can talk to people who can relate to my thinking and help me evaluate the good spots of my life." But sometimes it was hard to find people who would listen to them process being childless. Iris admitted that "No one wants to really hear about it. I've only talked to a handful of people, ever, about it—and you're one of them. I've been the square peg in the round hole." "Mothers can be very insensitive toward women like me," Angela told me. "It could be that mothers simply did not consider how their conversations might exclude women who don't have children." Other times mothers "talk in code or shared experiences that were very important to them but which alienated women like me who have no children," said Janice.

As a result of the tension that many of the women in this study have learned to expect, they engaged in a strategy of selective disclosure.[3] Mica reflected how "It's like there's two parts of me—one that really wanted kids and one part that's glad I didn't. When I'm with people who are really into kids, I can let my guard down and be all gushy about kids. We can have honest conversations about how it feels not to have them. But when I'm with women who are into their careers or lifestyle, who act as though kids would be a burden, I find myself agreeing and talking exclusively about that part of me that finds it convenient not to have them. Fortunately, most people don't see me in both settings—otherwise, they wouldn't understand and think I was a hypocrite, falling out on both sides of the kid-coin." Another woman who had been ambivalent about having children, Nicole, said "I know who I am, but it seems that other people have their own ideas about who I'm supposed to be and how I'm supposed to act." As a result, women developed ways to buffer their egos from attack.

Women in this study used corrective or preventive interaction strategies when they felt threatened or discredited.[4] Corrective strategies sometimes involved confrontation. Sylvia recalled: "When women ask me why I have no kids, I find myself explaining how my life is better and more productive than if I'd had them. I feel I have to bring their attention to how rude, how insensitive their comments are, and how they leave me out." But women found that when they tried to get others to understand their point of view, they became weary, angry, or frustrated. "I don't think at those moments I explained myself the best," Natalie acknowledged. "Most of the time, I don't think explaining things to them helps anyway," Angela agreed. "Sometimes it's easier to just avoid the whole child thing." Women used avoidance, concealment, and denial as preventive strategies to minimize being treated differently because they had no children. Childlessness is not immediately apparent to others, and women such as Toni "simply don't bring the issue up unless directly asked." Concealment is not a lie; rather, Toni found, it is "a convenient way to avoid unpleasant encounters." Concealment was used by most of the women at some time or another to reduce their isolation from others. Jennifer "would act like I was too busy with my job or other important things to have a child. By portraying herself as a businesswoman not bothered by child care responsibilities, she was able to protect herself from others knowing the truth. "If I show any feelings of remorse, I'm afraid I'll be vulnerable. Most of me is fine about not having kids, but there's part of me that's tender about it. I don't want others to go there," she said. Allie found that "it's easier to tell my family that we just aren't at a point in our lives where we want kids, instead of telling them the truth—that I can't get pregnant, that I've gone through all the tests, and that I'll probably never be able to give them grandkids running through the house. It makes me too sad to tell them the truth."

Sometimes concealment was used at work to preserve an image. Often this image was related to being "man enough for the job," as Tina put it. Kris discussed the dangers of telling co-workers that she wanted a child: "Motherhood is a dirty word in some circles. Companies don't want a professional woman who may put a child first over corporate needs. I'm sure that they wouldn't want to promote me if they thought I might get pregnant. So I wouldn't dare utter the baby word or indicate that I may actually want a child. The secretaries at work all talk about their kids, while the administrators all talk about their careers and their cultural endeavors. For a woman who wants to be up and coming, you learn pretty quick not to act like you really want kids, or that you're sorry that you don't have them, for fear that both sides will talk badly about you."

Yet being a "cold fish is no good either," Sue observed. "Part of being successful is to show empathy, a tender and gentle side as well as a tough and competent one. It's a hard balance to achieve," she said. Yvonne, an administrator, admitted that "I love kids and believe I would have been a great mom. I like to talk to my staff about their kids and I feel as if I know their entire families. They love me because I'm 'real.' But I find that while it's okay for them to talk to me about their kids, it doesn't feel okay for me to talk to them about my private life. I feel I can't look too vulnerable about the kid issue around them, because I'm afraid that—isn't this stupid—that I'll look too human, that I'll appear like I don't really have what it takes to be an administrator, because if they know how much I wanted kids, then they would look at me and feel pity instead of respect."

There is a thin line between concealing that you want kids and denying it to yourself. Missy didn't think she was denying her feelings about having children, but "my friends have confronted me with, 'you say you don't want a child, but why are you on the floor rolling the ball if you don't really like kids?'" Ellie admitted that she had denied how much she wanted children: "I say I don't want kids. But then why is it that I keep getting all mushy inside when I see little babies? Why is it that I feel so jealous when my friends get pregnant? Why is it that every time I think, 'hey, I've got it under control, all figured out,' that something will happen to make me realize that maybe I don't. And why in the hell am I sitting here crying, if I haven't denied the importance having a kid means to me?" It may take time for a woman to admit she denied part of her past, as shown in Lily's story: "I was gang raped when I was fourteen, and I never told anyone. I only told a girlfriend, 'Hey, I had sex,' like I was really cool and all. I stuffed all my fears and really never dealt with it. All my life I have been carrying it around. I felt like I was a promiscuous young thing because of it, so I had to prove to myself that I was in control of the situation, that I was in charge of me and my behaviors. It took years, until I was well into my adulthood, to realize that it was all untrue, that I had no control at all. I've been telling people for years that I never wanted kids, when what I never wanted was to have a child and have it go through what I did. Since I couldn't protect me, how could I protect a child? So I denied ever wanting one." Concealment is a cognitive decision, but denial may not be.

Although some women in the study avoided the topic of children by "closing your ears and turning down the volume in your head" (Janice), other women avoided people or events that had the potential of being emotionally difficult.[5] Kendra "avoided baby showers," Monica "avoided friends with newborns," and Sylvia "would never go to a matinee! There are always so many kids there." Yet the women found that they weren't the only ones who avoided talking about babies— their pregnant friends or family members may have too. Calina found that "Friends are hesitant to tell me that they're pregnant, and when they do I have to act all cheerful instead of crying. If I hear about one more person who is pregnant, I'm just going to lose it." Frances and her "best friend swore to each other that we'd never have kids. One day we were in the grocery store and she announced that she was pregnant. I was shocked. She'd made the choice in a vacuum after years of not having kids, without even talking to me about it. I was stunned—she got pregnant on purpose! I just left my grocery cart full in the middle of the aisle and walked out of the store. I left her there. I was so surprised. I didn't know how to process it." But Jeanne found that other women's avoiding the topic may be unwarranted: "My own sister was pregnant and didn't want to tell me because she thought it would make me feel bad. This was such a surprise to me—I saw myself as very happy for her! I love going to her showers and look forward to buying things for her, especially impractical fancy dresses for birthdays and Christmas. But she was convinced that I'd be upset, and it took a long time for her to accept that I really wasn't upset and that I really was deliriously happy she was bringing our family a baby to love."

Childless women did not want to retreat from people, conversations, or life experiences. "My experience of not having children is just as important as their experiences of having kids," stated Sally. "I want people to understand what I feel. I want to share all of me—my thoughts, my experiences, my longings, my delights—with my friends." And yet, many childless women felt they could not. If the Beatles were right, that you get by with a little help from your friends, then a lack of support from partners, friends, and family makes it harder to resolve tender areas around not having children.

Women confided that although their partners were usually supportive of their childlessness, often their parents were not. Parents may have expected their daughters to become mothers. "Mom thought motherhood was the best thing in the world, and she wanted the best for me too," said Elise. But she resented the pressure that "Mom put on me to become like other women." Elise resented her mother's "hurry up and get pregnant" attitude that asked directly, "When are you going to give me a grandchild?" Victoria "couldn't help but feel guilty when Mother would say things like, 'Who will carry on our family name if you don't have kids?'" Women whose parents were insensitive toward their childlessness resented it when their parents compared them with sisters and other relatives. Common statements included, "Your sister-in-law, who's only twenty-one, is going to have a baby before you do," or "You remember David and Becky? They just had twins." Nance remembered her mother saying that "I should have kids, even though she knew my marriage was in trouble. It was the ol' 'have a kid and save your marriage' thing, even though we know that seldom works. My parents were so insensitive. Mom didn't want kids for me. She wanted me to have kids to care for her." Toots found that her family treated her differently because she did not have children: "My brother has two boys, and I get jealous of the way he gets treated that my sister and I don't, just because he has kids. There was a time when I wouldn't go see my mom—I got so tired of her asking me when I was going to get pregnant, or after dinner when she'd say things like, 'You don't have to be married to have kids.' Always, with her, I feel I'm a failure because I know she'd want kids and I can't have one." Monique admitted that "it's been over ten years since I've seen my mother. When she phones, I make the calls brief—and I've learned to hang up if I need to. Phone answering machines help to screen her out. Do I ever think she is going to stop treating me this way? No. The only thing I can do is adjust my own behavior to safeguard my own mental health." Few women found that their families were very supportive of their childlessness. "They just don't understand it," Heather said. Homes in which the women were only children or only daughters put more pressure on them to reproduce: "I could have received a lot of pressure from my family, but I didn't. My brother had kids so that took the pressure off of me," said Tina. Calina's mother wished for her to have kids. "I know that motherhood was her most fulfilling act, but she's unable to see that I really am content with my life," she said. "I wish she would open her eyes and see that my life is good and that I'm happy, and be happy for me and celebrate life with me."

Friends as well put pressure on women to have children, in both direct and indirect ways. Direct messages were conveyed to women such as Amy, who "didn't know what to say when my niece introduced me to her friend as her 'old maid aunt.' It hurt so bad, tears welled up in my eyes. I couldn't speak, my throat just closed up. After she said it, she felt bad about it. But when she said it, she meant it. I've become today's version of the old maid." Lisa was surprised at how offended she felt when her friend, who had two small children, chided, "How in the world would you know what it's like to be a mother?'" Childless women felt deviant and alienated as a result of direct comments. Indirectly, women felt pressure to have children so that they "could be like" their friends. When women thought about their friends who were parents, they contemplated having children to be like them: "Having kids would give us the same base of experiences as our friends, so we could have new types of conversations and do things as families. It would be different from now, but it could be a lot of fun," said Melissa.

Some women found that being child-free enabled them to give insight and support to women who couldn't have children. Nance talked about a good friend who married for the second time and "went through everything you could possibly think of to get pregnant. My friend was desperate to get pregnant. But I told her that she could have a very good quality of life without children. I told her about the benefits of not having kids. There are lots of people who don't have kids, and so you should not feel different; nothing is wrong with you if you don't." Elise was pleased that she could be "a role model to girls who are considering whether they want to parent." Sally said, "Some women think they have no alternatives if they have no baby. But how many alternatives do mothers have if they have a baby?" By being with women with children, sometimes women found that their childlessness had been reaffirmed: "My best friend couldn't wait until she had kids," reflected Maura. "Then she had one and became constantly tired and broke. As her kids got older, there was always a conflict to mend. I think that I am happier than she is because I didn't have kids. It's so odd—for years we both felt sorry for me that I couldn't have kids and in the end, I think we both look at me and wonder if it wasn't me that had the better life."

As a result of not being understood, women in the study found it was more comfortable to build friendships with other women who did not have children instead of with mothers. "We are all free as birds to do what we want when we want. We can sit, uninterrupted, for hours on end, or pick up and go places. Now, doesn't that sound good?" asked Sylvia. Valerie found it "easier to be friends with others who don't. We can go sailing for weeks at a time, or I can call someone on the spur of the moment for lunch, or we can go shopping or to the museums and spend hours longer than we anticipated, without anyone getting upset with us. Mothers can't do that." Evie observed that "only now, as my mom-friends' kids are growing up and moving away, have we been able to establish really good friendships. When they had little kids, we were in different places, and they had so much going on in their lives that it was hard to connect. Now that they've got more time, their lives and mine are merging closer together, and we can become better friends."

Some women in the study discussed their friends' lack of empathy, but others talked about wonderful friends who generously shared their children. Sally was grateful to her pregnant friend "who let me go to all her doctor's appointments with her. I could listen to the baby's heartbeat! She let me feel the baby kick. I went through her whole pregnancy with her. I was her coach through labor and delivery." She beamed as she described how she had been the first one to hold the baby. Other women talked about how their friends made them godmothers, aunties, or co-parents or elevated their position so they were more than "just friends" to children.[6] "I will never have children of my own, and I feel like we raise the kids together. I have an important role in the kids' lives that no one else can have. They share all the ups and downs with me, and I struggle along with them about how to deal with nasty classmates, lost soccer games. I get to help the tooth fairy and be there late on Christmas Eve. My friends let me know that they are my kids too," said Barbara.

It was difficult for women when they did not receive the support they needed from their partners. When women who didn't want to be childless had partners who were insensitive to their desire, "I wondered if it was me that wasn't communicating or him who wasn't listening," said Lucy. "I put my entire life on hold, and he never seemed to understand or care. Kids were my dream, not his. He just never really cared at all, even though I had told myself that he did," said Catherine. "It's confusing when I thought he wanted children, only to find out I was living in an illusion." It was also difficult for women who were content to be childless who were with partners who desired children. "I told him I never wanted kids. I was clear about it. He wanted kids and figured that sooner or later I would change my mind. I didn't. It took years to go through this dance. When he couldn't accept my decision, we had to make a choice—either I had to give him kids I didn't want, or we had to split so we could both get what we needed," said Tanya.

Although Lucy, Catherine, and Tanya had experienced stress in their relationship with their partners over mixed communication and childbearing choices, other women had partners whom they described as "wonderful and understanding." Joanna recalled that during her infertility treatments and miscarriages, her husband "was going through the same things I was. His loss was as great as mine, and he was a comfort through dark days." Anne found that her relationship with her husband grew stronger from the loss of their sons. Barbara and her partner have "a loving relationship that grows better with time." The relationship was stable because "we both respect each other's decisions." But as Barbara pointed out, "it's easier to live with another person when you see eye to eye about" decisions such as childbearing.

Women felt that "even though my family and friends may not understand or be as sympathetic as I'd like, we share a history. They know me and what having a child meant," said Ahanna. Social contacts and work colleagues, on the other hand, "don't necessarily know me or care about me at all," Kendra observed. "I try to act like my co-workers' opinions don't matter, but really, they matter a great deal. I spend as much time there as at home." Josi commented that "I may like some people there, but I have to remember that work is work—it's a job, it's a competitive environment, and people have no obligation to care for each other there." Most often, people get to know just enough about those with whom they work that they believe they have insight into their psyches. Yvonne said, "A woman I worked with told me that 'if you had children, then you'd understand.' At some level, that woman was right. I can't know how it feels to be pregnant, or what it is like to nurse a baby, or the emotions involved in the care of your own child. But even though I've not known those feelings or had the mother experiences, I can still understand. I can have empathy, and I can help the young women I work with to make good decisions. There is not necessarily a relationship between one's childbearing status and good decision making. Our hearts are just as big, and we can love just as deeply."

Through routine conversations, women reevaluated their motivations for childlessness. Ramona said, "It's been tough. When I was first married and we became social with other people, most of our friends had children and for them to up and go, it was hard for them to do. I understood it. After finagling to finally get together, I found I could add to their conversation about kids going to school, but I became bored with it. I could be in their world, but they didn't seem much interested in sharing mine. Then I moved and became friends with a group of women who had waited to have kids. We had things in common—until babies came. After that, I didn't want to spend my time talking about potty training and 'isn't he adorable,'" she said. "I find myself impatient when women talk about breast feeding, and about how overwhelmed they were with kids. I found myself wanting to get away from these relationships because we had nothing in common anymore. In cities, there are more women without children, but they are so busy, I only see them when we are in the park when we are all walking our dogs." She hesitated, thought, and continued: "I bounce back and forth between all of this stuff. I don't know if deep down inside I did want children or if I did not want them, and then I think if I had one, I would love it as much or more than I love the dog. I don't remember crying because I wanted to be pregnant. If I did not have to think about it, I would probably be a great mother. I also believe that if moms weren't into their kids, then I'd be upset. I want them to raise great kids who can run the country. I don't know if I have shut my mind because that was the hand I was dealt. Now I'm just too tired."

Betsy felt that people in her professional network treat childless women differently: "I have experienced subtle discrimination because I am childless, and it doesn't feel nice. No one has all of life's experiences. When people say mean things, it's a hurtful way of keeping you out, of not including you. Sure, some people don't intend to hurt you by their words, but others do intend to make you feel bad. Motherhood to them is a club that you cannot belong to unless you have a kid. We're all responsible for each other and work toward the collective good. As a therapist, I spend hours with clients and with children, but these experiences don't seem to count for anything to them." Sarah said, "I've been told that 'you're selfish' and had this thrown at me since I was in my late twenties. People will even say hurtful things about my not having a child when they are talking in a group, and they say it so loudly they have to know I'll overhear. Yet they don't know the details of my life. They are totally unthinking remarks. But I never confront the person saying such things. It's so hurtful. I've decided I don't want to have anything to do with them, and I avoid them."

Although Betsy found that motherhood was an exclusive club that was difficult to enter, childless women sometimes found that they could became "legitimate" grandmothers. Usually, they became grand-mothers by marrying men whose children had borne children. Acquir-ing grandchildren seems to provide women with an important social role. As Gwen announced, "My husband and I spend lots of time, money, and energy talking about the kids, planning for them, and doing things with them. I feel like a real grandmother. I can now flash photos of grandchildren, just like the other grandmas—I too have stories to tell, so I have access to a new type of women's conversation that I was never privileged to before." Being a grandmother also pro-vided women with a channel for affection, stories, and gifts. "I always wondered who I could give my jewelry to, and now I have someone who will genuinely appreciate it," said Naomi. But most childless women do not acquire grandchildren. Interactions with friends who are grandparents "can be quite alienating. My friends flip out their most recent photos of their grandchildren, and regale me with tales of how Benjamin is doing this and how Jessica is doing that. And I can look at them politely, ask questions, and smile," Carol said. "I don't understand it, I can't relate to her excitement, and I sort of don't care about all the details. It's sort of like when one person reads a book or watches a movie that they're all excited about and they try to give you the blow-by-blow details of it, and try as you might, it's just not the same as having experienced it yourself. Most of us naturally check out of those types of conversations, no matter what the topic is," said Hannah. Inevitably in routine conversations, something can be said which is a "'gotcha,' one of those moments when it's clear that my not having kids permeates my entire life span," said Evie. "I miss somebody never calling me Mom. I don't know what it is to give birth. I can never plan for a wedding or anything for a child. I can't go to school for a meeting and be with the other mothers. And I'll never be a grandmother who bakes cookies and attends recitals who gets to be the first one to hear a kid's big news. It is a loss, no matter what you say."

The issue of becoming a grandmother, or not, was yet another reminder that a woman's childbearing decisions have life-long consequences. Ellie commented on her friends who were becoming grandmothers: " It blows my mind! They can watch the whole flow of their genes go from one generation to the next. I can't. It's interesting now that since my friends' kids are all grown up, no one focused on little kid things. People's lives center on other things, like politics, work, or their own creative processes. It's more fun to talk to others now about what they are doing to change themselves or changing the world. But now that my friends have grandkids, I find the conversations have shifted again, back to my not having a door into those kid conversations." Sylvia pointed out that if her grandparent friends "would quit making their family the main topic of conversation, and talk about things that's more important to the world, it'd be a heck of a lot easier to be around them. They have no idea how boring they can be, as they sit there in their smug pride. Just because they procreated, it doesn't mean that they're responsible for any of the good things, or the bad ones, their offspring generated."

Because the women in this study did not expect that their work and social acquaintances would know them very well, it was easier for the women to excuse their insensitivities than those from family or friends. Women felt hurt when their friends and family conveyed a lack of understanding of what childlessness meant to them. Wanting to help, family and friends may often fail because they don't understand the loss that accompanies infertility. "It's difficult," said Mary Margaret, "to really understand another person's sorrow. Sometimes people mean well but say the wrong thing. Quite by accident, they ended up hurting my feelings. In fairness, it appears that most of the alienating comments and behaviors occurred when people don't know what to say or do when they learned that I couldn't have kids." Vickie found that she would get angry at "the rude, insensitive comments that people would say. I never asked their opinion—they just volunteered their two cents about my reproductive life like they were making some public service announcement." Nance also found herself hurt and angered by the words of friends and family members "who should have known me better, who should have known what to say." She paused, reflected, then continued: "It took me a while to learn that what they needed from me was a roadmap of how to talk about these things. They needed guidance, since my experiences were foreign to them. It took me a while to recognize that my mom's feelings of loss and hurt were just as real and valid as my feelings not to have kids." Women found that it was easier to confront or ignore negative statements when they came from total strangers or acquaintances. There was less emotional investment in the people, so there was less likelihood to be disappointed. In those situations, Greta indicated that she was "more likely to walk away in frustration, rather than to angrily confront people."

After childless women dealt with the initial shock, hurt, or anger from insensitive comments, they tried to understand them. As Josi reflected, "If I think about it, I know that raising kids is difficult. You give up a lot to have folks who have them. I sometimes wonder—do some moms who put their careers on a back burner use criticism as a way to lash out at someone who embodies their own disappointments in life? When they make these hurtful statements, they must come from unresolved feelings of pain that they have. So I try to forgive them, because I've had my pain too." Elise reflected that "Sometimes when we aren't resolved with our decision, other person's statements hurt us. I'm comfortable with my decision. I teach that I'm voluntarily child-free and stand up in front of class to make my position public. If anything, I get the opposite kind of feedback that some women get. Students come up to me and say I'm a good influence for them. They say they're relieved to find someone they can talk with about their feelings. Not everyone wants to have kids and that's okay."

Processing childlessness was a roller-coaster ride for many women, complete with highs and lows, and unexpected twists and turns. It was particularly hard for women in the study when they had been excited for a sister who was pregnant, only to have the sister lose the baby. The babies of close family or friends provided some childless women with an opportunity to transfer their nurturing emotions. Sally's sister "is pregnant and has an extra chromosome. If the baby is born, it will die in a year. It's so sad and frightening for her. She's lost two babies and is unsure whether she can do this again. My sister's loss is mine as well. Being an aunt and loving my sister's child is the closest thing I'll ever get to being a mom." Tina found that when her sister miscarried, "I felt terrible. There's this sense that I lost a bit of myself when she lost the baby. I would be comforted if my sister had a child. I could really give to it in a way that made me feel like a mom." Kris's sister's baby was going to be born "with severe mental and physical defects, and the baby probably would have died soon after birth, if it had lived. After much agony, she decided to abort the fetus. It was the right thing to do, but it was so frightening, so sad. She was having our family's first baby, so it is also part of me. People don't understand why I've been so upset about it. Her loss is my loss. It was like losing a baby I never had."

Expressing honest feelings and being respected for them was just as important for women who chose not to have children as it was for women who wanted them but did not have them. Women who miscarried or lost babies found it particularly difficult to receive the support they needed. "My friends are so uncomfortable with my talking about it that they can't deal with what I've gone through. I end up supporting them, listening to them, pulling them together—when it was my issue. I'm the one that miscarried. I'm the one who can't have kids. In the long run, I've found that it's easier not even to talk to them about what has happened or how I am feeling," said Sherri. Joanna agreed: "Sometimes I need to cry or be upset. I need my friends to listen to me and support me. I wish they wouldn't avoid my hurt. It ends up with me taking care of my friends, instead of them listening to and helping me. I must have time to move through it all, to heal up. Instead of giving me encouragement, time, or even quiet, they give me this, 'Well, why don't you just go out and get a baby if you want one so much?' They don't react to the loss that I have over not having my own baby. I get this Band-Aid response instead of them letting me cry and help me explore my hurt. I know that they're trying to help, so it's okay, but it's easier to be with friends who understand."

Yet other women didn't want to confide in others. Sometimes this is because "I'm a very private person and childlessness is a very private issue" (Jeannie), they are "weary of trying to explain the unexplainable to those with no imagination" (Sherri), they are "sick and tired of people making not having kids some psychopathology when it's a totally normal thing for women to do" (Sylvia), or they fear that verbalizing a desire for a child "would put a curse on my having one," according to Nelly. "When you really want a baby, you just cannot help hoping that somehow you'll get pregnant," Nelly said tearfully. "I want a baby so badly you cannot imagine it. It's the one thing in my life that I've always wanted. And yet, one thing after another keeps happening that takes me farther and farther away from that dream. I'm terrified that it won't come true. I'm scared to even talk about it, for fear I will jinx it. So I just hold it all inside, and don't tell anyone really how I feel."

Another possible explanation for the isolation childless women experience, according to some researchers, pertains to the threat that childless women pose.[7] Mothers and nonmothers do not always communicate, not because they have little to say to one another but because of what childless women mean to mothers. Author Kathleen Griffen alleges that childless women, by their mere existence, force "a resounding silence" in which mothers must question the nature of womanhood. Childless women pose an implicit threat to traditional ideas about what women are supposed to be.

It was sometimes hard for women in this study to gain their own perspective on their childlessness because "families and friends have their own spin on what they think I should feel," said Tina. As a result, more than half of the women had seen counselors to help them resolve inner conflicts that were related, directly or indirectly, to childlessness. The issues women brought to therapy were complicated and intertwined; their feelings were complex. "When I was younger, I just dealt. But there came a point when I saw that my stuff was getting in the way of my living the quality of life I deserved. So I saw a therapist" (Jennifer).

Therapy helped women to deal with a host of emotions. "Not having a child bothers me most when I think about my family unit," said Toots. "My twin sister is contemplating a first child, my brother has a child, my cousins are having kids, and I get caught in the same issue of feeling bad that I don't have what they have. Then I turn around and kick myself for feeling so selfish. It's a Catch-22," she said. "I do a lot of this to myself, but it was my desire to have kids. Maybe I stayed in the marriage too long, wasting a lot of time hoping it would work out and things would get on track. I'm mad at myself that I stayed in the relationship so long. So now I do isolate from the kids issue and get caught up in the struggle with myself. I feel uncomfortable, even at my age, going to my gynecologist because he brings up the topic. He's as nice as he can be, but I just listen when he says, 'well, you're getting at that age when you better be thinking about it,'" she continued. "When married women would ask 'When are you going to have kids?' I always duck the question, laugh it off, always so embarrassed to say my husband doesn't want kids. I always had hope. It has affected me in ways I never knew it would. I get tired of putting up a facade to protect myself and my feelings—but this is a stupid way to live. I worry about it a lot because I don't want to withdraw . . . I don't feel like this all the time, but I feel stuck. It's not on my mind twenty-four hours a day, but it affects how I enter into future relationships."

Many of the women who were interviewed had seen counselors "for one reason or another." Some of their reasons for therapy were directly related to childlessness, but often the problems had nothing to do with reproductive issues. Although some women found therapy "to be a wonderful gift to myself," others found that psychotherapy was not always the answer to dealing with the emotional complexities associated with childlessness. "Sometimes you have to just get through the unexpected emotional moment, sometimes you have to confront people who make you feel bad directly, and other times you learn to avoid situations," Angela said. Although counseling may help people to manage their own emotions, it does little to control the behavior of others. Kris observed that "If I have the problem, then counseling helps. But if it's the other people who have the problem—that they try to impose on me—then they're the ones who need help." Toots also pointed out the limitations of therapy: "I've had it with counselors. I have a keen awareness of how I feel and the spot I'm in. I go from day to day, week to week, month to month, and think of things I could get involved in and do. That's okay, and it works for a while, but then I think how all this talking and doing isn't taking care of my woman thing. So I isolate myself for a while, and then later come out." But the women interviewed appeared to have a good sense of how they felt about not having kids, whether or not they had undergone therapy. "I wanted to get pregnant, and we tried and tried and couldn't. It got so bad that, even though I'm a psychologist, I had to go to a therapist to deal with my anger. The therapist's advice was 'you cannot control this one. You have to deal with the issues of control.' But I still get angry. Last week I had a sixteen-year-old client with a year-old baby. My client was telling me that her one-year-old baby told her he wants a brother, so she's trying to get pregnant again. Yeah, sure! I see clients who abuse their kids, and I want to tell their child protective service workers that 'you don't understand. I want a child, and yet these people have no trouble having them.' I can be professional in the session, but at home, I rant and rave, with such indignation. My husband will ask me if he should get the knives out yet." Joanna summed her views up in another way: "I am now doing the kind of psychological work that would make me a better mother, yet now I don't have that option."

As women struggled to identify their emotions around their child-lessness, they admitted that their interactions with others varied, usu-ally in response to a particular situation. Thus, their responses were not necessarily predictable. "People will ask me, 'Why don't you have kids?' and after all these years I still don't have a pat answer. It all depends on who I'm talking to, how I'm feeling that day, and how I want to tell my story. I might say, 'I had endometriosis and couldn't,' or I might say, 'my relationship wasn't working out,' or I have simply said, 'I chose not to have kids.' All of these answers are partially true, but I may not want the person I'm talking with to know all of them," Sarah said. Given that the causes of childlessness are complex, it stands to reason that women's responses to it are complex as well.

In sum, the childless women in this study were routinely confronted with difficult interactions with family and friends, work colleagues, and total strangers. Lesbian and inifertile women were those who found it most difficult to talk with others about the meaning of childlessness in their lives. It is likely that people who said hurtful things to them had no idea of the impact of their words. Irrespective of the cause of their childlessness, women have made it clear that they need greater support and respect.

CHAPTER 10 **Nurturing Others**

Even though female nurturing is typically associated with caring for children, most of the childless women I interviewed for this study incorporated nurturing of others into their day-to-day lives, whether at home, at work, with friends, or in their communities, and many pointed out that nurturing was an important part of their character. Helping others seemed to be a natural extension of life for many of these women. As Rose stated, "When I was young, I learned to feel responsible to, and for, others—and I am." Minnie acknowledged that "I may not have children of my own, but I am godmother for a whole bunch of kids. I've adopted certain people across the planet as my family. I care for them dearly, and I believe they care for me as well." Although she is not a cuddly woman, Minnie lives her life in the service of others. She sloughs off praise for what she does for others, because helping others for her "is no big deal. I'm just doing what people are supposed to do to help each other."

The women who were interviewed for this project were proud of the contributions they had made to family, friends, and their communities. Many had lived their entire lives anticipating that one day they would become mothers; unable to have children, they transferred their need to nurture from biological children to caring for others. "Even if I'd had kids, I'd still be taking care of others. It's the way I am," Hannah said. Through nurturing others, they gained a sense of fulfillment. Thus, nurturing others was an important part of these childless women's lives.

However, not all women who considered themselves to be nurturing desired children. Many had strategically decided against having children. As Ani stated, "I had a wonderful, loving family as I grew up, and I have a wonderful, loving extended family now. It just so happens that I didn't choose to have children of my own to be a part of those families. We build our families across time by adding people we love into them. There are many ways to love, and many people to love. My life is gloriously full and rich. I think I would have been a great mom, but I'm making lovely contributions to others in the life I have chosen."

Whereas well-nurtured girls may have found it easy to nurture as adults, women who were not well nurtured as girls sometimes described a different scenario. They did not witness the altruistic role-modeling that was essential for learning how to care for others. They could not draw upon a history of practical interaction patterns that were characteristic of being warm and empathetic. It was not that women didn't want to be nurturing—it was more likely that they did not know how or, if they knew what to do, they did not feel comfortable doing it. This lack of skill at nurturing had had an impact on women's decisions to remain childless. Some felt they would not be good mothers, others felt they could not give children what they needed, whereas a few felt that the personal costs of having children were too great. Feeling awkward and self-conscious, they chose childlessness as a more comfortable lifestyle. However, even these women frequently found different, more comfortable, ways to express their concern for others.

How did the nurturing experiences girls received growing up become transformed into nurturing behavior when they reached adulthood? How did nurturing skills vary among the different types of childless women? What were common types of assistance provided by childless women? What was the meaning of nurturing for women with no children? These questions form the basis of this chapter.

Most of the childless women interviewed for this study described themselves, or were described by others, as nurturing individuals. Many specifically stated that they enjoyed "caring for," "giving to," "assisting," "mothering," or "helping" children, spouses, friends, family members, animals, or even organizations. Betsy's description of herself is a good example: "I am the world's great Earth Mother. I mother my dogs, I mother my birds, I mother my friends, I mother my nephews, and I'm finding that now I even mother my mother." Even though a woman did not have children of her own, "I take care of everyone," said Barbara. "I'm a nurturing fool," Catherine announced. Randi laughed, "I'd give you the shirt off my back if you needed it. If you needed my blood, I'd cut open my veins and say, 'suck.'" They viewed nurturing as an essential activity that far surpassed the bounds of a parent–child relationship.

Nurturing may be a need. When one gives to others, one also benefits, according to psychologists. Erik Erickson indicated that a common midlife developmental challenge that confronts adults is to create generativity, that is, to act in ways that will have lasting benefit.[1] By contributing to others' lives, "we pass on a part of ourselves to the next generation in which our talents, attitudes, values, behaviors, and gifts are transformed by others," said Angela, a psychologist. By helping others, adults can more successfully confront the final stage of human development—aging and preparation for death. Women in this study who felt their lives had made a difference lived lives filled with optimism and confidence, whereas those who felt they had failed were haunted by feelings of despair and depression.

Part of women's presumed need to nurture may be socially induced. Social attitudes and institutions still support the "nurturing children if you can, and nurturing others if you cannot" assumption that women's ultimate role is motherhood, and that if women don't bear children, they are still expected to take care of others.[2] Nurturing others was also perceived to be a part of feminine spirituality. As Elizabeth put it, "The world is nurtured by mothers, so it is women who protect the heart of universe. Unless the nurturing part of us comes to inhabit the world, we're doomed. We're all children of God, and we need to give it to all of ourselves, even to adults, who are also children of the world. We must pour out energy into the world as it exists, and transform it. Feminine energy is Goddess energy, the creative energy," she said. Elizabeth found that "It's hard to describe with words, because some people will find fault with whatever words I use and put their own spin what I say. But I'm talking about the loving, positive energy. This energy and love must be given to every living creature on the planet in order for us to survive. If we all lived up this way, the world could be the wonderful place it was meant to be." Darlene asserted that "Every creature is part of the Divine. By taking care of even the smallest and seemingly most insignificant of beings, we nurture the greatness of creation. It is through feminine nurturing—which men could do too—that life is given and protected."

Nurturing may or may not be gender related. According to work by anthropologist Margaret Mead, some males exhibit more nurturing behaviors than do some females, who may be more masculine and aggressive than their male counterparts. Although it is convention to believe that females are more nurturing than males, the scientific reality is that it may not be so. Nurturing is arguably more of a learned, cultural trait rather than a genetically linked behavior. Throughout generations, a learned trait can enter the collective consciousness of women, according to some theorists. Chodorow writes that the mother–daughter relationship is shaped in the female psyche and that women nurture because of this psychological character formation. Her thesis is that women nurture not because it is a natural instinct or because of gender role formation or ideology but because of psychological character formation. Usually, she notes, women take care of everyone in the family, from infants to the elderly. It's not that men cannot nurture—it's that most of the time they don't, so little girls observe adult women being the caregivers: "Women mother. In our society, as in most societies, women not only bear children. They also take primary responsibility for infant care, spend more time with infants and children than do men, and sustain primary emotional times with infants. When biological mothers do not parent, other women, rather than men, virtually always take their place. Though fathers and other men spend varying amounts of time with infants and children, the father is rarely a child's primary parent."[3]

Chodorow posits that because of the nurturing they receive and are expected to give, girls define themselves more in relation to others: "The basic feminine sense of self is connected to the world, and the basic masculine sense is separate."[4] If women need to connect to others, and if children are the customary vehicles by which they make these connections in the family and the larger social environment, then it stands to reason that women who do not have children may find themselves feeling marginal, separated, or isolated. Childless women must struggle to develop an alternate female identity in place of the maternity they anticipated or were expected to experience. To be healthy, they must consciously or subconsciously process not having children and transform themselves, according to another theorist, Mardy Ireland. She asserts that "Faced with the reality that childbearing is no longer possible, she may consciously accept her own particular childless circumstances, letting go of her identification with her womb as the place to nourish a child so that another kind of creative child may be born. In this act of conscious letting go, a different path is opened. An inability to relinquish the unrealizable aspect of motherhood for the sake of something else, something often unknown, can result in a life pervaded by bitterness, disappointment, and a sense of failure."[5]

The act of caring for others can be altruistic; other people's needs may come first, but the act of caring can also fulfill a woman's personal agenda to be needed. According to Joanna, "When I nurture people, it's really always about nurturing me. When I tell people I love them, it's risky. Maybe I tell people they're important to me because they may say they love me in return, and maybe I need to hear it. Maybe I subconsciously do things for people because I want them to do those things for me."

From another perspective, the notion that women should carry on their shoulders the responsibility for the family's and community's well-being could have grown out of women's need to make themselves indispensable. In a patriarchal world in which men ruled the roost, women had to look for domains in which they could exercise power and authority. Caring for others created a form of reciprocity in which others felt obligated to return some sign of appreciation. In this view, nothing is free, not even love. When a mother gives to a child, she expects in return compliance, devotion, and affection. When women cared for husbands and home, the traditional view held that women did so because it was their job, in much the same way that men worked in a factory or shoe store. Care and nurturing were sometimes provided out of a sense of obligation, expectation, and concern to maintain the status quo.

Traditionally, providing expressive care, emotional support, and physically helping others were activities prescribed for women. Self-sacrifice was essential to this role, and it was deemed honorable and fulfilling to help others get what they needed. Thus, motherhood, nurturing, and self-sacrifice became intrinsically linked. But contemporary women witnessed women's social liberation from the traditional roles that kept them subservient to others.[6] Many women no longer felt that they had to serve coffee at meetings; rather, they were the ones who could be administrators developing policies. Girls learned that they were to find not just a job but a career. They wanted financial independence. They learned that they could be their own person, not "owned" socially or emotionally by husbands or parents. Within this new mind-set, nurturing was no longer mandatory. It took a back seat to personal development.

When women in this study were asked, "Are you a nurturing person?" their answers were fascinating. One group of women quickly identified themselves as nurturing and told stories of how they loved to take care of others. Ellen, when asked if she was nurturing, affirmed: "Absolutely—it's who I am by virtue of my genes and gender! And I'm proud of it. From a very early age I was praised for my nurturing behaviors. In kindergarten I befriended a classmate who had polio; when I was eight I began baby-sitting for my nieces and nephews. When I was in the sixth grade, the principal used to ask me to take care of her second grade class when she needed to leave the classroom. I baby-sat for neighbors' children at an early age. And I always felt like my younger brother's mother." Barbara, whose love was effervescent, talked of long-ago lovers, family members whom she adored, and how she sacrificed having a child in order to please her partner because "her needs are no less important than mine. If I love her, I need to do what will be good for her, that will make her happy." Sally, an interior decorator, made sure there were lace doilies under our teacups, because, she said, "even the littlest things let others know you care." Joanna, who had miscarried several times, wiped away her tears as she said, "I'm delighted to tell my story so that other women can learn what I went through, so they know they aren't alone." Rose was "absolutely a nurturing type. When I was young, I always needed to be needed. At the [residential facility that specialized in assisting children to overcome developmental disabilities]," Rose found that she was always "the helper. The nurses would all fight to get me—I helped dress the little kids and care for myself as well." Her desire to nurture others has continued into her adult life and her work with the physically challenged people who are her clients. Although physically unable to have children, she has assumed an active role co-parenting the children in her family: "Next month I'm taking my twelve-year-old nephew to Disney World. I try to spend special, quality time with each of my nieces and nephews," she said with pride.

It is important to note that childless women did not see a correlation between being employed and having kids. Mothers who stayed at home were not necessarily warm and nurturing; mothers who were employed full time outside the home were often loving, giving, and nourished their daughters' physical, emotional, and social needs. Nurturing was a personal attribute, an intimate characteristic that women felt intensely. Calina's parents both worked, yet she had a keen sense of being loved: "Mom and Dad were both very nurturing. I remember crawling up in my mom's lap all the time. She was always accessible and fused her work and home life. Dad would pile us kids in the car for ice cream, take us places, talk to us. He never hit us, and my folks would process everything with us. This had to serve as the forerunner to my going to school to be a psychotherapist. Friends recall my home as a warm, loving place. If I'd had kids, I'd have made the same kind of home for them," she said. Some nurturing mothers were stay-at-home moms, like Melissa's: "Mom was the nurturing one and we had fun in our family. Mom always encouraged others—she's an intuitive person. She stayed at home with me until I was ten, and only after all of us were in school did she go back to work." Audrey's mother worked part time, and she "got us up, had our clothes ready, made us cream of wheat, braided our hair, walked us to school, cleaned our rooms while we were away, and was there to meet us at 3:00. She brought us home for milk and homemade cookies, helped us with our homework, made good dinners, played games with us, got us our baths at night, and read us stories and tucked us in. Dad wasn't there most of the time, and when he was, he was a figurehead whose presence really didn't matter too much one way or another. His interest in the business world, instead of the home world, made him somewhat irrelevant to our everyday life. But Mama, she was everything." Rose saw her mother as "wonderful, and she did everything for us. She was a single mom, since my dad died when we were small. She packed shoes in a shoe shop for forty years. She worked hard, and eventually got sick and had to go on disability. All the time, she was there for us." Maggie's mother also worked full time and "was the most wonderful, giving, loving woman. I was so lucky to learn how to care from her. I think her working gave me a model to see that I could be a career woman with a loving heart to all the kiddos" she oversees as a school administrator—and a deliberately childless woman. Women often learned that family comes first, even when it means self-sacrifice. "I've dragged my little sister and brother around for years. I stayed with them when they were sick, I taught them how to read and cook, I studied with them under my feet, and I even took them on my dates," said Ahanna. These women had all learned the importance of nurturing—and they had opted not to have children.

Although these women seemed to have felt "totally loved in every way" by their parents, others resented having a mother who didn't enjoy parenting. "It inhibited my desires to have children. Mom resented us. Sure, she did things for us but we always knew her heart wasn't in it like other mothers," said Rhonda, who was deliberately childless. Valerie's mother "was more into her gardens than into having kids. She didn't nurture me. On the surface it looked like I should have had a great childhood, I never felt she loved me." Many recalled parental love as compartmentalized and pragmatic. "I can pinpoint exact incidents when my mom made me feel really loved," said Yvonne.

For women like her, affection was seen as one-shot occasions instead of a continuous stream of nurturing. They did not seem to experience the important accumulation of the everyday, minute, routine moments of care. Julie "couldn't recall any one particular thing that my parents did that made me know they loved me, since they always there loving me, and I knew they always would be." Yvonne recalled parental affection in a few isolated moments she could pinpoint, such as "the time my mom sat beside me when I was sick and stroked my head." It was the constancy of parents' behavior as nurturing or non-nurturing that was important in influencing their daughter's adult comfort with caring for others.

Well-nurtured women frequently wanted children because they felt a sense of nurturing competence. "Our home was so wonderful, full of people and laughter. I learned how to love there. I always dreamed of bringing my own kids home, and having them experience the joy I did. It makes me really sad that won't happen," said Laura. When well-nurtured women contemplated having children, they wanted "not just kids, but the way of life we had," Rose said. "Not having kids cuts off creating a lifestyle that I'd learned to love to keep. As a single adult, I spend much of my time alone. When you've got a family, there's always people coming and going, doing this and that, and it's vibrant and real. I can be busy with friends, but it's this sense of family, where you're really, truly needed that I miss the most," she said.

This notion that women missed not just children but the lifestyle associated with having them was repeated regularly. Many of the women had parents who "were the eternal well-spring of love," as Julie called them. "They showed they loved us in acts as simple as packing school lunches every morning and having sit-down dinners every night. They took time to ask about our day at school, listened about what was important to me, and they'd help me solve my problems. If I had kids, I'd do the same thing, because that's what parents are supposed to do," she said. Whether in routine acts as simple as Sally's mother "pulling me into her lap every morning for a cuddle and a kiss" or "big" events like Amanda's birthday party "when I got to have oodles of friends over, and chocolate cake with pink frosting, and my folks let me be the queen," girls who had learned how to nurture felt much more comfortable about doing so in their adult lives. "Taking care of others is what you're supposed to do," Veronica announced. "I don't think it has anything to do with whether you're a professional, career track or the mommy track. Nurturing isn't what you do as much as how you do it, or what you are, I guess. I wish I had kids, but I don't, so I do other things to take care of folks. It doesn't matter how busy you are—you make time to do it. I remember the summer when my dad organized all the neighborhood kids into a baseball league. It was so much fun. I think about doing the same thing myself."

To "make a family, we thought about adopting," said Laura. Women who wanted children considered adopting a child—but most they didn't. Some "thought about it for about half a second" (Missy), whereas others like Martha "debated long and hard about it." If so many childless women think about adopting, why don't they follow through? A few may adopt, but most are ambivalent or even reluctant about raising an adopted child.[7] Adopted children "often come with baggage they can't get rid of. It's hard enough to raise a child with everything going for them—it's a tough haul when you take in kids who need more than what a normal person can reasonably give," said Janice. "Many adoptable children have experienced some emotional trauma or have differences that may be a challenge for new parents. Knowing the types of troubles they come with, I knew adopting would require a great deal of time, patience, energy, and money," said Nora. "I just didn't think I had the wherewithal to do it." Tina confessed that "I think if I had a child and it wasn't perfect that I would accept it more easily than if I adopted a child whose needs were significant. I know that sounds terrible, but it's true. Somehow, the flaws of your own child are more lovable, or tolerable, than the flaws of someone you don't know, who may be someone you're not really like." Mary Margaret and Dawn considered adoption but found that support was not easy to get: "My brother-in-law said that he'd go for adoption if we could get a nice Caucasian baby. Race is not a factor for me. If a child needs a home, I don't care if it's purple or pink. But there's a long waiting list in the state for Caucasian babies, and my husband knows that his family wouldn't accept a nonwhite baby. They say, 'no black, Asian, or Hispanic babies.'" Emily contemplated adopting but didn't want to become a single parent: "Kids need as much as possible—and a strong sense of community. It's difficult for a single woman to have a child under these circumstances. If I'm going to go to all the effort and expense to have a child, then I want everything to be perfect for it."

Some women tried to adopt, but failed in the attempt. Sometimes situations "blew up in our faces" (Erica), sometimes a partner's "enthusiasm for the adoption waned" (Sherri), and sometimes "health conditions took precedence and we just never got back on the adoption track" (Ellie). Being "so close to calling a child my own" only to have something interfere with the adoption was extremely frustrating, as illustrated by Laura's tale. Laura was diagnosed with cancer and was unable to bear children: "Fortunately, my husband and I are good friends and that helped us get through those days. My cousin worked for a mountain clinic with unmarried, pregnant girls. In the fall, she called and wanted to know if we were interested in adopting a baby. At first we laughed and said 'no way.' But we decided we'd go for it. There was a possibility that the girl would have twins, so we decided to let it happen as it was meant to. We were all ready, but at the last minute, the mother decided not to give them up. We were disappointed, but now that we got warmed up, we started thinking more about adoption. About six months later, when we were settling back into the normal routine of life, we got another call about a girl who wanted to give up her baby. This girl had a good background, and we got really excited. We discussed names, ages, sex, all of it. We looked at things in the baby stores, but we didn't buy anything because I knew better than to get excited. Guess what? She kept the baby. Then it all happened again a year later. Three times! A girl at church wanted to give up her baby, and I was hesitant about it and tried very hard not to get excited about it. But she too decided to keep the baby. I told my husband that I couldn't stand losing three babies in a span of two years. We were happy before. At age forty-two, we decided to have no more thoughts or talk about babies. Then three years ago, a woman offered me a two-year-old girl.

The child had been abandoned. I thought of legal bills. The newspaper was full of stories about women who come back years later and take back their children. I couldn't stand loving and nurturing a baby and then have someone come years later and take it away from me. I simply said, 'I appreciate the fact that you think enough of me to offer the child, but emotionally I cannot handle it.' But I miss those children, my children."

Heather said, "I think any childless woman who doesn't think about adopting a child at one time or another is lying. Some of us disregard the idea quickly, while others of us decide that we will go for it, full speed ahead. But most of us hover in that gray area where we want to adopt a kid of our own, yet we are terrified to do it for a whole bunch of reasons. Ultimately, for me, I let my indecision reign and I haven't adopted yet. But sometimes, I say to myself, maybe one day I'll decide that's what I want to do. Adoption is neat that way; unlike menopause when childbearing decisions are over, the decision to adopt is never quite over—it can be postponed indefinitely." Tashi "always thought that adoption was conceptually a good idea. We always adopt others into our lives. I influence other people with my life. I thought about adopting a child at one point, but it is not anything I now want to do. I've got kids in my life. Older kids have so much baggage. I'm not into trying to do penance. I've done human services all my life. Now I want a healthy, full experience."

Well-nurtured women who chose to be childless were common, and they were less likely to contemplate adoption because they had strategically decided to live a child-free life. "I had a lovely family growing up," Maggie insisted. "There were many things I wanted out of life, and I felt there wasn't enough of me to go around for all of them. I thought it was better to go into a career where I could care for hundreds of children, instead of just one or two of my own. It seemed my attention would be better spent that way," she said. Her decision was made "Not because I didn't like kids—I think it's because I liked kids so much." Maggie's definition of childlessness expanded the term beyond the confines of the parent–child relationship into one that was more inclusive.

The issue of exactly what is nurturing, and who are nurturing people, is curious. Sometimes, girls like Maggie experienced forms of care that corresponded with conventional definitions of the term. But many experienced nonconventional forms of nurturing. Ramona confessed that "I'm not so sure that I know what nurturing is. I'm not a huggy kind of person, but if people have a problem they do always seem to call me." Culturally, some groups of women learned not to express softness and vulnerability—but that didn't mean they weren't nurturing. Joan reflected on the day her Native American grandmother told her that "in my world, we learned that in order to love our children, we had to be strict and strong. We could never be weak or soft. Sometimes it was difficult to be unbending and hard, when what my heart wanted to do was to swoop down like the wings of the eagle and carry them away from all bad feelings. But that would not prepare them for life, so I held my tears inside and forced myself to make them strong. Non-native people were surprised that I wanted children—they thought because I was hard on the outside that I wasn't soft on the inside." Joan's experience was not unusual. Hiding traditionally "soft" emotions and exhibiting "strong," masculine behaviors may have been mothers' attempts to prepare their daughters to assume leadership positions in their communities—to provide them with the internal skills needed so that they were not locked into traditionally oppressive feminine roles. Nurturing need not always be "hugs and kisses and cuddles and mushy stuff. I think you have to consider the source. For instance, my mom gave me what she could," Yvonne observed, "but she had been raped as a girl and wasn't physically demonstrative after that. She seldom hugged me, but she'd pet me sometimes. My mom acted in matter-of-fact ways and assumed that I'd do well. Not 'Good for you,' but 'Of course you should.' I got everything I needed but not everything I wanted from them. The result is sometimes I feel so clumsy when I try to hug people or show them affection. So while my folks were nurturing, and I think I am, I don't think my brother or I show it very well."

It was possible for women who didn't receive a great deal of nurturing to want children, "even though I'd have to learn how to do it," said Yvonne. Iris also wanted children but felt there was part of her that wasn't entirely comfortable knowing how to parent: "My parents both studied at an Ivy League school and became doctors of theology. My mother baby-sat for Reinhold Niebuhr's children. We were lily white, affluent, and lived in tract housing where the men would all go to the end of the street to catch the train to work. The black maids would come to work on the buses. We went to private schools before we were two, and the housekeeper kept us when we got home. We had all the material things, summer camps in France, trips to Europe. We were very privileged, and I can't think of a thing we didn't have. But my mother was never there for us. I remember I always wanted something to love—a kitten, a dog. I told Santa I wanted a kitten. But I got a Tiny Tears doll instead. My mom said that animals were too messy. So I trapped things—frogs, salamanders, bugs, a squirrel, rabbit. But they made pathetic noises so I let them go right away. And I drew and developed a real love of art. I drew paper dolls, dogs, houses, and made an animal kingdom. I was given dolls, but they're still in their boxes so they wouldn't get messed up. My mom's message was—don't get messy. Animals and babies were messy. But I wanted kids—maybe because I wanted to create in a child's life the world I wished I'd had."

Betsy also never felt nurtured as a child: "My mother was mentally ill and a chilly, not a warm and fuzzy person. I was the oldest of three kids. My brother was twelve years younger. I remember taking my books, purse, and brother everywhere. Even to parties. I used to wonder why I never fit in, and I figured it was because I had such big caregiving responsibilities for my brother so early in life and because I have a crazy mother. I felt very self-parented. Dad too had his needs and wanted me to care for my sister and brother. I never felt taking care of them was drudgery. I always felt responsible for them. I pushed my sister to go to college and even got her the application. I wanted to guide them to get all the help that my folks could never give me."

Often, women who had not been well nurtured remained deliberately childless. Toots's parents were "definitely not nurturing. We never had a lot of hugging. My mom felt uncomfortable with that. We weren't exactly deprived, but my mom seemed to have time to give my brothers attention, but not me or my sister. I resent the double standard." And Sally confided, "My mother hates me. Deep down inside, I'm sure of it. And I have learned to hate myself. I work over time trying not to hate me. I do therapy, run, and watch what I eat. But no matter what I do, I can't earn her affection. Some days I love me more. But most of the days I despise myself, if I must be scrupulously honest. So what man would want me? What child could ever really love me, and what in the world would I have to give to it?"

Daughters who were raised by relatives, nannies, or housekeepers because their parents were away "all the time" did not have the same warm feeling toward their parents. As Del pointed out: "I didn't get the normal parenting at home. I was an observer, watching other kids or kids on TV get it." Tashi resented her parents leaving her "with my grandmother to raise us. I learned how to care for people from her, not from my parents." Although both Del and Tashi said there were times when they wanted children, both focused their energies on building prestigious careers.

Women who described themselves as poorly nurtured said they had difficulty giving to others. Often, those who were not well nurtured appeared detached and reserved. Others were more likely to regard them as cool and aloof. Sometimes these women acknowledged that others sometimes regarded them as cool and aloof "and sometimes they're right," according to women such as Alicia. Alicia was guarded when expressing emotion, especially soft emotion. "Some people think I have a hard edge," she admitted, "but I find it easier to be critical, I guess, in my conversation than to be a sop." Some women in the study identified themselves as nurturing types, even though they appeared stiff and cool during the interview. "After learning from the master of aloofness, I guess it's inevitable that some of her rubbed off on me," Wendy admitted. Some women such as Nicole found that it was convenient to "build barriers around parts of myself, especially the parts of me that are vulnerable," and wondered if her emotional restraint was related to her uneasiness about having "to be emotionally available 24-7, the way you have to when you have kids." In general, women attributed their reserved emotions to their home life. Women who had had cool parents who had not nurtured them well tended to deliberately choose childlessness. Because of her history, Jane felt that "it's not part of my nature to be nurturing. I do think I'm sensitive, though, but I often don't know the right things to say or do. Some days I find it even difficult to take care of me, much less be responsible for a child. I can't imagine having the emotional wherewithal it would take to have kids and parent them right." Sylvia confessed that "I don't understand this mother-love thing. Mine sure didn't know how to show me the how-to's of doing for others. Now, I have great empathy, I really do, but it's hard for me to show it. It takes me a long time to feel comfortable with others. I rarely reveal my inner feelings to anyone; however, I'm always there to listen to them. It wouldn't feel natural for me to get all gushy with kids."

Women poorly nurtured tended to divulge themselves hesitantly and selectively to others they deemed safe and worthy. Natalie learned that "You don't give yourself away cheap to just anyone. Some people hug and act like they're bosom buddies one minute and cut each other the next, behind their backs. I'd give the shirt off my back to people I love—but I have enough self-respect not to do that with every Tom, Dick, and Harry. There are only a few friends who know the real me, and I can be myself with them." Invariably, a woman who was emotionally cool and uncertain about her ability to nurture children reported that she had "learned to build emotional walls around myself when I was little. It was safer that way. While part of me may want kids, when I think of the emotional cost, it's too much," said Jane. This may be one reason why women found it difficult to talk with others about emotions underlying their childlessness.

It is possible to learn how to nurture, but it is not always easy, and it may take time. Child abuse expert Ray Helfer asserts that when adults have been deprived of the normal experience of being well cared for, they must relearn those emotions and behaviors.[8] Often, it is through working with those who are vulnerable that adults acquire nurturing skills. Deborah, a physician, said she had to be confronted with the requirement to nurture others to realize that past experiences had influenced her ability to care. "I was in medical school and doing fine. Then I hit my rotation in pediatrics. There, I confronted babies and kids who needed me, who'd lift their arms up to me to take care of them, and it was like my face smashed into a brick wall. It was as if my arms were frozen down at my side, and I was physically, as well as emotionally, unable to reach out to them. It was then that my supervisors took me aside and confronted me about my behavior. And it was after that when I realized I had been sexually abused, and that I didn't want to be around kids because I couldn't protect them, because I hadn't been able to protect myself." Deborah realized that she should not go into pediatrics but that she needed to resolve her issues around her past in order to care for others.

In another example of how women are confronted with pasts they see they must overcome, Monique recalled, "I know both my parents loved me, it's just that my mom had an easier time showing me than did my dad. I am my mother, as they say. But I wish my dad had been more of a love, like my friend Annie's father," she said. She recalled how her friend's father "would pick her up, throw her over his shoulder and tickle her while she giggled madly. I remember standing there, wanting my dad to do those kinds of things for me. He never did. Once Annie's dad picked me up like he did her and threw me around. It was the most wonderful moment, I'll always remember how good it felt to have a man act like that with me. So here I am now, a grown woman, and I keep ending up with men who are like my dad, while I keep wanting guys that look and act like Annie's. I don't want to have kids with men like my dad—I want a dad for my kids like Annie's." Monique had "learned where my raw spots are," and she "spent hours trying to redress it."

Figuring out how their nurturing skills may have affected their childlessness was a long, arduous process, according to some of the women I interviewed. "I had to get into therapy to figure it out," said Sue. "It was driving me crazy—I heard one thing and I saw another, and I just couldn't make out which was real." Women looked to therapists or other women to provide them the positive maternal role modeling they had not received from their own mothers. Although, like Valerie, some women were able to understand their mothers' influence on their psyches and behaviors, still they found themselves unable or unwilling to become a mother. "I never had the ideal mother-figure to aspire toward. I can't relate to it; it is an alien thing to say things like some people do about "my wonderful mom.""

Women who felt a strong need to nurture often worked with other people's kids. "It gives me the chance to be around kids, and channel part of myself to them," Briana said. "It makes me feel good to go into the school and volunteer with them. I like to think I help them, and I know that going there helps me." Helene found that "Children gravitate to me, they climb on my lap and show me dandelion puffs and hoppy toads, or ask for me to listen to them because they know I want to. Sometimes I wonder if they are little souls sent from above, since they must be able to tell that I have a place in my heart that needs to filled up. So by giving to them, I get back what I need," she said.

It was common type for childless women to assume the role of godmother, aunt, co-parent, or special family friend.[9] Katie took her godmother role very seriously. "I will be in charge of the children if, God forbid, anything ever happened to their parents. It would be very hard on all of us if something happened and we didn't have a close relationship; you have to build love over time. You can't expect it to happen overnight." As a result, Katie has gone out of her way to remember birthdays and holidays, to attend sports events, school plays, and dance recitals. Jane and her husband are godparents to a friend's child. "I am so pleased that my friend allows me to share her child. I also have nieces and nephews, and my husband's daughter lives with us periodically." The designation of a godmother allowed childless women to have an official relationship with children they could call their own. "There are even Hallmark cards for godmothers. We count as an official caregiver of kids," asserted Sue.

The most common role assumed by this group of childless women was that of aunt. Most of the time there was a biological connection between the child and the woman but not always. Sometimes women were designated as the child's aunt because the term "friend" did not convey the close emotional bond between them. Within the aunt's role, a woman could assume great latitude for showering affection and attention on a child. "Every child deserves a childless aunt and uncle."[10] Jill's nephews come to visit her every summer. During that time, "We do nothing but kid things, and I have had wonderful times with them. They still are coming at ages ten and twelve, even though they are 'too cool.' This wonderful time with the boys has been good for us, and we get a chance to 'parent,'" she said. Lucy announced, "I love kids. I've always wanted them. There has never been any ambivalence about having them. I'm a kid magnet, always have been." As a result, even though she has no children of her own, she is a Pied Piper in her neighborhood. Tina, who works in a bookstore, loves "to give books to my niece as a present. When new books come into the store, I'll think, 'Oh, she'll like this one.'" Women such as Nelly found that they are also co-parents: "I drive in the nursery school car pool for my niece every Thursday morning. It helps my sister. I feel like I'm the lucky one. I feel bad for my sister because I get to hear all about my niece's day and listen to her talk about it right after it has happened. Then I get to tell her mom. Sometimes I feel like I'm the father to her." Her ten-year-old nephew came down with cancer, and the family fell apart. Everyone relied on Nelly to care for the younger siblings, as well as her single-mother sister. Nelly continued, "I've been having them both sleep with me every night. I keep one under each arm and they cuddle close—they need to know that I'm there for them. They need so much love right now, they're scared for their brother, and are too little to understand why he gets so much attention and why they don't get any. I'm the only one who has the time to give them what they need."

The unselfish giving to children was just as rewarding for the giver as it was to the receiver. By caring for other people's children, women gained a sense of being loved and a sense of being a competent caregiver. This was important, because even if women did not have their own children, they had acquired an intimate sense that they were good "mothers." "My friends always ask me if I want to go along to the amusement park or watch their kids for the weekend. They tell me that I'm like family, not guests, because the kids love me. I make the kids waffles, and I go to the children's museums and Disneyland with them," said Briana, who wanted kids but could not have them. Rose, who is always surrounded by children when she is at home, announced that her nephew called her Mama. "All the kids I cared for, no matter how many of them I had at once, were always clean and well behaved. I could take them anywhere and know they would act properly. I think I would have been a great parent." She loves "all my kids. I can't pick and choose between them. I could never understand how people mistreat children. I've got one nephew who was the ugliest kid in the whole world, and I just love him. It doesn't matter what the kid looks like, or what he can or can't do. It matters what they are. It matters that they are. And they all deserve to be loved."

Women also experienced emotional distress when children they cared about were hurt or sad. For instance, Mille was devastated when her niece, at age twenty, was in a bicycle accident and became brain dead. Millie and her sister grieved together, and her sister told Millie that "she was as much yours as ours." Millie felt as if "I had lost my own child." Her grief led her to become compassionate to others who have lost children. Millie, a former elementary education music teacher, became a minister, in part because "the church has something powerful to give to people who grieve." Millie provides religious services to people who have lost children, and she conducts an AIDS liturgy and a "service for a blue Christmas"—to provide support for people who are alone or grieving during the holiday season.

Women like Vicky were adopted as aunts by their friends' children and were grateful for the experience: "I'm so glad they let me be a part of their family and make me feel like their kids are mine. I can give advice to kids, since I'm not their parents. They listen to me. I correct kids right in front of their parents, and no one gets upset when I scold them." Julie agreed: "It's sort of like the Native American custom of everybody took care of one another's kids because you're all part of the same tribe anyway."

In some cases, women talked about how much they enjoyed being with the children of their friends but how glad they were to leave them in their parents' care. "I enjoy borrowing other people's children," announced Sue. "I like being taken into other people's hearts and homes and made an honorary godmother to their children. I love kids, yet I get my maternal needs taken care of in about three days of being with them."

Some childless women in the study became stepmothers, which, according to Sarah, resulted in "my becoming a mom." Randi disagreed. As a stepmother, "I'm not really being a mom, yet I feel different from women who don't have kids," she said. Today, more than 60 million adults and 20 million children—one out of every three Americans—belong to stepfamilies.[11] It can be difficult for a stepparent to automatically love a newly acquired child. Love takes time to grow. Yet cultural standards about mothering hold that remarriage creates an instant family, that stepmothers should automatically love their stepchildren, and that stepchildren will automatically love them. This is not necessarily true. It takes time and effort, patience and dedication to forge a sense of family among people who are thrust together by circumstance. "It's very hard when the kids live with their mother and visit us every other weekend—I feel like the evil stepmother every time I try to enforce any sort of discipline," Randi said. Julie "resent[s] being the spare mom," she said. "We don't see the kids much, yet they're the only kids that I'll ever have. It's hard to build a relationship with them when they live with their mom, because I cannot imagine trying to call them up there and have their mom answer the phone. She's their real mother, and I'm only their stepmother. I have to know my place. When they're here, I feel we do okay, and I try to be their friend or big sister. But it's not a very big place, given that I only see them once or twice a year." Dawn affirmed that "the role of stepmother puts me in the position of never doing anything right. No matter how hard I try, I cannot compete with their biological mother. It's not that I'm trying to, but I feel that their mother will always come first in every way. Sometimes, I'd like to have some little piece of a relationship with my stepson that was just ours, that didn't belong to anyone else. But I'm irrelevant to him, really. Sure, I cook and do laundry and take him places and listen to him, but forever and always, his family unit will be he and his dad, and he and his mom." Another woman, Ruth, found that "His kids don't see me as their mother. They shouldn't because I'm not. But I've gone out of my way to hold my tongue and do special things for them.

It's as if whatever I do can be sloughed off, because I really don't count. I can do things for the kids and my husband gets the credit, not me. I resent them at those moments, and I resent him. It's really hard." It is particularly difficult for women who wanted to have their own children, "and the closest thing I'll get is parenting some other woman's kids," said Leanne. "Sometimes I just wish my husband's kids would throw their arms around me and tell me they love me," she sighed. "It's not very gratifying to want kids so much, and to have some almost at my fingertips, yet be unable to really be their mom. They seem totally unwilling to really let me hold them, cuddle them, smooch them, the way a real mother could to her little ones."

They are not alone in her frustration. In nine out of ten cases, children live with their mother after divorce and visit their fathers—and stepmothers.[12] Acting as a weekend mother can be more stressful than full-time motherhood because the role is ambiguous and there is less opportunity to bond with the children. Even when children live with their stepmother, it takes time to build a relationship.[13] According to Rosette Signore-Gossett, stepmothers "put in hours of worry, communication, and counseling to do their job well trying to be sensitive to children and ex-wife issues. Among the many issues to deal with are the unresolved anger, hurt, and guilt from the first marriage, the lack of awareness in schools, and discipline and loyalty issues."[14] Stepfamilies are fragile and issues of how to parent contribute to the failure of remarriages.[15] In this study, women with stepchildren reported sometimes feeling estranged from their husbands. Nance said, "I'm always the third wheel. His kids always come first. I'm glad when they're gone visiting their mother. Then I get his undivided attention. No matter what I do, I never do it right in their eyes. And when they're around, my husband sides with them. So do I want kids of my own? I should say not, from what I've seen with them!" Alissa, who lives with her husband and his fifteen- and seventeen-year-old sons, said, "I live with teenage kids and sometimes I'm fearful of them. There is sometimes a sense of relief that I don't have one." But women like Sarah found that her stepdaughter is "one of the greatest blessings in my life. It's been much more frustrating, challenging, gratifying than any other relationship with any other person in my life. I don't feel any different about her than any parent would toward her child. It's the most incredible relationship that I have with my stepdaughter. I'd throw myself in front of a train to save her," she said. Frances, too, found that stepparenting was very rewarding. She had married a foreign pilot who was almost twenty years older than herself. "I was his fourth wife and was a young girl in an adult world. It was an exciting life. He had two daughters, ages twenty and eight, and the youngest one came to live with us. I was her mother, for all practical purposes, and a friend to the twenty-year-old." At one point in their marriage, they talked about reversing his vasectomy and having a baby. "All I could picture was sitting in the hospital bed with rosy cheeks and a new baby, being the adored mother. But this image didn't last too long." After the divorce, she married a carpenter who had two children. They were together for nine years, and "I parented his children. By this time, I figured it was my role in life to be a stepmother, not a biological mother. It was okay that I didn't have kids. He became an alcoholic and violent, so we divorced. I've remarried a nice man who wanted children, but by then, I didn't."

Although it was difficult to be a stepmother, women in this study found it even more difficult to give up that role when they broke up with their partners. The stepchild had enabled some women to assume the role of a mother for a while. But when a couple divorces, it is common that the relationship with stepchildren is severed as well. When Debbie's husband asked for a divorce, she knew his children would naturally side with him and that she had "in one split second lost all rights and entitlements to being a mother." Once divorced, she never saw them, "despite making efforts to. They didn't want to see me. I was always the outsider. The kids and their dad had a bond that I couldn't enter into. As a simple example, during dinner their conversations were really with their dad. I was just there. I was not talked to, or asked questions." Sarah, however, has maintained contact with her ex-husband's daughter "because I wasn't divorcing her."

Ironically, some childless women found that when they married men who had children, they could suddenly become "a grandmother when those children had children. It was so weird—I had missed being a mom, but I was a legitimate grandmother to the new baby," Dawn observed. "When the kids come with their little ones, it seems natural for them to come in with hugs for me, as well as my husband. I get to make cookies and snuggle them for stories, and do the things I always would have if I'd been a mom."

The most common recipients of women's nurturing were their partners, friends, and family members. Laura confessed, "I spoil everyone around me, whether it's animal, vegetable, or human! It comes from my background. I enjoy doing for others. If I'd had a child, it'd be spoiled rotten too." Louise "dotes on my husband," Barbara's "focus is Suzanne," and Elizabeth is her family's "Mr. Fix-It—anytime anyone needs anything, they call me." Amanda found that "instead of taking care of kids, I've ended up taking care of my parents." Childless women did extraordinary things to care for others. The extent of love and concern they exhibited seemed to be boundless. For instance, Valerie talked about visiting an old college friend who was dying from cancer. "We sat and laughed and cried together. We shared cups of tea and long walks. We laughed so hard when I was helping her shower and I got soaking wet too." She admitted that her goal was to "help her live a little bit before she died." Some women confessed that they exhibited nurturing behaviors for complex reasons. "I guess I displaced my nurturance during those days. I took in a stray kitten, then another stray cat and an abandoned dog. I looked at my choice in husbands and realized that I took care of them without getting my needs taken care of," said Catherine. "What I needed was a baby." Catherine nurtured others because she wanted to, but she also resented not getting what she needed out of life. Ahanna felt the same way: "I'm expected to be my parents' caregiver. They don't have much money and have extensive physical, emotional, and financial needs. But what about my job, my marriage, my needs, my choices?"

A large number of childless women transferred their nurturing needs to pets. Sometimes nurturing animals was seen as preparation for parenting. "If I can't be successful raising a dog, I've got no business having a kid. A dog is really a good trial run for parenting, and for me to see if I can put the dog's needs before my own," said Nicole. Pets were often regarded as children. Calina called her cat as "my baby sur-rogate. I love her. Want to see her photos?" Allie "found a child replace-ment—a boxer. I named him Joy, because he's totally happy to be alive. I found him in a shelter, and he's as ugly as sin." May considers her dog "the baby of the household. Today was his third birthday. I gave him a wonderful breakfast, then we went for a long walk in the park. I thought about getting him bones, but he really doesn't like them all that much. But I got him a new squeak toy—he really loves those." One childless woman, Amanda, felt there was a spiritual connection between childless women and their pets. She wondered, "Do you choose animals or do their spirits choose you? The animals in our lives are there for a purpose." Although pets may mean different things to different people, it is clear that they have provided the women in this study with companionship and an outlet for affection.

Women who had been brought up in nurturing families tended to select occupations in which nurturing was a key element. The majority of women interviewed happened to have careers in the fields of edu-cation, social work, health care, child care, secretarial support, and the arts—jobs that historically have been labeled as nurturing, or women's work. Others chose jobs in which nurturing was not a major focus, such as business, law, accounting, or advertising. But on the job, these women often found a niche in which they could care for their col-leagues or clients. Thus, in this study it was not so much what a woman's occupation was but how she did it that was of interest. Per-haps a woman was a personal nurturer in a non-nurturing profession, a professional nurturer, or a personal nurturer in a professionally nur-turing occupation.

A significant number of women in this study were teachers, from preschool through college level. For all of its changes, teaching is still a female occupation. The women talked about how teachers nurture their students: "We teach children how to drink from a cup, how to tie their shoes, how to go to the bathroom by themselves, how to color, how to be nice to their classmates—we teach them how to do every-thing," according to Barbara. Elise "expected to have children and always envisioned that I'd marry and have kids. This probably led me into teaching. I loved kids, always baby-sat, was always around babies and kids of all ages and was comfortable with them." Teaching took the place of motherhood for many childless women. Leanne loved "teaching the little kids. They are so honest, so wonderful. I can hold them and make a difference in their lives. I come to know their family situations, and all the things, good and bad. I can give them advice and help not just the kids but their entire world through them. It's a great feeling. But it's a short feeling, because they leave me and go on. Then another group comes in so that I can do it all again. I wonder, in the long run, if this is enough, if I can make enough of a difference in a lot of kids lives, or whether I would make more of an impact if I had just one or two that I gave my life to." Maggie, a public school administrator, had developed an answer to Leanne's dilemma. "I felt I had to decide if I was going to have kids or teach kids. I didn't feel I could do both adequately. So I decided to teach them. And now, instead of having only one or two kiddos, I counted up and figured up that I have hundreds of kids who are mine each year, and that over the years I've had thousands of kids. I think I've made a good investment, now, don't you?"

Teaching, like all forms of nurturing, is a reciprocal behavior. When one gives, one also receives. Valerie loved teaching because "there's something in the teaching relationship that takes the place of having kids. I taught high school for twenty-five years. The kids would write or visit me, long after graduation. They'd stop by and tell me their problems. You come to like them and they like you. When I moved, I lost my teaching job. I missed not working, but mostly because I missed the relationship, the human contact." Missy, an elementary school teacher, found that "I have a niche working with kids. When kids say to me, 'I'm going to be a teacher just like you when I grow up,' I feel great. If I can make a difference, even if only in one or two kids, if I can help their self-esteem, I will have mattered. I want to make kids feel they're special people just for who they are—they don't have to do anything to be special—they already are." Laura said, "I wanted to have my own kids to teach but now realize that teaching was a good outlet for me. I hope I leave a little bit of me with everybody—

the children I taught maybe will think of something that I gave them and maybe it will go on to their children and theirs too. Many of the kids I taught lived in situations where their lives weren't very good and the only feelings of self-worth and safety they got was in my classroom. I always felt safe so I was able to give that to them. Education was important, but my kids had to be in a good state of mind so that they could learn. Only after they felt good about themselves could I teach them anything that mattered," she reflected. As a college professor, Elise realized that when she taught her students, she was often the first openly childless woman her students had ever met. "I found that after class, young women would stay after class to talk with me. They wanted to know what it was like for me to not have had children. Sometimes they would confess their 'secret' to me—they weren't sure they wanted to have children. I became a sounding board for them to express their own thoughts." Barbara was a professional parent educator. Although she had no children of her own, she had spent her career understanding child development and parent–child interaction. She prided herself on "being able to talk to new parents and give them advice—they often do not know what to do, and are so pleased that I would listen to them." Was the fact that she had no children a liability? "Of course not," she said flatly. She saw herself having "perspective that they may not because they are so close to the situation." Teaching became an outlet for these women's nurturing behavior, and their students became extensions of themselves.

Many women I interviewed had been baby-sitters or day care providers at some point in their adult lives, because, as Nelly stated, "I just love kids." Most believed that one day they would have children of their own and that exposure to children would help prepare them for when they did become mothers. However, for all of the many reasons outlined, each woman remained childless. Sometimes women decided to care for children in order to satiate their nurturing needs. For instance, Mary Margaret was working at a local department store and found herself in charge of the children's section. "I really enjoyed trying to help people figure out what types of clothes would be best and what sizes they needed." But working in the children's section only made her "heart ache worse for a child." Her minister encouraged her to open a day care center so that she could express her nurturing qualities with children in a constructive manner. So she quit her "sales job and began taking children into our home." She and her husband befriended the families of the children as well and would regularly drop by their homes to visit or to give children gifts and help them with chores. Mary Margaret would pull kids on sleds through the snow in the winter and take them to the pool in the summer. "I just love them to pieces." Her face radiated with delight as she talked about being with them, but just under the surface, her pain over not having her own child was always there.

A few women decided to be child care providers because they had made deliberate decisions that they would never have children of their own. Barbara "adores kids, I just love them, love them, love them," and she wanted to devote her professional life to "helping them to grow and thrive and be everything they could dream to be." Children and their parents flock to her. She sings and dances, is spontaneous and creative, and people will stop on the street to watch the sweet interaction between Barbara and her "little friends." To her, children are the most important thing. When forced to choose between interacting with kids or adults, she would choose to talk to the children first. "I am enraged that some people feel that early childhood education is not as important as elementary, high school, or college level teaching. Children must be given the attention they need early in life—early childhood education in so many ways is the most important of all educational times." Despite having no children of their own, women such as Barbara were active child advocates.

A disproportionately large number of childless women were in human service occupations such as social work or psychology. These occupations seemed to appeal for various reasons. "I want to help others"; "I wanted to understand myself"; or "It's the best way for me to care for others and care for myself simultaneously," were common answers. Mary became involved in domestic violence work because she had been a sexual abuse victim, and "I now work helping other women to avoid being sexually abused." Rose was born with a genetic

condition that left her physically challenged, and now she works helping other physically challenged people. She feels she understands their
problems and that she is a good role model because she has learned
how to overcome, or live with, her limitations. Veronica works in
human services, especially with Alzheimer's patients. "I like to take
care of others. I guess it makes me feel needed," she said. Yvonne
found herself "working with young women to help them make good
decisions for themselves." Demaris, an author, was writing a children's
book "and the animal characters are like kids, each with unique personalities. I've used no pronouns to describe any of the animals by
gender so children can be empowered to mentally construct the animal in accordance with the personality and behavioral traits each
exhibited. I want children to believe they can be anything they want to
be," she said.

Human services provide intimate interpersonal contact. The
importance of reciprocity in the relationship was a common theme in
interviews with childless women. Greta said, "I can offer so much to
others because I don't have any kids. I can now help many kids instead
of one, and I have the ability to have a larger focus and do more for the
world than I could by producing one child." Tina said, "There are lots
of ways to contribute the same thing that parents do without being a
parent. I can provide caring to other people through other means."
Angela, a psychologist, talked about the day a child client asked her if
she had children of her own. "I told him I did not, and a big smile
spread across his face. He told me he thought it was good that I didn't
have kids—he said, 'if you had your own kids, you probably wouldn't
have room in your heart to love kids like me.'" She went on: "He
helped me to understand this is what I am supposed to be doing, caring for children like him. If I had my own, perhaps he's right—perhaps
I wouldn't have as much time, or energy, or dedication to help children
like him."

Working with children through human services was also a way for
childless women to capture some of what it is like to be a parent.
Theodore Miller, a pediatrician, once told me that one of the most
important reasons to become a parent was to recapture one's own

childhood. In being with children, one can be a child for a moment, and in so doing, adults have the opportunity to rewrite their own childhood. "This is critically important in helping us to become what we really wish to be," Angela said. "I became a therapist and really enjoyed working with children in my practice. I could help the ones who were getting lost, create opportunities, and be a positive role model for them. I find it satisfying and totally delightful that I can be childlike with children and put away my adult agenda for a while." Working with children was a way for these professional women to work out their own issues. Rhonda was emotionally mistreated by her parents, and she now works teaching adults how to be better parents. Toni was physically abused and now works for a child protective service organization. Amy lived in a home in which her parents had problems with alcohol, and today she works as a therapist focusing on substance abuse clients. Calina works for a hospice organization as a bereavement counselor. "It evoked certain issues for me—I miscarried a baby that the doctors said would have died shortly after it was born. There is a sense of relief that at least I didn't have to go through what some mothers have to go through. While some people can't understand how I can do this kind of work day after day, I can only say, I don't know why, but I can. It is a part of who I am, a gift that I can give to others."

Women were drawn to health care occupations "because I was interested in helping others," according to women like Deborah. She is a family practice physician who would have "loved to have found Mr. Right and gotten married and had kids, but it didn't happen. So my life is my patients." Nikka announced, "I'm a nurse—surprised? I have a management position in a home health agency. I have a strong social network of mostly women friends and do have many children in my life. My friend's children have always enriched my life and lessened the void of not having children. Some of these children call me aunt; others have always let me know they wanted to spend time with me. There was a time when I couldn't look at a pregnant woman without wanting to burst into tears. It was very different when I was in my thirties and close friends were pregnant. I am happy with my life as a single woman, partly because of the inner peace that I finally feel, and partly because when I look at the alternative of being in a compromised marriage or dependent relationship. I'm content to have my life as it is." Allie is an occupational therapist and works with "seventy-five-year-old kids. There's a part of me that wishes we had kids, but you can't cry over split milk. It will ruin your relationship, and we have gone through too much for that." Elise spent seven years providing direct services to families because "I wanted to do things to help people, and this was related to the sixties mind-set of helping to make the world a better place. It was also another way of meeting my own nurturing needs instead of having kids and family of my own." Ultimately Elise began "teaching young women about human sexuality. I'm on the board of directors for a family planning clinic. I run institutes on HIV. The epidemic became an impetus for me to remain involved in the field of human sexuality." Whether women were teachers, psychologists, social workers, or health care providers, the common thread was that they all felt their work nurtured others.

Other women decided to go into business. Although the corporate world is typically regarded as impersonal and profit-oriented, childless women such as Del tried to bring "a more humanistic, caring approach to business." From top-level chief executive officers to secretarial support, women without children set a tone for their work environments. Upper echelon CEOs such as Del "tried to make work an extension of home for my employees. I want them to feel supported here and that we can work together like a family." Administrative assistants such as Jude tried "to help the people in my unit to get what they are entitled to, and to help them when things don't run right." As a secretary, Mary Margaret found that she got to "know all the students and faculty, their private lives, their ups and downs. I try to give them a smile or a cheery word, and they seem to appreciate it. The students all call me Mom," she said with pride. Women such as Del, Ruth, and Chi candidly discussed how, at the administrative level, they attempted to humanize their workplaces. Del, who built a million-dollar business over the past decade, reports that "My company is my baby and my employees are my family. Many of my employees have kids, and I have a fantasy of opening a day care center here at work. It's the way I run my company—all for one and one for all. You can't just work here. You become family here." Women who have no children invested heavily in the creation of their businesses. The organizations that they built with their own hands from the bottom up were not just vehicles for making a living; they were also extensions of themselves. As a result, the administrators wanted their businesses to be more than just a place for their employees to work. They hoped that by providing employees a supportive environment in which to work, employees would bring both a professional and personal dedication to the firm. Fanny opened a gourmet restaurant "that nurtures the body and the soul of both the people who eat here and those who work here," she said. "I want the people who eat here to have a wonderful experience and come back again and again. I want my restaurant to have great food, served in a pleasant manner, and served in a comfortable atmosphere. And I want my employees to feel a sense of dedication. In order for my place to be what I want, I need to have my employees happy and productive, so I make this a good place to work."

Del discussed how this type of environment takes time to build. She compared the development of her firm with the growth of a family: "My company has gone through all kinds of stages, similar to a child. So I feel I have gone through all kinds of parent stages with it. At first, it was totally dependent upon me. Then it grew and I had one or two employees. It grew stronger and bigger. During the company's teenage years, it went through a teenage rebellion stage, when it would act up whenever I was away. I tried to turn it over to someone else, but it didn't want to go. It didn't do well without me, even though I thought it needed more independence. Then there was the phase when we considered a merger and it was like a daughter who wanted to marry the wrong partner. I had to step in and make it right. We are now having our best year ever. The company is my child, and it even acts like me. So I better treat it like a child, love it, and give it all the attention it needs."

Chi reflected on how she wished she had better nurturing skills; if she did, she speculated, perhaps "I'd be a better administrator. I'm a corporate administrator in financial services and my job is very demanding. I wonder if I'd be a better manager if I was a mother, because mothers may have learned patience and skills that would be applicable to building self-esteem, encouraging performance, and guiding people successfully." But these women wanted more than being a parent to their businesses. They wanted their work environments to be symbiotically nurturing. They didn't mind putting their all into their organizations, but they expected something more than just money in return. "I've nurtured my business to the point of burnout. I got too involved in it. I spent the long hours, hired the best people, praised them, encouraged them, and helped them along in the next step. It got lonely though, because it got one-sided. Now I want more nurturing relationships. I demand something from all relationships now. Otherwise, I won't mess with it if it doesn't help me grow or feel good," reported Monica.

Nurturing a business has both economic and emotional implications, and it improves the quality of life for both employees and those they serve. At the other end of the corporate ladder are the secretaries, supervisors, and line workers; when those workers do more than "just their jobs," they contribute to the creation of a positive work environment. Women who do little things to let others know they care make a priceless contribution to people's attitudes about work. Jude, a deliberately childless administrative assistant, prided herself on "remembering to have a card for each employee's birthday, throwing baby showers, or sending flowers when a loved one dies." Helene, an area supervisor, referred to herself as a "rabbit who hops around and watches over my co-workers, especially the younger ones who need to talk. People have so much going on personally in their lives that it can't help but effect the workplace. Sometimes people only need a little bit of an outlet to make all the difference in their productivity. When someone is sulking, patting them on the shoulder and gently saying, 'Bad day?' will let them know we care, without interfering."

This concern displayed naturally by childless women appears to have been embraced by the corporate community as good business practice. The business world has come to realize that women who nurture colleagues at work make valuable contributions to the overall work environment. Coleen Keast, former president of the Whirlpool Foundation, found that women are redefining what nurturing means both in and out of the workplace. These nurturing women are highly coveted employees because they transform the work environment into one in which employees feel more comfortable. "Work mothers" are enormously valuable in the workplace because they do more than nurture others—they empower. According to researcher Gail Letherby, "These women make everyone feel connected, and five good things happen in the workplace as a result. Everyone around them feels more energy and zest, more self-confidence; they are clearer in their thinking, better able to do things, and they want to do more. They bring people together and make team effort work. Women typically create community in the workplace."[16]

The women I interviewed nurtured not only people and pets but also groups such as community organizations. Minnie "gave a dozen Walkmans and six boom boxes to be distributed in the Christmas baskets. People remember little kids, but they don't give age-appropriate gifts to teens. I thought they'd feel better about themselves if they got gifts that could help them to be in style. I gave a gift certificate for some free CDs with each one. I also bought twenty turkeys and ten hams to be distributed in the baskets too. I don't have family here, besides my husband, and it's nice to be able to give to the kids in my community who need help." Fern helped her community by serving as a volunteer church organist. Yvonne coordinated services at a planned parenthood facility. Mary and Louise worked at shelters and with sexual assault centers. Women such as Ruth walked miles to promote breast cancer, whereas Toni rode her bicycle in a rally to help AIDS victims. Patricia worked with schools developing Junior Achievement programs, Laura helped start a new program at her library, and Ellie made quilts for children with AIDS. Mary collected stuffed animals to be handed out at the domestic violence shelter, whereas Betsy rocked infants in the hospital and Rose went to Washington to march for Children's Rights with Marion Wright Edelman and the Children's Defense Fund. Briana "was a scout leader, and my husband was the baseball coach. Sometimes we would look at our voluntary acts and wonder why we were acting as parents for these kids when their own parents weren't involved." Vicky "is on the town council, and she loves being a caregiver to the city that she loves." Veronica reflected on her activity in so many organizations and mused, "I have found many ways to spend my life—holding a career, being involved in volunteer organizations, building my relationship, and my spiritual life. By not having children, I've been able to offer time to volunteer organizations where others could not." Giving to others, from individuals to organizations, was important to childless women. "I don't have kids, so I can care for other people's kids through these actions, and it makes me feel happier," said Briana.

There is an old saying that claims you can't give to others what you don't have inside yourself. Childless women, as a whole, were concerned about how to improve themselves. They had "made a commitment to become more aware of the still, small voices that spoke deep inside" (Iris). Many of the women, such as Josi, who had deliberately chosen to remain childless to pursue a lifestyle with more time for self-development found that "by parceling out time for myself, I'm in better position to give to others." Whether or not religion played an important part in their lives, most of these women sought a greater kinship with what could be called their spiritual side, or their feminine intuitive self. Amanda talked about the importance of nurturing herself in order to make the world better: "I cannot understand how I can heal the world if I cannot heal myself. I know that if I am good and full, then I will rub off on every person I meet."

Many of the women were concerned with nurturing their bodies as well as their minds, and physical fitness was important. "I know that people may say it's selfish to want to spend time on developing myself instead of a child, but I disagree. I think that if I'm healthy and centered, then I'm in a much better position to do for others," said Layne. Women were involved in activities that included running, volleyball, dancing, boating, cycling, swimming, karate, kickboxing, hiking, and skiing. "Fitness takes a certain amount of discretionary income to pay for classes or equipment, as well as time," said Tanya. "If I had kids, I wouldn't have either! My friends with kids certainly don't have money or time. Kids schedules must come first, so most the time they have to wiggle fitness in with parenting. I find that by the time I get to where I'm going to work out, suit up, do my program, clean up, and get home, at least three hours have gone by. I can understand where people with kids wouldn't have that time, especially if they have to work! I enjoy the use of my body, and I am proud that I look nice and feel good," Tanya said.

Many childless women were employed in occupations that dictated a "well-turned out image," Heather said. "I think that the way I feel about myself is apparent in what I wear and how I carry myself. When I'm feeling sick or tired, I don't care how I look. But when I'm feeling good and I'm excited about doing something, I dress nicer, do my hair and make-up better, and look much more attractive. There's nothing wrong with that, is there? But if you look at women with kids, sometimes they don't look as trim and tidy, probably just because of everything it takes to be a mom." The care they expressed toward others was reflected in the manner in which they cared for themselves. Betsy is a good example: "I'm generous and nurturing—but I am to myself too! I try to take care of myself as well as other people. I'm not necessarily selfless, for I have definite boundaries. For instance, I have left relationships that weren't good for me, and I left my career as a psychologist because I got too burned out. Leaving things is sometimes what's best for you. Saying 'no' to some things doesn't make you selfish; sometimes you have to pick which things you can and can't do, since you can't do or be everything."

Many childless women were involved with the arts, music, and other cultural pursuits. Many played instruments, particularly the piano. As a child, Vicky took both piano and ballet lessons. "Daddy loved ragtime and bought me a piano if I'd play the '12th Street Rag.'" He went with her to all her recitals. Eventually, she studied piano at the Royal Academy of Music in London. Fern is a classical pianist and would have loved to have spent her life as a musician. "But my parents did not approve, and I became a lawyer instead. But my passion is still music." She plays for civic organizations, and each summer she attends a music camp where she can live and play with others all day, for weeks at a time. "One day I'll leave my piano to that music camp." Leanne enjoys singing, and although she "was never good enough to be a professional," she works with the local theater and music organizations to promote musical endeavors. Tina has actively pursued her art since she retiring after twenty-six years from GTE. She began taking classes and today regards herself as a painter. "I can't say I have any talent in it, but with practice and training I believe I can do it, and it brings me great joy." She takes Spanish classes, redecorated her house and gardens, and does "all the things I never had time to do before. It's absolutely blissful." Valerie is an art historian who has "a keen eye for how to mount pieces of art. Selecting the correct frame and matting and locating the art in the right place brings me enjoyment and creates pleasure for others as well." Joyce is a seamstress, "real June Cleaverish, but I really love to sew." Yvonne is a weaver and has a four-harness loom in her home on which she creates her masterpieces. Kendra is an interior decorator who specializes in creating tasteful environments that address her clients' needs. "Beauty needs to be everywhere, so I determine what my clients want, and then design, shop, purchase, and install the materials in my own style." Suzanne is a landscape architect, and she "designs stunning yards for home owners." She also works with businesses but prefers to "work with individuals who want to bring peace and beauty to their everyday lives." Jude spends "hours in the gardens" and has "planted perennial flower beds with interesting designs in color, style, and shape of plants. My plants are timed so that there are blooms of color in the yard throughout the spring and summer." May also enjoys her flower and vegetable gardens. "Maybe some people don't care, but I enjoy weeding and making the yard look good. I have stones on a path through the garden, and I am building paths on the land with hints of color, bird feeders, or interesting things to look at every so often, to make the walk interesting."

Literature was also important to many of the women, and they nurtured themselves through reading. "Moms don't get a chance to read much, and I devour books," Tina said. Many women were writers, although few had published their work. "But sharing my thoughts with others is a way to nurture the world too," Mica said. Women conveyed an interest in culture and knowing more about people who were unlike them. Travel was an active part of many of their lives, and some women had traveled extensively throughout the world "which I couldn't have done if I had kids," said Elizabeth.

"No single person is responsible for making the world a good place—rather all people have a responsibility for improving our communities and social order," said Hannah. It is the view of some of these child-free women that by not having children, women have a new opportunity to create social change. According to Evie: "I've decided that I'll make a difference. I plan to pick certain people out and love them and teach something that they might not find elsewhere. I want people to rely on me, just as they rely on the fact that the sun will rise tomorrow. I will make time to share myself with others. I'll make time to learn about them. I'll make time to open my wallet to give them what they need. Kids need both biological and nonbiological mothers. We have different things to offer them. If we are all a part of the Earth Mother, then we have an obligation to care for each other. People shouldn't have to ask. I should just do it, and if I do, then maybe other people will help too. Wouldn't that make for a lovely world?"

When asked if they had advice for other childless women, Kendra asserted, "'to thine own self be true.' If you're glad you didn't have kids, help others to understand that you're a really neat person. If you're sad about it, then find ways to do something about it. Life is too short. Since you can't please everyone anyway, get out there and please yourself." "Let nothing stop you," said Sue; "Have an unshakable belief in yourself." Chi advised, "If you've listened to your inner voice and have decided that having a child is really what you want to do, then do it. I have a friend who wants a baby so much. My advice to her is don't wait. If you want a child, don't talk about it. Just do it." Joanna said, "I hope my experiences will help other childless women to understand that the hard times they experience are normal. I know there are lots of other women out there like me, but I know it's been difficult to get the support I need. So I advise women to talk openly with others. Be honest with yourself, and don't be afraid to share yourself with others. Women like me would really have appreciated it." Rose hoped that "my story will help other women to see that childlessness doesn't have to be bad," and Mica hoped that hers would help women to see "how wonderful a child-free life can be." Amanda advised women to "quit beating ourselves up about not having kids. Only when you stop second guessing yourself and trusting yourself can we become okay with our decisions. There's a reason for everything. Just give yourself time and space to figure it out."

CHAPTER 11 Childless Women
Growing Older

Many of the women in this study found that the "crisis" of childlessness led to opportunities for new self-understanding. "When I was
young, I was so ambivalent about having kids that I had frozen feet. I
never decided to have children, but I never decided not to. I hung in
limbo and didn't know why," said Missy. "Now that I'm getting gray
and I know people my age who are dying, I have to confront things that
I was willing to pass over, things that kept snagging me up—like
whether to have kids. There's less time to deal with things than I imagined. There are fewer tomorrows and more yesterdays. Since we only
have today, I figured I'd better get down to the business of getting my
emotional house in order. I need to reflect upon why I've done what
I've done, why I didn't have kids even though I said I wanted them. I
need to sort through what it all means."

These women were surprised at how "not having children kept
creeping back into my life," as Ramona put it. "I thought it was only
going to be an issue when I was thirty or so, when I was trying to decide
whether or not to have kids. But it was also an issue when I was about
forty-five when my friends' kids were graduating from high school; it
was an issue at about fifty when I hit menopause, and again when I hit
fifty-five when my friends became grandparents and I wasn't. I didn't
expect to get hit with these waves of emotion over something I
thought I'd resolved years ago." Women understood there would be
implications for not having children, but "I never realized that this deci-

sion would confront me until my dying day," said Kendra. "As I've gotten older, I now see the full extent of my decision not to have kids."

Ramona at age fifty-five and Kendra at age forty-nine are not old by gerontological standards. With life expectancy continuing to increase, women as a group can expect to live another twenty years after age eighty.[1] There has never been an elderly population in the history of the United States that has been as large or diverse as today's; some have had their first child at age sixty, whereas others have had great-grandchildren at that age. Among this population childlessness is common: one in five women in this group did not have children.[2] By the time women are in their mid-forties, the reproductive decisions they had made earlier in their lives usually become permanent. The women interviewed for this study were generally between the ages of forty and sixty. Although they are not elderly according to today's standards, the women themselves felt "mature, even old, since my childbearing years are basically over," said Louise.

When confronted with the fact that they were too old to have children, many of the older women I interviewed found that this "was a shock, even to me who never wanted to have kids," as Natalie put it. Catherine found herself "very sad about it. I grew up in a lovely family and now it's certain that there will be no more of us to carry on the family line." Sylvia, on the other hand, found that "it was a profound relief when I hit menopause. I never have to worry about having kids again!" Usually, however, even deliberately childless women had some difficulty accepting that their childbearing years were over. "Even though I've chosen not to have kids, I still feel like I'm in control because I have my periods," said Maura. "I use contraception on a regular basis not to get pregnant. When the day comes that I can't have kids and won't need to use contraception, it'll be weird. I'll be glad I don't have to use it anymore, but I'll be sad that I won't need to use it too. My sexuality is wrapped up with my ability to reproduce. Just because I don't want to use my equipment, it's still nice to think that I'm woman enough that I could put it to use if I wanted to," she said. Other women identified with those sentiments. Sarah said, "I might still have a chance to have kids, if I really want to." Vicky hopes that

"I'll get pregnant in the future, even though I know I'm growing older and approaching the point of no return."

"Waiting until you're older to become a parent could be a good thing," Ahanna stated. "When I was young, when many of my friends were having their first babies, I was in no way prepared to be a good mother. My relationships were in flux. I was working hard to make ends meet. I was immature. I wanted to play. I had too much ego and wouldn't have been able to put the needs of a child first—even though my big ego said, 'of course I could.' Now, I'm more quiet inside. I have more time since my job and money and relationships are stable. I've become a woman, instead of a girl. As a woman, I know better what's important." Janice reflected that "We grow from babies to girls to adolescents to women with people always taking care of us. We get taught we should have babies, but most of us aren't full-fledged women when we have them. It seems that babies would be cared for best by those who have dealt with all the petty stuff that developmentally you have to go through in order to grow up. Now that I feel like a full woman, I'm ready. But it's taken a long time to become that." Lauren agreed. "It has been hard for me to be whole. I've been on a quest for my own spiritual development. I'm settled now. Up until now, I never felt I wanted to settle down. Now I have an understanding about what it means to be in a relationship. Now I can consider having a child."

These women are not alone in their interest to have first children late in life. Demographers indicate that more older women today expect to have a child than did women in this same age bracket twenty years ago, probably as a result of new reproductive therapies and a general trend toward older women having children.[3] But "even if I had kids now, people would think I was odd. Can you imagine my being on the maternity ward with some sixteen-year-old mom?" Lucy was concerned that because she was older, her childbearing would be out of sync with that of most women, who have children when they are significantly younger.

As women struggled to understand the causes of their childlessness and transform its meaning, their understanding of childlessness changed. When they were younger, the women in the study reported, they were more likely to blame external sources, such as their partners and relationships. They accused their bodies, or the bodies of their partners, for being unable to bear a child. They ascribed their emotional discomfort around children to their own parenting, to family dysfunction, or to their lack of exposure to children. They attributed childlessness to external constraints of money, time, work, and school. There were always reasons that influenced why they did not have children. However, as women aged, they acknowledged that they had much more control over their childbearing than they had originally thought. "I allowed myself to give in to my husband's not wanting children. I never forced what I wanted," said Beverly. "I could have been more assertive about our having children," reflected Monique. "I could have demanded we go into counseling or I could have left the relationship to find a man who did want a family. I could have gone through artificial insemination or adopted a child on my own. But I didn't. You can only blame other people so long—one day it hits you between the eyes that it was you making the decisions about what happened in your life. You can only be a victim if you let yourself be one. At some point, you have to accept personal responsibility for your actions, as uncomfortable as that process may be."

Emotional issues about having children became stronger as women listened to the ticking of their biological clocks. "I feel the clock counting down," said Heather. "It's now or never." The pressure to become pregnant "before the clock runs out," as Heather put it, was greatest among involuntarily childless women whose situations had prevented them from having the children they had expected. Sally had always wanted children, "but it wasn't until I was forty that I felt psychologically whole and ready to have them." Fern, who had never wanted children and had had several abortions when she was younger, found that when she turned forty, she "wasn't using birth control anymore. I'm in my forties, and if kids happened now, it would be okay." Louise "didn't meet the right person, and at age thirty-five I began processing not having a child. This was very hard. I'd thrown myself into my career, schooling, and volunteer work. I decided to ban travel, date more, and worry less. At age forty, I got married. He was older than me and not interested in having children. He felt he wouldn't be a good parent, and he wanted me to himself. I was much more on the fence about this, but I went along with his decision. It was a big surprise for both of us that I really desired a baby so much in the early years of marriage. It all came tumbling back. It was a reaction to everything not happening on time, and now that I was safely married my desire resurfaced." Betsy is a therapist who worked with abused children, and she and her husband had busy personal and professional lives. "We were so busy with our careers that we did not talk much about kids. It was always viewed that we would 'one day.' Then 'one day' I realized I didn't have that many more days left." Some women felt that it had taken so long to find the right mate they were no longer interested in having children. Jeannie had waited for her Prince Charming, but "when he came along, he was older than I expected he would be, and he didn't want children. By that time, my biological clock had run out." Greta met her boyfriend when she was thirty-eight years old. They talked about having children, and "both of us found our desire to have kids was waning." Women who wanted children felt they if they were going to do it, they "had to act soon."

Some women perceived themselves to be too old to have children because they were past the customary age when women have babies. Many older women feared their bodies would let them down. Allie said, "The older I get, the more scared I am that my body will not function right if I should meet someone I wanted to have kids with." She was concerned that her "old eggs" might be "defective. I wouldn't want to have waited all this time to have a baby, then find myself with a Down syndrome baby or one that wasn't right. That may sound awful, but it's true. When I think of having a baby, I dream of it being healthy, perfect—not deformed and a source of sadness and strain instead of joy." Elise found that "Now that I'm perimenopausal, I don't mourn for a baby, but I think about not having a teenager. I think this is because all the women in my age group have teenagers." Nicole said, "I think I'm too old to raise a child now. I don't know if I want to get up several times each night to feed a baby. Chasing after a toddler and keeping her out of trouble would take so much energy that there would be little time left for me and my partner. When kids get older they can be handfuls. It's hard to put all your energy and hopes and dreams into a kid. There's so much to worry about—drugs, violence, sex. I don't know if I have the strength to endure going through all that." Women were aware of both the physical and psychological demands of parenthood—and those that accompanied being child-free.

Some women felt that by not having children they became psychologically older than women who were mothers. "I feel old—out of touch," said Louise. "Kids keep you young. I live a very adult world, a world of work and adult conversation. Sure, I have recreation of all sorts, but they too are adult-centered. When I see parents out playing with their kids, going sledding in the winter or making sand castles at the beach in the summer, I'm envious. I'd feel silly to do that by myself. You need to be with a kid to justify acting like one." When women age, their perspective about themselves and what is important in life changes, according to Fern. "The little girl next door talked to me while I worked in my flower garden. After I finished, I invited her in for lemonade. As we drank, I said, 'Whew! That was so much fun to work in the garden.' She looked at me as if I was daft. 'How could that be fun?' she asked. I told her, 'Just wait and see.'" But some childless women found that getting older wasn't always fun or complimentary. "Sometimes I think about my spinster aunt who lives by herself. I wonder if I'll be like that, all alone with people feeling sad for me because I have no children. I don't think I will end up that way, but I do think about it. But maybe that old mold won't be true in the future because there are so many of us around," said Nance. Not all childless women felt like Louise and Nance. "Because I have no kids, I'm physically fit," Missy said. "I feel younger because my body is still in good shape. I haven't had the wear and tear on it like women who have kids. I still have a small waist. Maybe it's because I have enough time to work out and take good care of myself. Some of my mom-friends are so busy making sure their kids get what they need that they don't have enough time to care for themselves the way they'd like. I work to keep myself attractive. I still have a waist, see?" she laughed. "I also have enough time to shop, and enough money to buy great clothes." Whether a woman felt older or younger than others her age could depend on their social network, according to Janice: "I think the biggest reason why some of us who don't have kids do well while others of us don't is related to who you live with. I live and work with a bunch of kids and they keep me young." The benefits of being child-free were not just physical but psychological, according to Betsy: "When we get together, I feel so much younger than my friends with kids because I'm out involved in the world. I'm out there going places and doing things and meeting interesting people. I've got great stories to tell. Their world seems smaller. It revolves around kids and school. When we're in social settings, people seem to enjoy talking with me more because I've got interesting things to say," she confided. Lifestyles and interests "keep you young," according to Julie. "My world is full of people of all ages and types. I think part of it is because of who I am, and part of it is because I've reached out to make other people my family. My house is a magnet, my e-mail is always full, and my phone is always ringing. I have to hide if I don't want company. But I do. Being involved keeps me interested and interesting." Women indicated that whether one felt old or young as they passed the menopause mark was largely due to self-perception. Amanda said, "While my mother mourns not being a grandmother, I feel young and attractive because I haven't experienced the wear-and-tear that comes with motherhood. I can't imagine myself as a grandmother, although some of my friends are."

Whether women in the study had deliberately decided not to have children or have always longed to become mothers, it was inevitable that "someday soon we'll all be physically unable to bear children. It's part of the natural plan," Sue said. Yet, Sue said, "I can hear my biological clock ticking louder and faster as I approached the doomsday of menopause. Up until this time, I could say, 'oh, I haven't found the right guy yet,' or 'I'm not ready yet,' but clearly it was with the intent that someday I will. It's not totally impossible to have kids. I could probably still have one if I wanted to." Then she added with a sigh, "I guess having a child now is pretty much out of the question." As women age, "it takes time for the realities of it to sink in," said Ellie. "When I was young, I had a choice. But since menopause, I no longer have a choice.

It has all been taken out of my hands." Menopause implied more than an end of childbearing; it also signified a loss of youth, choices, and dreams of what could have been. Sarah said, "I've heard my biological clock ticking, and let me tell you, if I could find it, I'd smash it over someone's head!"

Menopause heightens sensitivity to childlessness for women and their partners. Although it signals the end of worry over unwanted pregnancy and the inconvenience of birth control, women such as Kendra did not look forward to that liberation. "While I've complained my whole life about having my period, now that I don't have it I feel less womanly. While I'm wiser and smarter now, there's still this sense that those twenty-five-year-olds can give men something that I can't. And that something is a baby, or the chance of a having a baby. There's something quite sensual and provocative about having sex and trying to beat the odds by not getting pregnant. That roulette makes sex exciting. Safety may be comforting for some people, but when a guy knows he can't knock you up, some of the adventure is gone." Natalie and her husband had talked about having kids one day, "but when I became menopausal, it was clear we wouldn't be having any. You can't know when you're going to go into menopause—it just happens, and for me it happened earlier than I thought it would. I adjusted to not having kids but he didn't. Before long, he said he wanted a divorce—that he had found someone else." Although they maintained a cordial relationship, she discussed "the ultimate blow, when my ex brought pictures of his new baby to show me. He was very excited to be a dad. Because we've remained friendly since the divorce, I guess he thought my seeing the pictures would be okay. But it wasn't, let me tell you. I still feel the knives in my heart," she said.

Menopause, as a developmental stage, often occurs about the same time that women confront another life challenge—the loss of their parents. "I had been fine about not having kids until my dad died," Catherine said. "When he died, I realized there would be no one left to carry on our family name, and no one to whom I could pass on his photography equipment. Then my mom's health declined, and it became clear that I was the end of our family line. I remembered all the fun we had when I was little. I found I wanted to give kids things that I'd learned or collected during my lifetime. As I buried my folks I realized how much I wanted kids." Betsy found that "when I hit forty, death, which had never been a part of my life before, became a constant theme. My dad died, I got divorced, then my mom died. Looking at all of the endings around me, I couldn't help but wonder—should I have had a child?" Evie confessed that "when my parents and cousin died, I had this overwhelming sense of loss—not just the loss of them, but the loss of everything that I'd held dear. I was confronted with the endings of life. Up to this time, I saw life as full of beginnings, of possibilities, that I could become anything. I had come to expect that tomorrow would be a lot like today. But that's not true. When they died, human limitations smacked me in the face. Not having a child hit me all over again. I regretted my decision, and beat myself for why I didn't have one when I had the chance. I felt all alone in the world."

Childless older women experience the same biological declines and social-psychological challenges as do women with children, but the impact of these challenges may be more severe if a woman is alone. Although, when younger, childless women have been found to be happier than those women who were mothers, as childless women age, they experience more loneliness, smaller social networks, and less neighborhood integration, compared with those of women who have children. Children naturally involve their parents in school and community programs, which enables them to meet more people casually. Most problems concomitant with aging are mitigated if one has social support, particularly from family members. Older childless women appear to have fewer familial supports, which is likely given that children are the major source of support and assistance for older persons. Childless women who have fewer resources to help them cope may find their social worlds shrinking as their physical needs are increasing, and they have a tendency to become isolated, lonely, and depressed.[4]

"If I don't have children, who will be there for me as I grow older?" asked Hannah. "I think about the whole of a normal woman's life as she shifts from being a single woman to wife to grandmother, and I wonder what milestones will mark the years of my life. Who will pore over the traces of my life, searching for meaning and a sense of connection? In a world in which ancestors are universal, what will it mean to be a woman without descendants?" This issue confronted childless women such as Vicky, who said, "It's hard to watch kids grow up when I know I'll never have anyone to care for me when I get old. I have two cousins that I call nieces that I've helped raise. It was hard to see the older one get married, and the younger one is pregnant and experiencing something I'll never know. They'll check on me when I get old, perhaps, but I have no one to take care of me, the way I take care of my mother." Laura worries about the future. "My brother has two sons who will take care of him and I wonder down the road, who will take care of me. My husband and I work in the nursing home and I see so much loneliness. I don't want to die alone and lonely."

The women I interviewed considered what the end of their lives would be like as childless women. When women have children, they assume their children will help them—physically, emotionally, and financially. "My brother says that's why he had five kids—he figured that at least one of them would be around to help," said Belinda. Yvonne contemplated the benefits of the extended family, "where one generation would care for the next. My folks took care of my grandparents, I'm taking care of my folks, but there is no one to care for me."

Women have learned that although historically older people could expect that their children would take care of them, this may no longer be the case in contemporary society. In part this may be the result of people living longer, healthier lives, and in part this may be the result of the cues women have received from their own parents. Jane noticed that "I don't think I'm expected to provide for my mom during her older years. She doesn't expect it from me, and I don't envision myself doing that. I don't think one should have kids just to care for me as I get older. I don't see many people my age taking care of parents— Social Security works for them. I assume that I will take care of myself." Deanna concurs: "I live in New England, and my parents live in California. I see them twice a year. My aunt has three kids, and none of them lives near her. One lives in Europe and the two others live thousands of miles from her. Even though she has kids, she's on her own." Even if women have children, there is no guarantee they will live close enough to be of help. "No one has any guarantee of having any-one else care for them when they get old," asserted Mary. "I figure that everyone ought to make their own independent plans for who will take care of them when they get old." Many childless women have enough money saved so they can purchase assistance from health care providers.[5] As Sylvia said, "When it comes time, I'll simply hire people to help me run errands and do chores." She continued: "If people have a good social support network—and I do, then they can give me the emotional support, advice, and physical assistance I might need. There's no requirement for help to come from family members." Hav-ing money and support gave them options. "There's a whole group of us who plan to live together and take care of each other when we get to be little old ladies," said Tanya. "And when we get to the point we can't take care of each other, we'll hire someone. And when we can no longer live at home, either we'll go to an assisted housing facility or we'll figure what ice floe we want to go out on." Many of the women in the study were adamant about taking care of themselves for as long as they could. Although some women such as Sylvia anticipated hiring help when they get older, some such as Tanya or Laura considered whether they might wish to end their lives. Laura and her husband are still young enough to live full and independent lives. But they are child-less and "decided we'd better make plans for our 'golden years.' Most of our friends are in the same situation, so we decided that we would live in a communal living arrangement. We're serious about having a place where we take care of each other. But this solution will only work for so long. Many of us will live to be one hundred, and what will our lives be like then? There is the expectation that we will end up alone, especially as our friends grow old and pass on. We talk about getting old a lot. My husband (a doctor) will make it easy for me to die. We've discussed euthanasia. I think that a lot of people our age look at their lives, the health care situation, and what life will be like when we are very old and ill. We take the attitude that 'I'll do it for you, and you do it for me.' Euthanasia is a part of our future." Laura then turned philosophic: "I've looked at death in the face, and it's not the worst thing that can happen to you. Living is a gift; every day is a gift. I refuse to be a burden to my family or anyone else."

Although women such as Laura had given a great deal of thought to the end of their lives, death was not an easy topic for women in the study to discuss. "But I think my generation does it much better than my parents' generation," said Sue. "I don't want to die for a long time. I still have lots that I want to accomplish. People with kids may not want to die because they have to raise their kids; I don't want to die until I have done the important things in my life that will make a difference." Childless women did not want to be a burden to others, but they did not want to be alone. Julie doesn't want "to die by myself. In my culture when you die, you always have family with you, helping you leave this world to travel into the next. I don't have kids, so who will help me make that journey? I'll have to impose myself on my nieces and nephews, which isn't the same." Dawn said, "I'm frightened by growing old, getting sick, and ultimately being alone. People with partners or kids always have someone they can count on to help and to care. I'm afraid there won't be a soul I know who will volunteer to take care of me. I'll have to pay strangers to be with me at the end of my life. But you know, perhaps it is better that way. Why would you want to inflict your misery and dying on people you love?"

Death is inevitable. As childless women contemplated their passing, typically they predicted one of two scenarios. One predicted the she would be alone. Leanne said, "I don't want a funeral. Funerals are supposed to be for the living to grieve. I don't think I'll have any kids to grieve me. Can you imagine having a funeral and nobody coming to it?" Deborah was sad that "there will be no children to say kaddish for me when I die, no one to visit my grave." Rose wondered, "as the youngest of my string of brothers and sisters, what will happen to my memory when the youngest of the nieces and nephews die? Who will put flowers on my grave? I wonder sometimes, how far should you carry on family memory? No one in my family remembers where our extended family is. But they existed. They created us. We are here for a purpose. But we don't remember them. Yet, if my nieces and nephews have kids, and they have kids, and so on, somehow my brothers and sisters will be remembered. But what about me? Sometimes I wonder, is it important, really, that someone remember us down the road? There are days I say, no, it doesn't matter. But there are other days when I feel so bad that no one may ever know I was here."

Other women, however, anticipated that when they died, their contributions would be long lasting even though they never had children. Dawn said, "People will remember me by being funny, for making them laugh. I keep saying that when I die, I want them to go to the funeral home and boo-hoo, but what I really want is for people to tell funny stories. I try to find something funny in the worst situations possible." Maggie said, "I have made a difference. I have a whole list of things that I've accomplished. Many of the things I've created, no one knows I've done. I've been like a shadow for some people, helping other people to run with my ideas and take the credit for them. But I know what I've helped to build. Sometimes I've enjoyed taking the credit and receiving the awards that people so generously have bestowed upon me. But what I've done hasn't been for me, you know. It is for us, it's for making the impossible possible." Although many women could take stock of their social contributions, other women felt that it would take years before their actions took "root and bloomed." Women such as Sue reflected that "even mothers don't have any certainty that their kids will grow up, or grow up to honor her, or make a good difference in the world. They could grow up to be murders or bring her and the world sadness. Whether you're a mom or like me, we work hard today cultivating activities that may bring good things in the future. Maybe they won't take full form until much later, perhaps after I'm dead. I'm like the character in the book *The Man Who Planted Trees*.[6] I sow ideas and lay foundations so what I dream about today can become a reality tomorrow." Jane observed that "you never know when you do something whether it will have lasting importance or not. You do what you think is the right thing and sometimes you find these major efforts we undertake don't matter at all. Other times, we do simple, little things that end up having tremendous impact." Ramona said, "I gave birth to my organization but I'm not sure if I'll be there to see it grow up. Yet I believe that it's an important thing to do, so I will do it and hope one day it will fly on its own."

As the women in the study reviewed the meaning of their lives, many found that for all their uniqueness, they were perhaps no different than women with children. Toni said, "I am a grain of sand on the beach. I'd like to think that I've mattered, but in the sum total of it all, I know I won't matter any more than any other grain of sand. We're all important in our own way. Together, we create an environment that can sustain life. I think it's the natural order of things." Elizabeth felt that her life story was far from complete: "When I contemplate my future, I question what it all is for. I look at my faith, my family background, my past, my present, and my future. I've had wonderful training and great gifts—but for what? I believe I'll have a story to tell, I just don't know what it is yet. Perhaps my legacy is not through children or what I have done, but through something that is yet to happen."

It is how you live life, not how long you live or whether you have offspring, that is the true measure of worth, many women reiterated. "No one wants to be around people who are morose, who feel they are failures, or who are bitter and sad. You get to decide how you will live. One day I saw two older women walking down the street. One walked slowly with her head down, while the other looked so perky and cheerful. Their walks told their stories, of who they had been, and what their futures were going to be like. There was no doubt which I'd rather be with, or which type I'd rather become," said Belinda. "I've made decisions in the past that put me where I am now. But I still have choices to make. I don't have to be haunted by the past unless I allow myself to be. I have learned the hard way that I am the pilot of my ship, and that I still have a journey to complete. I've decided to make it a wonderful adventure."

CHAPTER 12 Reflections
on a Childless Life

As the women in the study reflected on their lives, most were content
with how their lives were turning out. Many were philosophical when
discussing what childlessness meant to them. "Of course I wish I had
become a mother and done it in those unconscious years when so
many women I knew were doing it. Fantasizing in this way, I can easily
skip over all the hardships and frustrations that mothers experienced in
the past ten or twenty years of raising their children. Still, I can actually assert a certain amount of pride in the way I have chosen to lead
my life. I am pleased that I withstood the pressures, that I kept my independence, that I did not give in to the myths which surrounded me.
I did not conform but instead kept myself apart and independent in
some essential way. None of this is ever very simple. There are pleas-
ures that one gives up when one decides not to have children. But as I
keep telling myself, you can't have everything. Choices have to be
made, and consequences have to be lived with. The act of choosing
inevitably brings loss. It is a difficult lesson to understand and accept."[1]
Rose wished that "if only I knew back then what I know now—that
things work out they way they're supposed to." Childless women need
not be regretful or sad; they can be fulfilled and joyful with the way
their lives have turned out. As Natalie said, "I've enjoyed every moment
of my life—just some more than others. Not having children could
have been the best thing that happened to me. I've had an opportunity
to get to know myself. I've had a chance to decide what I wanted to

become, and I've been able to do things for others. Kids can be great, but this life has been wonderful, too." Iris summed up her thoughts by saying: "The older I get, the more I rationalize that the universe wanted it this way." Jeannie observed that "The only thing that really matters in life is whether you love. If you love others, then you become loved. It is as simple as that."

Every woman must find her own context for understanding her childlessness. Many women put their childlessness into a spiritual context. Greta, who believes in reincarnation, felt "I had kids in another life. This time, this life, maybe I'm not supposed to have kids. I'm here to focus on my relationship with the Creator." Mary Margaret felt that sometimes "we are put on earth to care for kids that aren't our own. One of my friends is an unwed mom with a beautiful five-year-old daughter. We're now a big part of her life. We help her and by doing that we are helped. God puts us where we're supposed to be." Toni said, "I find my healing in action on behalf of others. I volunteer, I'm on boards of directors, I use my professional role to pave the way so that others will have an easier road. By doing things to help others I have helped pay off any karmic debts I've owed, and hopefully I'm building up karmic benefits that will one day be returned to me. Who knows—maybe next time I'll have kids." Kris felt that "if I'm supposed to be pregnant or have a child, the Universe will find a way for me to parent. It's the only explanation I have, to believe in the higher power. Turn it over to the Goddess, to someone has more control and insight than I. If I didn't have that kind of spiritual base, I couldn't do well."

Childless women were more likely to view themselves as spiritual rather than religious. "Organized religion often offers only one way of doing things, and it's responsible for so many of the negative views about women who don't have children. Yet I can accept two things that appear contradictory because two things can be true but different at the same time," said Veronica. She continued: "I have problems with the 'either/or' doctrine. I don't have children, but I'm enormously caring about other people. I'm feminine even though I don't have kids. I'm doing a good job about living a right life. I desire to live communally, like the Shakers. You know, the 'hands to work, hearts to God,' approach. I am not a churchgoer. Like my dad, I find God in the outside. The interpretation of the Word can be a problem—but for me it's where living, thought, loving action came from." Rachael said, "I have a firm religious foundation, but it's one where all faiths converge. It doesn't matter if you are Christian or Jewish or Muslim or Buddhist—they all teach basically the same thing, if you listen carefully. I have little patience with those people who want to push one type of view down other people's throats. Especially for us (child-free) women, we have the opportunity to tune into our feminine side of Creation. When I was younger, I felt like I had to be one type or another—like a mother or a career woman, like they were worlds apart. I was taught that God wanted women to act a certain way. Now I see that everything is one, all religions are one, they are all about the One, just as we are all one." Women such as Anne found "great comfort" through her faith, which helped her "to survive the loss of my babies." Women such as Mary, who struggled with infertility, wondered "if you don't have faith, how can you make sense of the senseless, how can you find hope to go on?" Sara summed up her feelings by saying, "Everything that happens to you can be a blessing, if you let it be—even when you don't like what happens. Women without children have been given the gift of time, time to think, and time to be alone. We must listen to our female energy—and if we listen carefully we will ultimately find God."

Childless women "struggled with divergent messages about who I was supposed to be that rattled around in my head for years," according to Lucy. "I wanted to come to a peaceful place about not having kids. I've made it, but it took a long time to get there, and some of that journey wasn't very pleasant." Some women felt they had failed a critical life test by not having children. Belinda admitted, "In some ways, I feel like a failure by not having kids. I'm cutting off my family line by my decision. Inadvertently, I'm not just rejecting having children, but in some ways I am rejecting my whole family lineage. And it's this feeling that I don't know what to do with." Women such as Catherine were sad that "when I die, it will be the end of our family line." She explained, "When you have a lovely, loving family, you'd like to pass it on. There were so many riches in our family that I'd love to have kids to share and give to their grandkids. It makes me so sad to think our family's contributions will end with me." This loss was felt most poignantly by women who were only children or whose siblings did not have children. "All the wonderfulness of our family will be over, since neither my brother or I had kids," Jennifer observed. Deborah was haunted by the implications of her decision to be childless because "it violated my parents' survival of Holocaust concentration camps. They struggled to keep both their bodies and faith alive so that future generations of their family could survive. Sometimes I think that since I have no children, my parents' struggles were in vain." Tashi, whose relatives were slaves, felt similarly: "As an African American woman, I am the beneficiary of enslavement and of all those who suffered before. I have arrived. I am their dreams. Women who came before me paid dues that I have never had to pay. Our kids are so privileged; they are born into the light. It would have been nice to have brought a person into the world who could have grown up from the beginning knowing that their lives here could make a difference. I wanted a child to make whole the circle," she said. "My mother, grandmother, and all the women before me have made unbelievable sacrifices for me, even though they never knew of me or how their actions may change the world for me. I'm the first generation to graduate from high school, and I got my bachelor's, master's, and my Ph.D. I am a privileged person who is free from all the oppression they suffered. If I had a child, I could raise the first generation of minority children who has no residue of being less. But life is about a continuation of that which is important. I plan to leave the planet changed, not by genes, but by teaching others."

Most of the women in the study did not feel they were failures because they did not have children. Amanda said, "I'm sure there was a greater purpose for my not having children. I was not allowed to know what it was at the time. Now that I'm older, I have the opportunity of looking at the sweep of my life and trying to figure out what it was. I have not turned bitter, and I am not lonely; I am happy and productive. I have plenty of people in my life to love, who love me in return. I think I passed whatever test it was the Creator had for me." As

Sarah reflected on her life and the emotionally difficult times she had because she was childless, she said, "I believe that everyone has a different path to walk. We can't know what it is like to walk down someone else's road. I think that everyone has contributions to make. Hopefully we'll all reach the same end."

And what is that end? "I want to leave this earth knowing that I did something for someone that mattered," Louise said. "Everything in life is a compromise. If you take one road, you get something different than if you took the other. This doesn't mean that something is ever resolved. I think that there is always nostalgia, you wonder what life would be like if you took another path. But you acknowledge the path taken and spend time making the choice work for you." "We always affect things and people. It doesn't have to be our own kids that we impact—it could be friends and neighbors or those we work with. Even short-term relationships are valuable, and there is pleasure getting to know someone and caring for them, even if it is in a fleeting way," said Betsy. "It's silly to value one choice over another when both contribute and add something important. There have been lots of famous women who have had no children. Maybe they wouldn't have made their contributions if they had borne children," she said.

Many women such as Evie, when reflecting back on their lives, noted that one of the most important challenges they faced was "to leave the world a better place than I found it." They wondered, "What will be our legacies to the world?" Although this question confronts all people, it seemed particularly difficult for the childless women in this study. They wanted to make contributions of lasting value that proved their lives had mattered. Mothers naturally assume their children will be the bridge between yesterday and tomorrow. Children are typically those who will acquire family possessions, stories, and legacies. Women who have no children must find other repositories of their heritage. Some legacies are material in nature—money, property, photographs, collections, or cherished items passed down from one generation to the next. Legacies can also be reflected in the contributions made at work or in one's profession, as well as to organizations or community groups. Other legacies are personal, in which family and friends recall the intimate challenges, successes, and personality characteristics of those who have died. Of course issues of inheritance and legacy are not unique to childless women, but many of the women in this study seemed to have their own ways of describing and thinking about these issues. Their stories help others to understand how these women think about their own childlessness in relation to how it influenced their emotions and decisions about what they leave behind. According to women in this study, perhaps the most important legacies are those that reflect family history, reputation, and heritage. "If you have children, you naturally assume they will get your stuff and remember your birthday or the Christmases you gave them when they were small. You assume kids will remember things about you, the way I remember how my great-grandmother smelled like vanilla and had a white hair that grew out of a mole on her chin. I remember my daddy being the guy other guys called for advice. I remember his laugh. But when you're without kids, you wonder about who should get what, or if what you have is even worth passing on to others. You wonder what people will remember about you, if anything," said Betsy. It was the stories that mattered most to childless women. "I want to be remembered for the things I stood for, the things I did, and perhaps the things that I dreamed about doing but never got a chance to accomplish," according to Amanda. Amy hoped that "one day people will tell stories about me. Funny stories, or stories about things I did, or how hard I tried. Someone told me, 'You are a person who acts with courage and integrity.' Our stories are the most important things about us, really," she said. There is something special about sharing one's intimate stories with others who will care, according to Vicky: "I can tell stories to my friend's kids, but those kids can't relate to them with the same interest or intensity as would family. It's almost as if the good things you do gets passed on, sort of like it's genetic, although I'm sure it's not. But family members take pride in one another, and claim each other's successes—and failures—as their own. I'm an outsider—a lovable, fun auntie type, but an outsider nonetheless. I am not kin."

Families pass on their unique histories, stories, experiences, contributions, and legacies to each new generation through tales, be they

fiction or factual. The truthfulness of the tales is not really of consequence. The stories convey important family events as well as values and
beliefs. They describe people who have been important to the family and
provide a way of answering the age-old questions Who are we? Why are
we here? and Where are we going? Stories link generations with each
other. Natalie, who knew "I will never have children," was "delighted, so
very excited" when she learned that her sister was pregnant because
"through my new niece or nephew, the stories of our family will get carried on. The child will learn about us, who we were, what we were like,
what we did, and what we wanted the world to be like. Sometimes I
think my dreams can become realized, my unresolved, undone parts of
myself can become whole when I pass them to the baby. In this way, perhaps, we are able to advance new generations and, indeed, the world.
Maybe in this way I will have mattered in ways that I never expected."
Monica looked forward to her cousin having a child because "now I will
have someone to tell my secrets to, someone to whom I can give the
things that matter the most to me. It's so odd—while I'm surrounded
with people every moment of every day, there's all these parts of me
that no one really knows. I'd like to make sure those parts of me don't
get lost. So my new baby cousin will give me that opportunity."

Some of the women I interviewed pondered who would be the one
to best understand their stories. "I hope to pass on my stories and values through my examples and discussions with others while I'm living,
rather than expecting others to preserve them after my death," said
Lucy. "After I die, all that will be left are my things. While they have
some utility, they're not who I am." Although these women found their
stories to be their most important legacy, they were also concerned
about who should be left the tangible remainders of their lives. "I have
property, a house, my car, stocks and some savings, a piano, and little
things that have meant a lot to me," said Nance. "Perhaps I have more
than some women because I've worked all my life, and by not having
kids, I've had a chance to acquire more things. If I had kids, I probably
would have left everything to them and not thought another thing
about it. But since I don't, I've seriously considered who should be the
recipient of my sweat, my luck, my frugality."

Contemplating who will be the beneficiary of their material life "hit me in the face when I went into work and had to fill out the beneficiary list on my insurance papers. It was yet another reminder that I don't have kids. Parents almost always pick kids. I sat there for the longest time trying to figure out whom to put. I should outlive my spouse, so he may not be the best person to put on it for the long run. I inevitably started thinking about kids—nieces or nephews or friends of kids that I'd like to leave something to. But then, I found myself wondering if I wanted to lay a bunch of money on some kids who really don't really know me or what I did in my life," said Sherri. Sometimes women found themselves choosing their beneficiaries by default: "By not having kids or having a significant other to name, and not being close to either my mom—and my sister doesn't know who I am—I don't know who to pick. I have a cat that I love, but I guess I can't leave things to it. I trust my sister more than the others, I guess." Joanne and her husband have "been extremely fond of a friend's son, and we plan to leave him a millionaire. He doesn't know this, of course. But he's a good kid and we think he'll do well with what we leave him." Evie countered, "I could leave my niece a very wealthy person, but I don't think that's a good idea. It would spoil her rotten. She would fail to use her talents and ultimately squander everything away, from my hard-saved money to her own talents. There must be a better way to distribute my estate," she said. Paula has remembered all of her godchildren in her will and has tried to leave equal amounts to each, "although I'll give each one something special that was mine, things that I believe they'll understand and appreciate." Victoria "put my parents as my beneficiaries, but they died. I put my husband, but we divorced, and I sure as hell wouldn't want him to have a penny of my estate now. I put down my sister but realized she would likely die before I would. So I started thinking about how much easier it would be if I had kids." Yet Laura wondered, "maybe throwing your estate at your kids just because you have them is a cop out. I think we spend a lot of our lives not thinking about issues like beneficiaries and inheritance."

Often, these women expressed some hesitancy about leaving their estate to their husbands when the men had children from previous marriages. Nance said, "My stepson has a mother and a father who will be leaving everything to him. Why should I? I'd rather leave my estate to someone who won't be getting anything from anyone else. It seems more fair to me. But I don't think he'd see it that way." Leanne confessed that "I like his kids fine, and I'm happy to leave them something. But I don't want to leave everything I have to them. There are other people in my life whom I love and want to remember." "While I feel close to my stepdaughter, I feel more drawn to my niece and nephew," said Randi. "They're an extension of myself, so I want them to have my things. There's a genetic, family track that resides inside of my brother's kids that makes us closer than I could be to my stepdaughter. My sister and I grew up together, enjoyed and endured the same set of parents, remember talking late into the night, sitting on the same bunk beds with the plaid bedspreads. This thing of blood being thicker than water is true. While we've had our troubles throughout the years, ultimately, we're cut from the same cloth. I cannot imagine anyone else knowing me like they do, on the cellular and historical levels," she said.

Childless women such as Sylvia were concerned that leaving their monetary estates to "kids who would fritter away my money because it really meant nothing to them, because I really meant nothing to them, well, that would seem a pretty stupid thing to do." Briana admitted that "I want what I leave to make a difference to someone. I did not scrimp and save during my lifetime so that someone else could go out and buy a Ferrari or take a vacation to Paris. I want my inheritance to be used to pay for someone's college education, or to start a worthwhile business, or to do something that is of value." Some women thought they would leave their money to philanthropic organizations that could decide where their money would do the most good. Some women selected organizations that benefited particular groups of people, such as children, sexual abuse victims, the elderly, or the homeless, whereas others identified animals or the environment as beneficiaries. "This way I have a better chance of making a long-term contribution to the world, rather than giving cold cash to people who I'm afraid will spend it on tasteless cars and blow it on vacations in the

Caribbean," said Lucy. Josi decided to contribute her assets to needy families: "Children need all the help they can get. I watch the government cutting programs for them, and I see how many are poor or sick or in need of good education and I want to help. The problem is," she admitted, "I don't know how. Where do you start to figure out where the best place is to do the most good?" Women also named local organizations in their wills. Some of these included churches, museums, schools, and clubs. Toni plans to leave money for renovations to her church; Rachael is leaving money to her synagogue; Betsy plans to leave money to protect a nature area; Julie states she will be leaving funds to support UNICEF and refugee programs; and Valerie wants part of her estate to fund a center to promote artistic development "since the government has massacred the funding for arts and humanities." Elise is leaving a large part of her estate to groups such as the Audubon Society, Sierra Club, and the Humane Society, "because I feel committed to ending animal suffering. We support about twenty-five different organizations," she announced. Brianna gives "a lot of money to the Children's Defense Fund. It's a wonderful organization. It was interesting—when I thought about my giving, I realized I give most of my charity dollars to children, instead of flood relief programs. I guess I've prioritized kids without even realizing it. In some way, I will live in the lives of children who don't even know I exist." Hannah commented, "There are all kinds of people who spend phenomenal amounts of money on things that have no lasting value. For example, consider that guy [Dennis Tito] who spent $20 million to go for a ride into space. Just think about all the long-lasting good that much money would do if it was spent on education, on the homeless, building a community center, or the like. If we are wise, we will use our lives and money to create benefits that can improve life forever."[2]

Although women such as Briana may give the bulk of their estate away "since they are just things," inevitably there were some material objects to which the women had a sentimental attachment. They wanted those objects "to go to someone who would appreciate them and understand what they meant to me," as Josi said. Calina said, "My nieces and nephews are the kids I never had. My nieces will get my jewelry that belonged to my mother and grandmother. Girls always get the jewels, you know. And the china and crystal. The boys will get pieces of furniture, with my admonition not to let their girlfriends or wives have the pieces should they get divorced. Things need to stay in the family." Nicole has "over five thousand photographs of the family, and I like the idea of giving my nieces and nephews the photos because they'll mean something to them. Some they'll really cherish." Heather said, "When I'm dead and gone, I doubt that anyone who really knows me would want the oriental carpet or the Haviland china. Rather, they'd know to find me in my dog-eared poetry books I've read so often that they're falling apart. They'll find me in the plastic barrettes I've saved ever since I was a little girl, or in my beveled glass hand mirror that I look in every morning. Things only have meaning when they help you to remember," she said. "When my grandmother died, all I wanted was her kitchen spoons and pans. I remember watching her use that wooden spoon every meal, and when I use it I think of her. It brings her close and I get flooded with memories of her. So is a spoon just a spoon? No. It is an object that has minimal economic value but tremendous emotional importance. It's not the object that's important. It's the set of memories associated with it."

Some of the women in the study reported that they didn't have anyone special to leave material objects to and that it influenced how they live their lives today. "When I go to buy something nice, I find myself looking at it and wondering, should I buy it? I'm getting older, and while I might like it, I don't need it," Catherine said. "It would be different to buy it knowing that it would be passed on to someone who would care for it like I do. But knowing there's no one, why should I buy it?" Toots agreed: "I collect those pretty little houses. They're expensive, and I have a hundred of them. One day it hit me—when I die, who will want them? They don't mean anything to anyone I know. That has occurred to me as I have gotten older, and it discourages me sometimes from some of the hobbies I used to have, because I don't know who I would pass them on to. No one is going to care about all these houses like I do. I have thought about selling them to a friend who collects them. I have wondered who I would give other things to, and it saddens me. I've pushed these thoughts aside, because it won't happen for a while. It's a source of struggle and upset," she said.

The issue of who should get family heirlooms was a symbolic one that reflected how integrated women felt in their social networks. Women such as Ellie had "dear ones who will remember me and they'd want my things," so deciding who would carry on their memory was clear-cut. But women who felt more isolated had difficulties deciding who should be their beneficiaries. This process was arduous, even painful, for them. Yvonne, who was adopted and not voluntarily childless, "never knew my biological family, and I have no children to make me a family now." Her adoptive "grandma gave my dad the family Bible to be passed on. She carried the first Bible across the Appalachian Mountains. I don't think I should take it. It wouldn't be right for me to have that Bible. I don't have any kids to pass it on to. It should go to a real Smith, not to me. So I made sure my aunt has the Bible, and she can give it to her children." Yvonne has lived on the margin, feeling as though she never belonged. "It's been hard, and it makes me sad," she said. "I've not had a bad life, but there was so much more I wanted out of it. The issues of relationships, of being needed, of having someone to give yourself to—these are what I miss the most. If I had had children, maybe it would all have been different. But it's too late now, and it does no good to second-guess decisions that were made so long ago."

Regret. Contentment. Frustration. Satisfaction. Laughter. Loneliness. Togetherness. Separateness. The lives of these childless women have been filled with the passions of life. Their lives have not been uniformly easy or difficult. Their childlessness occurred after a series of influences and decisions that occurred over a span of perhaps forty years of life. These women could have become mothers if they had really wanted to. But as Mica stated, "behavior speaks louder than any words I said. Behavior counts. If I had really wanted children that badly, I would have had them. But I didn't. I made countless decisions that assured my childlessness. Time after time I had opportunities to pursue a life with children, and I made decisions that led me a different way. I may have blamed others for those decisions, but ultimately those decisions were my own. It has taken me a long time to grow up and accept myself. Part of my being me is couched in the way I have led my life. In order to get to where I am today, I had to do what I've done. There's a reason why some of us have kids and some of us don't. It's not for me to know exactly what everyone's reason is. I don't think that as women we are all that different from each other. I have lots in common with friends who have kids. I think it's us that make the difference. We get chips on our shoulder, or we think our way's better than other people's, or that we know what's right. We get into pity parties or we get envious of the way other people live and get into the 'if only' kind of thought that makes us discontent with our own majesty. My friends who have kids sometimes wish they had my world, the same way that sometimes I wish I had theirs. The beauty of it all is that if we can put our egos aside, we can truly share one another's experiences and celebrate our gifts."

Where does this journey through the lives of this group of childless women leave us? Perhaps other women who are childless and child-free have found comfort in the insights of these women. Perhaps those who are not childless have gained an understanding of and a sensitivity toward childless women. For those women who are considering whether to have children, these stories may offer information that will help them make the right reproductive decision. As we have seen, there are benefits in whichever decision a woman makes. A woman who lives a childless life can be subject to emotional upheavals from time to time, but these stories of childless women also indicate that there are mean- ingful occupational, relational, and personal benefits to be gained. As Nance stated, "no life is perfect, yet every life is perfect within that imperfection."

These stories, of course, have been seen through my lens. I have tried to capture them accurately and to reflect the larger meanings associated with them. It may be that other childless women have expe- riences that are different than those told here. Every woman will have her own unique tale to tell. However, as I interviewed childless women across the United States, I found that themes began to emerge from their stories. Although I may use a quote from a particular woman to describe an experience, usually that quote incorporates similar experiences of many other women. I have learned that these women's experiences and emotions are not so different from each other, nor in many ways are they so different from those of women with children.

This project has led me back to my starting point—trying to understand my friend Fran's life, and mine. I will soon travel to Alaska, where Fran lives now, and I will take a copy of this book with me. She has no idea that I have spent four years of my life researching and writing it. I have not told her that I have gently delved into the lives of 125 women from coast to coast so that I can understand her experience, the life of my friend. But now I have a greater sensitivity and understanding. We don't have the luxury of thinking we have all the time in the world. We have grown up. We are fully women now, and we are not allowed insecure evasiveness, as is common in youth.

I will walk with her, quietly, among the scrub pine where the Alaska caribou run. Her golden hair, once the color of birch leaves in autumn, is turning silver. Her face wears the lines of life's laughter and sorrow. She is a woman of substance, a friend as solid as the granite beneath my feet. I know why she is childless, but I haven't understood how she felt about it. I've watched her nurturing my babies into their adulthood with constancy and faithfulness. Her love for us has never wavered, even when she's been angry or frustrated with us. She takes care of other people's children all the time, from the children of her siblings to the kids in her community. She befriends the needy. She regularly sends gifts around the world so that children she cares about will know that she loves them. If she had children, maybe she would have been just as giving, just as wonderful. But the fact is, she didn't have children—and we are all the better for it.

So I will put this book into her hands, and we will talk.

About the Interviews

Before I began this study, I conducted an intensive review of the literature on childlessness, infertility, and other relevant topics. I looked at
hundreds of books, reports, and articles, of which only a small number
are included in the notes. The literature review provided me with both
conceptual and methodological information to guide the initial stages of
the research. It was clear from an analysis of the literature that some
exploratory work had been conducted on childless women, but little of
it was based on large samples or used empirical analyses. I decided to
look at childless women who were baby boomers—they were old enough
not only to have made definitive childbearing decisions but to have had
the opportunity to assess how those decisions had affected their lives.

Because of financial constraints and sampling concerns, I decided
that a nonparametric sample was the most feasible and proceeded to
select a combination of a social networks and snowball sample. I chose
this strategy because it would clearly and quickly identify women who
had no children, thereby limiting the need for a costly, multistage survey
of a large random sample of all women in order to narrow the focus on
those who were childless. During preliminary sampling tests, I found
that although women with children tended not to know many women
without children, women without children usually knew a significant
number of other childless women. Because of the social mobility in
American society, women were just as likely to have close friends who
lived in another state as they were to have friends who lived nearby.

I interviewed the women either in person or on the telephone. The interviews generally lasted about two hours, although some ran longer or shorter. Women were informed that they did not have to answer any questions and that they could terminate the interview at any time. None of the women refused to answer questions, and none terminated the interview early. All of the women seemed to genuinely appreciate the opportunity to answer questions about being childless. They reported enjoying the chance to reflect on what their childlessness had meant as well as to provide information they hoped would be of assistance to other women.

Both qualitative and quantitative data were collected. Initially, a dozen childless women were interviewed; each of these women was asked to identify other childless women, who, in turn identified others. By the end of the project, 125 women throughout the United States had been interviewed. Women from almost all fifty states were represented in the study; they came from the Northeast (Maine, New Hampshire, Vermont, Connecticut, Rhode Island, New York, and Massachusetts), the South (Florida, Georgia, Texas, South Carolina, Virginia, and Louisiana), the Midwest (Indiana, Iowa, Michigan, Minnesota, and Wisconsin), and the West (California, New Mexico, Oregon, Alaska, and Washington). Because of the social networks component, that is, women tended to refer their friends, who were similar to themselves in some way, the sample of women was composed primarily of white, middle- and upper-middle-class, employed, and highly educated women. Most of the women had a college degree or some sort of specialized training. All major racial and religious groups were represented, as well as some women who were extremely wealthy and some who were not. Although it is possible that the views of women in this study are not representative of all childless women, the views are representative of those held by the types of women that Middle America comes in contact with on a day-to-day basis.

Using a grounded methodology as advanced by Barney Glaser and Anselm Strauss,[1] I began by asking a limited number of open-ended questions. These core questions included the following:

Why are you childless?

What was your childhood like? Did you think that you would have kids or not?

What were your mother's attitudes about having kids?

Have you ever been pregnant? If so, what was the outcome of the pregnancy?

Were there times you wanted a child?

Were there times you did not want a child?

What have been the easy times associated with being childless?

What have been the difficult or challenging times associated with being childless?

How have you processed your childlessness over time?

What legacies do you plan to leave?

What words of wisdom do you want to give others about being childless?

As respondents answered these questions, I was able to confirm whether the questions were useful. In a grounded methodological approach, if the questions are useful, they should continue to be used; if, after a reasonable number of interviews, questions cease to be useful, they should be eliminated from the interview schedule. Thanks to pre-tests of the interview items, I was able to use all of the initial questions for all 125 interviews. The interviews were structured in such a way that women could add information they deemed relevant but that had not been asked. Over time, as common themes emerged, a few new questions were added to the interview schedule. In this way, women had the opportunity to address the same core questions as well as provide unique and personal information. During the interviews, respondents provided new insights and information that formed the basis for future questioning. After approximately twenty-five interviews, I had developed a well-structured interview schedule. I continued to conduct detailed interviews until no new themes were identified and patterns of responses were clear.

After no new themes were identified through interviews, I considered the data collection part of this study to be complete. Although the themes reported by the respondents were well established by the end of the seventh-fifth interview, I interviewed an additional fifty women to make sure that I was observing the patterns and trends in the data accurately and to reduce the chances of any skew or bias in the sample. To assure confidentiality and anonymity, I assigned each woman a pseudonym so that the real name of the woman could not be linked with her story. Several women selected their own pseudonyms, and several chose the same name.

Data analysis consisted of both qualitative and quantitative forms. For qualitative data analysis, each interview was kept as a unique file so that composite histories of each woman could be kept. Patterns were then identified and a file of quotes around a given topic was created, for example, on abortion, impact of career, or relationship with mothers. Quotes were then analyzed by comparing them with findings in the literature, and statistical analyses of the interview data were completed. Fifty variables were identified through the interviews, and a data file was created using SPSS (Statistical Package for the Social Sciences). Each interview was coded according to the respondent's answers to these variables. The data were then statistically analyzed, and descriptive and inferential statistics were calculated. Given the sampling strategy and the primarily nominal- or ordinal-level variables, the statistics were carefully analyzed so as not to overstate relationships. The statistical calculations gave validity to the ethnographic data provided by the women. It is thus with confidence that I present this information about childless women.

Once the data were collected and analyzed, theory was developed to correspond with what I had observed. The findings led to the development initially of twenty chapters of material, which have been synthesized into the dozen chapters that now make up this book. Throughout the book I have referred to "many" women or used other terms to indicate that a significant number of women had a particular experience or felt a particular emotion. It is important for the reader to understand that I made those statements only when data indicated overwhelming trends, usually those that were statistically significant at the .05 level or smaller. In this way, I have attempted to provide representative information about experiences of childless women in a readable way.

To enhance the understanding of these statistically significant trends and to bring them to life, I have used the women's quotes throughout the book. It is easier for most people to understand a phenomenon when a story is told or when a real person's experience is explained in everyday language. The quotes, then, are representative not just of the opinions of those to whom the quotes are attributed; they also usually convey the similar experience of a larger group of childless women.

It is possible that this baby boomer age cohort may have had experiences that make the findings unique. Therefore, although the data seem to correspond to trends found in other research, future research in this topic is encouraged.

Notes

Chapter 1   Childlessness in America

1. Julia Wood, *Gendered Lives* (Belmont, CA: Wadsworth, 2001).
2. Kathleen Griffen, "Childless by Choice," *Health* 10, 2 (March-April 1996): 98–104.
3. Rita Rhodes, "Women, Motherhood, and Infertility: The Social and Historical Context," in *Infertility and Adoption: A Guide for Social Work Practice*, ed. Deborah Valentine (New York: Haworth Press, 1988), 5–20.
4. Mather quoted ibid., 7.
5. Viviana Zelizer, *Pricing the Priceless Child* (New York: Basic Books, 1981).
6. Diane Eyer, *Mother–Infant Bonding. A Scientific Fiction* (New Haven: Yale University Press, 1992).
7. Ibid., 2.
8. Nancy Theriot, *Nostalgia on the Right: Historical Roots of the Idealized Family*, Monograph Series I (Cambridge, MA: Political Research Associates, 1990).
9. Betty Farrell, *Family: The Making of an Idea, an Institution, and a Controversy in American Culture* (Boulder, CO: Westview Press, 1999).
10. Nancy Hoffnung, "Motherhood: Contemporary Conflict for Women," in *Women, a Feminist Perspective*, ed. Jo Freeman (Palo Alto, CA: Mayfield, 1984).
11. Rhodes, *Women, Motherhood, and Infertility*, 15.
12. Sigmund Freud, *A General Introduction to Psychoanalysis*, as quoted in Carol Tavris, "Goodbye to Momism," *New York Times Book Review*, May 3, 1998, 16.
13. Helene Deutsch, *The Psychology of Women* (London: Research Books, 1947).
14. Barbara Harris, *Beyond Her Sphere: Women and the Professions in American History* (Westport, CT: Greenwood Press, 1978).
15. Janet Ruand and Karen Cerulo, *Second Thoughts: Seeing Conventional Wisdom through the Sociological Eye* (Thousand Oaks, CA: Pine Forge, 1997); Stephanie Coontz, *The Way We Never Were: American Families and the Nostalgia Trap* (New York: Basic Books, 1992).
16. Griffen, "Childless by Choice"; Sara Ruddick, "Maternal Thinking," *Feminist Studies* 6 (1980): 70–96.

17. Betty Friedan, *The Feminine Mystique* (New York: Dell, 1963); Shulamith Firestone, *The Dialectics of Sex: The Case for Feminist Revolution* (New York: Bantam, 1971); bell hooks, *Yearning: Race, Gender, and Cultural Politics* (Cambridge, MA: South End Press, 1986).
18. Ellen Peck and Judith Senderowitz, *Pronatalism: The Myth of Mom and Apple Pie* (New York: Crowell, 1974).
19. Lesley Novack and David Novack, "Being Female in the Eighties and Nineties," *Sex Roles* 35, 1–2 (1994): 57–72.
20. Meredith Maran, *Notes from an Incomplete Revolution: Real Life since Feminism* (New York: Bantam Books, 1997), 2.
21. Susan Douglas, *Where the Girls Are: Growing Up Female with the Mass Media* (New York: Times Books, 1995), 17.
22. Ibid., 15.
23. Katherine McCleary, "A Working Mom's Toughest Job: Her Marriage," *USA Weekend*, September 11, 1998, 10; Patricia Edmonds, "What Women Want Now," *USA Weekend*, October 23, 1998, 16–18.
24. Janet Hunt and Larry Hunt, "The Dualities of Careers and Families: New Integrations or New Polarizations?" in *Family in Transition*, ed. Arlene Skolnick and Jerome Skolnick (Boston: Little Brown, 1998), 275–289.
25. Kathleen Hughes, "Pregnant Professionals Face Subtle Bias at Work as Attitudes toward Them Shift," *Wall Street Journal*, February 6, 1991, B1–6.
26. Hunt and Hunt, "Dualities of Careers and Families," 283.
27. Diane Lewis, "Homeward Bound: Many Are Trading in Long Hours, Little Satisfaction for Family Time, Peace of Mind," *Boston Globe*, March 29, 1998, C1.
28. Tony Allen Mills, "Female Big Quitters Fuel War of the Sexes," *London Sunday Times*, March 8, 1998, A21.
29. Griffen, "Childless by Choice."
30. J. Allen, "Motherhood: The Annihilation of Women," in *Mothering: Essays in Feminist Theory*, ed. Joyce Trebilcot (Totowa, NJ: Rowman and Allanheld, 1984), 315–330.
31. Peck and Senderowitz, *Pronatalism*.
32. Dan Fost, "Childfree with an Attitude," *American Demographics* 4 (April 18, 1996): 15.
33. Manan Paux, *Childless by Choice: Choosing Childlessness in the 80's* (New York: Doubleday, 1984); Elinor Burkett, *The Baby Boon: How Family-Friendly America Cheats the Childless* (New York: Free Press, 2000); Madelyn Cain, *The Childless Revolution* (New York: Perseus Books, 2001).
34. C. Wright Mills, *The Power Elite* (New York: Oxford University Press, 1956), 126.
35. Marsha Somers, "A Comparison of Voluntarily Childfree Adults and Parents," *Journal of Marriage and the Family* 55 (August 1993): 643–650.
36. Rosemarie Nave-Herz, "Childless Marriages," *Marriage and Family Review* 14, 1–2 (1989): 239–250.
37. Charlene Miall, "Community Constructs of Involuntary Childlessness: Sympathy, Stigma, and Social Support," *Canadian Review of Sociology and Anthropology* 31, 4 (1994): 392–422.
38. Erving Goffman, *Stigma: Notes on the Management of Spoiled Identity* (Englewood Cliffs, NJ: Prentice-Hall, 1963).
39. Griffen, "Childless by Choice," 101.

40. Somers, "A Comparison of Voluntarily Childfree Adults and Parents."

41. Karla Mueller and Janice Yoder, "Gendered Norms for Family Size, Employment, and Occupation: Are There Personal Costs for Violating Them?" *Sex Roles* 36 (1997): 207–220.

42. Irena Klepfisz, "Women without Children/Women without Families/Women Alone," in *Politics of the Heart: A Lesbian Parenting Anthology*, ed. Sandra Pollack and Jeanne Vaughn (Ithaca, NY: Firebrand Books, 1987), 55–65, quotation at 56.

Chapter 2   The Pushes and Pulls of Childlessness

1. Nave-Herz, "Childless Marriages."

2. Gail Letherby, "Nonmotherhood: Ambivalent Autobiographies," *Feminist Studies* 25, 3 (fall 1999): 719–729.

3. Stephanie Dourick, ed. *Why Children?* (New York: Harcourt Brace, 1980).

4. Molly Peacock, *Paradise Piece by Piece* (New York: Riverhead Books, 1998).

5. Ingrid Connidis and Julie Ann McMullin, "To Have or Have Not: Parent Status and the Subjective Well Being of Older Men and Women," *Gerontologist* 33, 5 (1993): 630–636; Victor Callan, "The Personal and Marital Adjustment of Mothers and of Voluntarily and Involuntarily Childless Wives," *Journal of Marriage and the Family* 49 (November 1987): 847–856.

6. Susan Hays, "The Mommy Wars: Ambivalence, Ideological Work, and the Cultural Contradictions of Motherhood," in *Family in Transition*, ed. Arlene Skolnick and Jerome Skolnick (Boston: Little, Brown, 1998); Shelley MacDermid and Ted Huston, "Changes in Marriage Associated with the Transition to Parenthood," *Journal of Marriage and the Family* 52 (1990): 475–486; Lewis, "Homeward Bound," C1.

Chapter 3   Impact of Body, Mind, and Family Interactions

1. Joyce Abama, Anjani Chandra, William Mosher, Linda Peterson, and Linda Piccinino, *Vital and Health Statistics: Fertility, Family Planning, and Women's Health: New Data from the 1995 National Survey of Family Growth*, series 23, no. 19 (Hyattsville, MD: U.S. Department of Health and Human Services, 1997).

2. James Henslin, *Sociology* (Needham Heights, MA: Allyn and Bacon, 1999).

3. Nancy Chodorow, *The Reproduction of Mothering: Psychoanalysis and the Sociology of Gender* (Berkeley: University of California Press, 1978).

4. Nancy Friday, *My Mother, Myself* (New York: Delacorte Press, 1977); Elisabeth Badinter, *The Myth of Motherhood: An Historical View of the Maternal Instinct* (London: Souvenier Press, 1981).

5. Susan Abramowitz and Ellyn Kaschak, "From Mother to Daughter: Conceptions of Parental Heritage," *Smith College Studies in Social Work* 53, 1 (1982): 1–14; Joan Smith, *Different for Girls: How Culture Creates Women* (London: Chatto and Windus, 1997); Louis Leiderman Davitz, *Baby Hunger: Every Woman's Longing for a Baby* (Minneapolis: Winston Press, 1984); Sheila Rowbotham, "To Be or Not to Be: The Dilemma of Mothering," *Feminist Review* 31 (spring 1989): 82–93; ETR Associates, "Am I Parent Material?" (Santa Cruz, CA: ETR Associates, 1999).

6. Friday, *My Mother, Myself*, 39.

7. Davitz, *Baby Hunger.*

8. Rhodes, "Women, Motherhood, and Infertility"; Frank Cox, *Human Intimacy: Marriage, the Family, and Its Meaning* (Belmont, CA: Wadsworth, 1999).

9. Rowbotham, "To Be or Not to Be"; Sharon Begley and Martha Brant, "The Baby Myth," *Newsweek*, September 4, 1995, 38–46.
10. Chodorow, *Reproduction of Mothering.*
11. Ray Helfer, *Childhood Comes First* (East Lansing, MI: Ray E. Helfer, 1984).
12. Carolyn Morrell, "Intentionally Childless Women: Another View of Women's Development," *Affilia: Journal of Women and Social Work* 8, 3 (1993): 300–317; Judith Lorber, Rose Coser, and Alice Rossi, "On the Reproduction of Mothering: A Methodological Debate," *Signs* 6, 3 (1981): 482–514; Phyllis Moen and Mary Ann Erikson, "Their Mother's Daughters? The Intergenerational Transmission of Gender Attitudes in a World of Changing Roles," *Journal of Marriage and the Family* 59 (May 1997): 281–293.
13. Friday, *My Mother, Myself,* 1.
14. Coontz, *The Way We Never Were.*
15. Rhonda Mahony, *Kidding Ourselves: Breadwinning, Babies, and Bargaining Power* (New York: Basic Books, 1996); Elizabeth Menaghan, "Psychological Well Being among Parents and Nonparents," *Journal of Family Issues* 10, 4 (December 1989): 547–565.

Chapter 4   Consequences of Partnerships

1. Andrew Cherlin, *Marriage, Divorce, and Remarriage* (Cambridge, MA: Harvard University Press, 1992); Linda Waite, "Does Marriage Matter?" *Demography* 32 (1995): 483–507.
2. Leonard Caragan and Matthew Melko, *Singles: Myths and Realities* (Newbury Park, CA: Sage, 1982); Bryan Strong and Christine DeVault, *The Marriage and Family Experience* (Belmont, CA: Wadsworth, 1998); American Demographics, *Report on Childlessness,* October 1993; American Demographics, *American Households,* Desk Reference Series no. 3, July 1992; Dennis Ahlburg, and Carol DeVita, "New Realities of the American Family," *Population Bulletin* 37, 2 (1992): 1–3; Margaret Ambry, "Childless Chances," *American Demographics,* April 1992, 55–56; William Mosher and Christine Bachrach, "Childlessness in the United States: Estimates from the National Survey of Family Growth," *Journal of Family Issues* 3, 4 (December 1982): 517–543.
3. Kyle Crowder and Stewart Tolnay, "A New Marriage Squeeze for Black Women: The Role of Racial Intermarriage by Black Men," *Journal of Marriage and the Family* 62, 3 (August 2000): 792–818, quotation at 796.
4. Nancy Polikoff, "This Child Does Have Two Mothers: Redefining Parenthood to Meet the Needs of Children in Lesbian Mother and Other Nontraditional Families," *Georgetown Law Journal* 78 (1990): 459–575; Marcia Bedard, *Breaking with Tradition: Diversity, Conflict, and Change in Contemporary American Families* (Dix Hills, NY: General Hall, 1992); Caragan and Melko, *Singles: Myths and Realities;* Lynn White and John Edwards, "Emptying the Nest and Parental Well Being: An Analysis of National Panel Data," *American Sociological Review* 55 (1990): 235–242; Carolyn Morell, *Unwomanly Conduct: The Challenges of Intentional Childlessness* (London: Routledge, 1994); Susan Cohen and Mary Katzenstein, "The War over the Family Is Not Over the Family," in *Feminism, Children, and the New Families,* ed. Sanford Dornbush and Myra Strober (New York: Guilford Press, 1988), 25–46; Sharon Houseknecht, "Voluntary Childlessness," in *Handbook of Marriage and the Family,* ed. Marvin Sussman and

Suzanne Steinmetz (New York: Plenum, 1987); Jean Veevers, "Voluntary Childlessness: A Review of Issues and Evidence," *Marriage and Family Review* 7 (1979): 1–26.

5. Menaghan, "Psychological Well Being among Parents and Nonparents."
6. Somers, "A Comparison of Voluntarily Childfree Adults and Parents."
7. Jill Smolowe, *An Empty Lap* (New York: Pocket Books, 1997).

Chapter 5   Lifestyle Choices

1. Morell, *Unwomanly Conduct*; Jane Bartlett, *Will You Be Mother? Women Who Choose to Say No* (London: Virago, 1994); Laurie Lisle, *Without Child: Challenging the Stigma of Childlessness* (New York: Ballantine Books, 1996); P. Ziman and B. Aria, *Motherhood Optional: A Psychological Journey* (Northvale, NJ : Jason Aronson, 1998).
2. Griffin, "Childless by Choice," 103.
3. Mary Corcoran, Greg Duncan, and Martha Hill, "The Economic Fortunes of Women and Children: Lessons from the Panel Study of Income Dynamics," *Signs* 10 (1994): 232–248; U.S. Department of Labor, *Employment and Earnings* (Washington, DC: Government Printing Office, 1998); U.S. Department of Labor, *The Employment Situation* (Washington, DC: Government Printing Office, 1998); Jean Veevers, *Childless by Choice* (Toronto: Butterworth, 1980).
4. Elisabeth Menaghan and Toby Parcel, "Determining Children's Home Environments: The Impact of Maternal Characteristics and Current Occupational and Family Conditions," *Journal of Marriage and the Family* 53 (1991): 417–431; Claire Renzetti and Daniel Curran, *Women, Men, and Society* (Boston: Allyn and Bacon, 1998); Susan Faludi, *Backlash: The Undeclared War against Women* (New York: Crown, 1991); Diane Crispell, "Planning No Family, Now or Ever," *American Demographics*, October 1993, 22–23; Nicolaus Mills, *The Triumph of Meanness* (Boston: Houghton Mifflin, 1997); Leonard Beeghley, *What Does Your Wife Do? Gender and the Transformation of Family Life* (Boulder CO: Westview Press, 1999); Betsy Morris, "Is Your Family Wrecking your Career?" *Fortune*, March 17, 1997, 71–90; Renzetti and Curran, *Women, Men, and Society*.
5. Barbara Ehrenreich, *Nickle and Dimed* (New York: Holt, 2001); Sylvia Ann Hewelett, *A Lesser Life: The Myth of Women's Liberation in America* (New York: Morrow, 1986).
6. Arlie Hochschild, *The Second Shift* (New York: Viking, 1989); Felice Schwartz, "Management Women and the New Facts of Life," *Harvard Business Review* 67, 1 (1989): 65–76; United Nations, *The World's Women, 1970–1990: Social Statistics and Indicators*, series K, no. 8 (New York, 1991); Jenny Anderson, "The Overworked American," *Institutional Investor* 35, 4 (April 2001): 120; Barbara Gutek, "Comment: The Biological Clock Confronts Complex Organizations, *Journal of Management Inquiry* 4, 1 (March 1995): 66ff.; Mary Ann Lamanna, *Marriages and Families* (Belmont, CA: Wadsworth, 1994).
7. "The Cost of Children," *U.S. News and World Report*, March 30, 1998, 47–51; Reuters, "Mom, Dad and the Money Pit: Cost of Child Rearing on the Rise," *Boston Globe*, March 23, 1998, A3.
8. Esther Buchholz, *The Call of Solitude: Alonetime in a World of Attachment* (New York: Simon and Schuster, 1997), 2.
9. Laura Shapiro, "The Myth of Quality Time," *Newsweek*, May 12, 1997, 62–69.

10. Nancy Adler, Henry David, and Gail Wyatt, "Psychological Factors in Abortion," *American Psychologist* 47, 10 (October 1992): 1194–1204.

11. Rita Townsend and Ann Perkins, *Bitter Fruit: Women's Experiences of Unplanned Pregnancy, Abortion, and Adoption* (Alameda, CA: Hunter House, 1992); Nada Stotland, "The Myth of the Abortion Trauma Syndrome," *JAMA* 268 (1992): 2078–2079; Nada Stotland, "Letters to the Editor: A Reply," *JAMA* 269 (1993): 2210; Robert Blake, "Letters to the Editor," *JAMA* 269 (1993): 2209–2210; Finn Egil Skjeldestad, Jens-Kristian Borgan, Anne Kjersti Daltveit, and Erik Nymoen, "Induced Abortion: Effects of Marital Status, Age, and Parity on Choice or Pregnancy Termination," *Acta Obstetricia et Gynecological Scandinavica* 73 (1994): 255–260.

12. Kristine Baber and Christine Allen, *Feminist Families* (New York: Guilford Press, 1992).

Chapter 6 Infertility, Miscarriage, and Infant Death

1. Lynn Wilcox and James Marks, *From Data to Action: CDC's Public Health Surveillance for Women, Infants and Children: Infertility* (Washington, DC: U.S. Department of Health and Human Services, 1996); Susan Borg and Judith Lasker, *When Pregnancy Fails: Coping with Miscarriage, Stillbirth and Infant Death* (London: Routledge and Kegan Paul, 1982).

2. Mary Beck, "Baby Blues, the Sequel," *Newsweek*, July 3, 1989, 62–63.

3. Wilcox and Marks, *From Data to Action.*

4. Boston Women's Health Collective, *Ourselves, Growing Older* (Cambridge, MA: Boston Women's Health Collective, 1996); Terence Monmaney, "Risks Detailed for Older Mothers," *Boston Globe*, January 1, 1999, A3; British Broadcasting Corporation, "Late Arrivals," television show, aired in London, March 10, 1998; American Demographics, *American Households*; Griffin, "Childless by Choice," 100; Barbara Katz Rothman, *Recreating Motherhood: Ideology and Technology in a Patriarchal Society* (New York: Norton, 1989).

5. John Collins, "A Proportional Hazard's Analysis of the Clinical Characteristics of Infertile Couples," *American Journal of Obstetrics and Gynecology* 148 (1984): 527–532; Robert Benson, *Handbook of Obstetrics and Gynecology* (Los Altos, CA: Lange Medical Publishers, 1983); F. Gary Cunningham, Paul MacDonald, and Norman Gant, *Williams Obstetrics,* 20th ed. (Stamford, CT: Appleton and Lange, 2000); Denise Grady, "New Data on Babies of Women with Birth Defects," *New York Times*, April 8, 1999, A18.

6. Grady, "New Data on Babies of Women with Birth Defects."

7. Mary Lou Ballweg, *The Endometriosis Sourcebook* (Chicago: Contemporary Books, 1995).

8. Monmaney, "Risks Detailed for Older Mothers"; Grady, "New Data on Babies of Women with Birth Defects."

9. Mardy S. Ireland, *Reconceiving Women: Separating Motherhood from Female Identity* (New York: Guilford Press, 1993), 18.

10. Esther Fein, "For Lost Pregnancies, New Rites of Mourning," *New York Times*, January 25, 1998, A1.

11. Jennifer Downey and Mary McKinney, "The Psychiatric Status of Women Presenting for Infertility Evaluation," *American Journal of Orthopsychiatry* 62, 2 (April 1992): 196–205.

12. Barbara Menning, *Infertility* (Englewood Cliffs, NJ: Prentice-Hall, 1977); Sharon Covington, "Psychosocial Evaluation of the Infertile Couple: Implications for Social Work Practice," in *Infertility and Adoption: A Guide for Social Work Practice*, ed. Deborah Valentine (New York: Haworth Press, 1988), 21–36; J. Paulson, B. Harrman, R. Salerno, and P. Asmar, "An Investigation of the Relationship between Emotional Maladjustment and Infertility," *Fertility and Sterility* 49 (1988): 258–262.

13. Edward Freeman, Carol Garcia, and Karen Rickels, "Behavioral and Emotional Factors: Comparisons of Anovulatory Infertile Women, Fertile, and Other Infertile Women," *Fertility and Sterility* 47 (1983): 618–625.

14. Menning, *Infertility*, xi.

15. Freeman, Garcia, and Rickels, "Behavioral and Emotional Factors; Adria Schwartz, "Taking the Nature out of Mother," in *Representations of Motherhood*, ed. Donna Bassin, Margaret Honey, and Meryle Kaplan (New Haven: Yale University Press, 1994), 242; Downey and McKinney, "Psychiatric Status of Women Presenting for Infertility Evaluation"; Victor J. Callan, "Childlessness and Partner Selection," *Journal of Marriage and the Family* 45, 1 (February 1983): 181–186; Paulson et al., "Investigation of the Relationship between Emotional Maladjustment and Infertility."

16. Paulson et al., "Investigation of the Relationship between Emotional Maladjustment and Infertility"; Covington, "Psychosocial Evaluation of the Infertile Couple."

17. Steven Holmes, "Black Birthrate for Single Women Is at 40 Year Low," *New York Times*, March 18, 1998, A1; Irene M. Thomas, "Childless by Choice: Why Some Latinas Are Saying No to Motherhood," *Hispanic*, May 1995, 50–54.

18. Janice Raymond, *Women as Wombs: Reproductive Technologies and the Battle over Women's Freedom* (New York: Harper Collins, 1993); Margie Manning, "$1 Billion Spent on Infertility treatment," *St. Louis Business Journal*, September 15, 1997, 13; Esther Fein, "For the Infertile, a Treadmill of Despair," *New York Times*, December 14, 1997, A1.

19. Kate Johnson, " Fertility Clinics Report Treatment Outcomes," *Family Practice News* 29, 9 (1997): 7; Kelly Kershner, "In Vitro Fertilization: Is Conceiving a Child Worth the Costs?" *USA Today* 124, 2612 (May 1996): 30–33; Robert Franklin and Dorothy Brockman, *In Pursuit of Fertility* (New York: Henry Holt, 1990).

20. Nave-Herz, "Childless Marriages"; Fein, "For Lost Pregnancies"; Davitz, *Baby Hunger*; Schwartz, "Taking the Nature out of Mother."

21. Laura Mansnerus, "In Search of a Child: The Baby Bazaar," *New York Times*, November 26, 1998, A1.

22. Robert Paulson, "Fertility Drugs and Ovarian Epithelial Cancer: Is There a Link?" *Journal of Assisted Reproduction Genetics* 13, 10 (November 1996): 751–756; Farak Kostreski, "Infertility Coverage," *Family Practice News* 29, 11 (1999): 53; Aimee Ball, "Ovarian Cancer: One Women's Fight," *Harper's Bazaar*, September 1994, 20–65; Alice Whittemore, "The Risk of Ovarian Cancer after Treatment for Infertility," *New England Journal of Medicine* 331, 12 (1994): 805–806; Mary Ann Rossing and Janet Daling, "Ovarian Tumors in a Cohort of Infertile Women," *New England Journal of Medicine* 331, 1 (1994): 771–776; Ball, "Ovarian Cancer"; Raymond, *Women as Wombs*; M. Steven Piver and Gene Wilder, *Gilda's Disease: Sharing Personal Experiences and a Medical Perspective on Ovarian Cancer* (Amherst, NY: Prometheus Books, 1996).

23. Amy Sessler, "Miscarriage: A Grief That's Like No Other," *Boston Globe*, August 18, 1997, C1.
24. Ruth Carroll and Carol Shaefer, "Similarities and Differences in Spouses Coping with SIDS," *Omega* 26, 4 (1994): 273–284.
25. Sessler, "Miscarriage," 4.
26. Dennis Klass, "Solace and Immortality: Bereaved Parents' Continuing Bond with Their Children," *Death Studies* 17, 4 (July-August 1993): 343–368, quotation at 344; Covington, "Psychosocial Evaluation of the Infertile Couple."
27. James Naiman, "The Impact of a Child Death on Marital Adjustment," *Social Science and Medicine* 37, 8 (1993): 1005–1010; Carroll and Shaefer, "Similarities and Differences in Spouses Coping with SIDS."
28. Elizabeth Kubler-Ross, *Death: The Final Stage of Growth* (New York: Simon and Schuster, 1997).
29. Fein, "For Lost Pregnancies"; Stephen Smith, "Infertility I and II," National Public Radio, broadcast aired November 20–21, 1997.

Chapter 7 Choosing to End Family Dysfunction

1. Veevers, *Childless by Choice*.
2. Children's Defense Fund, *The State of America's Children* (Washington, DC: Children's Defense Fund, 2000); National Commission on Children, *Beyond Rhetoric* (Washington, DC: National Commission on Children, 1993).
3. Yvonne Vissing, *Out of Sight, Out of Mind* (Lexington, KY: University of Kentucky Press, 1996); Deborah Daro, "Child Sexual Abuse," *Child Abuse and Neglect* 15 (1991): 1–5.
4. Chodorow, *Reproduction of Mothering*; Paula Caplan, *Mending the Mother–Daughter Relationship* (London: Routledge), 1999; Edward Cohen, *Mothers Who Drive Their Daughters Crazy* (New York: Doubleday, 1997).
5. Friday, *My Mother, Myself*, 3.
6. Erving Goffman, *The Presentation of Self in Everyday Life* (New York: Doubleday, 1959). Veevers, *Childless by Choice*.
7. Mary Movius, "Voluntary Childlessness—The Ultimate Liberation," *Family Coordinator* 25, 1 (January 1976), 58; Mary Gerson, "Feminism and the Wish for a Child," *Sex Roles* 5, 6 (1984): 389–397.
8. Murray Straus and Richard Gelles, *Beyond Closed Doors* (Garden City, NY: Anchor Books, 1986).
9. Diane Eyer, *Mother Guilt: How Our Culture Blames Mothers for What's Wrong with Society* (New York: Random House, 1996).

Chapter 8 Processing Childlessness

1. Gail Sheehy, *The New Passages* (Thorndike, ME: G. K. Hall, 1996).
2. Erik Erikson, *Childhood and Society* (New York: Norton, 1963).
3. Robert Kavanaugh, *Facing Death* (Baltimore: Penguin, 1972).
4. Karen Burgwyn, *Marriage without Children* (New York: Harper, 1981), 167.
5. Michael Leming and George Dickinson, "The Grieving Process," in *Understanding Dying, Death, and Bereavement*, ed. Michael Leming and George Dickinson (New York: Holt, Rinehart and Winston, 1994), 495–506; Menning, *Infertility*; Betty B. Alexander, "A Path Not Taken: A Cultural Analysis of Regrets and Childlessness in the Lives of Older Women," *Gerontologist* 32, 5 (1992): 618–626.

6. Smith, "Infertility I and II."
7. Burgwyn, *Marriage without Children*, xi; Covington, "Psychosocial Evaluation of the Infertile Couple"; Callan, "Childlessness and Partner Selection"; Kenneth Doka, *Disenfranchised Grief* (Lexington, MA: Lexington Books, 1992); Griffin, "Childless by Choice."
8. Kenneth Doka, *Death and Spirituality* (Amityville, NY: Baywood Publications, 1993).
9. Davitz, *Baby Hunger*.

Chapter 9   Child Haves and Have-Nots

1. Ann Landers, "No Kids Creates Controversy," column, *Boston Globe*, December 2, 1996, D7.
2. Goffman, *Presentation of Self.*
3. Menning, *Infertility*; Miall, "Community Constructs of Involuntary Childlessness."
4. Goffman, *Presentation of Self.*
5. Miall, "Community Constructs of Involuntary Childlessness."
6. Andy Steiner, "Childless with Children," *Utne Reader,* January 2001, 72–79.
7. Griffen, "Childless by Choice."

Chapter 10   Nurturing Others

1. Erikson, *Childhood and Society.*
2. Letherby, "Nonmotherhood," 525.
3. Chodorow, *Reproduction of Mothering,* 3.
4. Ibid., 169.
5. Ireland, *Reconceiving Motherhood,* 69.
6. Renee Loth, "Relativity Redefined," *Boston Globe Magazine,* July 7, 1996. 5.
7. Gerson, "Feminism and the Wish for a Child."
8. Helfer, *Childhood Comes First.*
9. Steiner, "Childless with Children."
10. Ball, *Ovarian Cancer*, 50.
11. Marianne Dainton, "The Myths and Misconceptions of the Stepmother Identity," *Family Relations* 42 (1993): 93–98; Myriam Misrach, "The Wicked Stepmother and Other Nasty Myths," *Redbook,* July 1993, 88–92; Rosette Signore-Gossett, "Stepmoms: A Mother's Day to Remember," *Stepfamilies* 18, 1 (spring 1998): 6.
12. Susan Hoffman and Ronald Levant, "A Comparison of Childfree and Child-Anticipated Married Couples," *Family Relations* 34 (April 1985): 197–203; Dainton, "Myths and Misconceptions of the Stepmother Identity."
13. Emily Visher, "Emily Visher's Dream: Fantasy Expectations of Life as a Stepmother," *Stepfamilies* 14, 4 (winter 1994): 15–18.
14. Signore-Gossett, "Stepmoms," 6.
15. Pearl Ketover Prilik, *Step Mothering: Another Kind of Love* (Los Angeles: Forman Publishers, 1988).
16. Letherby, "Nonmotherhood," 525.

Chapter 11   Childless Women Growing Older

1. Betty Friedan, *Beyond Gender: The New Politics of Work and Family* (Washington, DC: Woodrow Wilson Center Press, 1997); Sara Rimer, "Kicking and Screaming, Baby Boomers Begin to Talk about Aging," *New York Times*, March 30, 1998,

A10; William Cockerham, *This Aging Society* (Englewood Cliffs, NJ: Prentice-Hall, 1997); Robert Atchley, *Social Forces and Aging* (Belmont, CA: Wadsworth, 1997); "Hillary Clinton Turns 50," *Parade Magazine,* July 7, 1996.

2. Abama et al., *Vital and Health Statistics*; Joyce Abama and Linda Peterson, "Voluntary Childlessness among U.S. Women: Recent Trends and Determinants," paper presented at the annual meeting of the Population Association of America, 1995; Griffin, "Childless by Choice"; Nave-Herz, "Childless Marriages."

3. Lisa Belkin, "How Old Is Too Old?" *New York Times Magazine,* October 26, 1997, 34–50; Betsy Garrison and Lydia Blalock, "Delayed Parenthood: An Exploratory Study of Family Planning," *Family Relations* 46 (1997): 288; Mary Leonard, "Boomers Try to Stop Time," *Boston Globe,* October 5, 1997, E1.

4. Linda Beckman and Betsy Houser, "The Consequences of Childlessness on the Social Psychological Well Being of Older Women," *Journal of Gerontology* 37, 2 (1982): 243–250; Christopher Lasch, *The Culture of Narcissism* (New York: Warner Books, 1980); Judith Rempel, "The Childless Elderly: What Are They Missing?" *Journal of Marriage and the Family* 47 (1985), 343–348; Cockerham, *This Aging Society*; Atchley, *Social Forces and Aging.*

5. Beckman and Houser, "Consequences of Childlessness."

6. Jean Giono, *The Man Who Planted Trees* (Chelsea, VT: Chelsea Green Publishing, 1985).

Chapter 12   Reflections on a Childless Life

1. Klepfisz, "Women without Children," 65.

2. Daniel Quinn, *My Ishmael* (New York: Bantam Books, 1997).

About the Interviews

1. Barney G. Glaser and Anselm L. Strauss, *The Discovery of Grounded Theory: Strategies for Qualitative Research* (Chicago: Aldine Publishing Company, 1967).

Index

abortion, 80, 103, 128
abuse, of children, *see* child maltreatment
acceptance, of childlessness, 82, 108, 127, 130, 148, 167, 212, 225
adoption, 182–184, 192
alcoholism, 61, 118, 126

benefits of childlessness, 128, 208–210
Bible, 8, 89

cancer: as cause of infertility, 85; as consequence of infertility treatments, 95
careers, 50, 67; economic considerations of, 69–70, 73; influence of mother's employment on daughter's, 48; nurturing, 84, 198–206; relationship to childlessness, 26, 67–71, 125
child maltreatment: consequences of, 46, 121; emotional abuse, 117; lack of affection, 115, 186; neglect, 118, 180; physical abuse, 118; sexual abuse, 120, 122
child-free movement, 20
childlessness: benefits of, 66, 79, 119; by choice, 25, 27, 55, 62, 65, 79; definition of, 83, 128; drawbacks of, 22, 148; history of, 7; involuntary, 28, 52, 85, 100, 121; temporary, 28, 32, 56; voluntary, 21, 29, 55, 66, 79, 119
Colonial America, 9

communication, about childlessness, 56–59, 97, 105, 139, 150–160
consumerism, 236; infertility treatments and, 21, 92; in the 1950s, 13
contraception, 13
co-parents, 162, 184
cultural influences on childbearing, 42, 54, 175

death, 222–224
deliberate childlessness, *see* childlessness: voluntary
demographic changes in the family, 10, 52, 214
discrimination, 23, 152, 164
divorce, 59, 63
domestic violence, 119

economic costs: of children, 9, 26, 56, 68, 71–73; of infertility treatments, 92, 94
education, 48, 73, 197, 229
emotions: alienation, 96, 139, 164; ambivalence, 18, 33, 130, 155; anger, 87, 107, 134; avoidance, 158; concealment, 156; contentment, 66; denial, 132, 157; depression, 93, 99, 108, 135; frustration, 58, 88; grief, 61, 101, 133, 135, 168; guilt, 98, 103, 141; jealousy, 138; loneliness, 96; longing, 137; loss, 88; regret, 134; relief, 76; surprise, 131

About the Author

Sociologist Yvonne Vissing is a professor at Salem State College in Massachusetts, where she is coordinator of the Center for Child Studies. She also provides a variety of research, consulting, and public speaking services for those in education, health, and human services. Her previous books include *Out of Sight, Out of Mind: Homeless Children and Families in Small-Town America* and *Finding Information about Children: Use of Electronic and Human Resources.*